3

MO   NO 14 '89

CO   JA 23 '90

KI   OC 26 '90

RI   JE 16 '89

SW   MR 11 '91

UP   JE 14 '90

4

ER   FE 10 '89

CS   AP 03 '90

HL   AP 14 '89

PI   AG 31 '89

BE   DE 27 '90

BL   AG 24 '90

SK   MY 02 '91

THE BOOK OF TZIRIL

A Family Chronicle

By Bess Waldman

ADAMA BOOKS
NEW YORK

3331485

Library of Congress Cataloging-in-Publication Data

Waldman, Bess.
  The book of Tziril.

  Reprint. Originally published: Marblehead, Mass.:
Micah Publications, c1981.
  1. Freedman, Tziril Miriam. 2. Jews—Soviet Union—
Biography. 3. Jews—United States—Biography.
4. Immigrants—United States—Biography. I. Title.
DS135.R95W24 1988 973'.04924 [B]   87-35146
ISBN 1-55774-016-X

This book was originally printed for my family. It was patiently researched, edited and typed by my beloved granddaughter, Debra Milamed. I wish to also thank Roberta Kalechofsky for her editorial expertise.

Acknowledgements—
Book design and typesetting by Miriam Milamed.
Glossary and technical assistance by Robert and Roberta Kalechofsky of Micah Publications.
Photographs from the collection of Bess Waldman.
Cover Design by Miriam Schaer

Adama Books
306 West 38th Street
New York, NY 10018 Printed in Israel

In Loving Memory of My Parents, Hinda and Avrum
and My Beloved Husband, David

My gratitude and thanks to —
My daughters for their aid and encouragement,
My sisters for their interest and their memories,
My granddaughter, Debra, for the manuscript of
the "Family Printing."

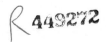

*A glossary is appended at the back of this book
for your convenience.*

Prologue

The month was January, the year 1948. We were having one of the worst winters ever recorded in the New York area. Outside, an endless storm was raging with winds and driving snow. My mother, who had lately been in poor health, had come for a visit.

Her nights, never quiet, became more and more restless, and my own nights were wakeful as I sat by her bedside trying to lull her to sleep. Soon her nights became more troubled, as she took to wandering from her bed in walking visions of despondency, certain her death was imminent.

"Nobody wants to believe me," she would declare mournfully. Before the storms had begun, my sisters and brother had visited her often. Her spirits had been high when she was surrounded by her children, but as soon as they had departed, she would claim that she had been deserted and abandoned.

Then the day came when she could not get out of bed.

"Where are all my children? Why are only you here? I had so many children. Where are they? Why must I be alone now that I am dying? Where is my son – how can he neglect me when he knows how sick I am?"

"It's the snow," I said. "It's impossible to drive, Mama. Just listen to that wind. Besides, the buses aren't running, and even some of the telephone lines are down."

"Lies!" she snapped. "Don't make excuses! Phone my son. Now. It is important that I see him. Tell him his mother is dying."

But after that she never mentioned her son. Her dark eyes were barely open as she lay there on the raised pillows, and her breathing was labored. The violet circles under her eyes were

1

almost black. Yet hers was still a beautiful face – she was close to eighty years, but only the sagging folds beneath her chin betrayed her age, and there was little gray in her masses of light brown hair.

During the next few days, before she lapsed into a final coma, she spoke incessantly of the long life which was re-enfolding before her heavy lidded eyes. She spoke of her child-hood in what was now called Lithuania, and of the beauty of the River Niemen, where the women of Kovno had washed their linens, and of the distant places where she had played as a child. She recalled what had been the most exciting event of her early years, and retold in vivid detail the story of her jour-ney through the Caucasus Mountains with her mother (she had called it "Kafkaz"), where they had gone to visit an aunt who owned a *drucke*, or printing press.

Tears had streamed down her cheeks as she recalled her father's departure for America.

"I was asleep. I was awakened in the middle of the night. He was bending over me, kissing me. My face was wet with his tears. My poor mother – she was also crying as she stood be-hind him, holding the lighted lamp. I'll never forget that night, when my father kissed me and said, 'Goodbye, Hindele. You'll come to me, to America, with Mama and the baby.'"

Since my childhood I had heard that story many times. My grandfather had fled conscription in the Russian Army, a long exile that my grandmother had always described as "a deadly curse."

She became suddenly quiet, but not for long.

"Bessie," she finally whispered. "Bessie. Promise you'll write my story. You're the only one of my children who ever list-ened. How often I would say to them 'listen, my children,' but did they? I don't want to be forgotten. Promise me you'll write my story."

I was greatly moved. My mother had a memory which spanned generations, and she was the repository of her mother's memories as well as her own. I had been listening to her stories since my childhood, though, to be honest, there had been times in later years when I had sat there in silence without really pay-ing attention as she rambled on. But I had heard it all, many times over.

Actually, I had heard many of the same stories from my grandmother. When I was a child, it had always seemed strange and exciting when my mother spoke of the past, but the same stories took on a note of tragedy when related by her mother. Bubbe, as we had always called her, would punctuate them with tears and deep sighs.

"Where would I begin?" I finally asked, thinking that I had been assigned an impossible task.

"Begin with Dvera, my grandmother," she said. "I was the first one named for her. Of course, I had two names, Hinda and Dvera. Hinda was the name of my father's mother. In fact, my parents had their first serious quarrel over my name. He wanted me to be called Hinda for his mother, and my mother insisted that I be called Dvera Esther for her mother. The rabbi had to be called to make peace between them. So I was named Hinda Dvera for both grandmothers, and they named my little sister Esther. But all my life, I have thought of myself as Dvera."

Bessie Lipschultz Waldman
Riverside, Pennsylvania
September 4, 1974

1
Dvera and Zalman Yitzchok
St. Petersburg: c. 1850

Dvera, widow of Zalman Yitchok Gordon, was led from the courtroom in shock and disbelief. Her long ordeal was over, after nearly ten years of litigation in the courts of St. Petersburg, capital of Imperial Russia. The highest civil courts in the land had unanimously rejected their suit for reparations for Zalman's vineyards in Kafkaz which had been confiscated some fifteen years before.

Until his death, Zalman had persevered, despite the advice of well-meaning friends who had warned him to drop the case and keep whatever funds remained after his fruitless battle with Imperial bureaucracy. Dvera, his wife, had continued the case after his death, even though she could no longer afford the services of a lawyer. She had been forced to stand before the tribunal alone, with the moral support of her dead husband's friends as her only counsel.

She had collapsed in despair when the final verdict was announced. As consciousness returned, the old, familiar pain in her chest became an agonizing reality. Fumbling in her satchel, she found her vial of pills.

"The pain – it's nothing new – it comes and goes," she told the cluster of friends who rushed to her assistance. Later, as they escorted her to the railroad station, they could find no words of comfort. Dvera had lost everything. Even the permit which allowed her to reside in St. Petersburg had expired at the end of the trial, and official regulations demanded that she, a Jewess, return to her home in Vilna immediately.

Dvera bade farewell to these old comrades of her husband, certain that she would never see them again, Some were professors at the conservatory of music who had known her

5

husband in his student days, long before the troubles of the Jews in Kafkaz, and the confiscation of his property when Russia began to consolidate her position in their native land after a series of wars with Turkey. As her funds began to dwindle, they had all advised her to drop the case, but Dvera had maintained that her husband had believed in the validity of his claim, since the vineyards had belonged to his family for generations. To have admitted defeat after so many years would have been a betrayal and an act of disloyalty to her dead husband.

She had been Zalman Yitzchok's second wife, but despite the difference in their ages it had been a happy marriage. They had met in the office of the government agency that had processed the claims filed by Jews who had been forced to leave Kafkaz during the turmoil of the 1830's, when Russia had strengthened her foothold in the region between the Black and Caspian Seas. Dvera's parents, who had died in St. Petersburg, had also lost their property.

Both Dvera and Zalman Yitzchok were descended from the Sephardic Jews who found a haven in Turkey after Spain's mass expulsion of the Jews at the close of the fifteenth century. After years of hardship, their ancestors had settled in Turkish territory, and had lived there in peace and prosperity for nearly three hundred years until their lives were disrupted by the expansion of Imperial Russia. In the fertile valleys to the south of the Caucasus Mountains they had planted vineyards near the ancient city of Tiflis. They had built schools and synagogues and raised their children as Jews in the midst of strangers – Georgians, Armenians, Turks and Circassians – but all things considered, they had done well.

Later, when Russia acquired large tracts of land from Poland at the close of the eighteenth century, Jews from Vilna and Kovno, Grodno and Minsk, came to settle on the fertile banks of the Kura River, bringing a newer tradition which mingled with their own. The Russian government had always grown uneasy whenever shifting boundaries and territorial gains brought large numbers of Jews within its borders. By siphoning off some of the Jews from the newly acquired Baltic region, two purposes could be accomplished at the same time. The Caucasus region would become more urban and westernized, and the diminished Jewish population in the old Polish provinces would constitute less of a "threat."

But it proved increasingly difficult for Imperial Russia to maintain her control of the areas only recently acquired from the Turks, since not even the Ottomans themselves had been able to completely subdue the native population of Kafkaz. During the wars against Turkey and the Pasha of Egypt, and during Russia's intervention in the Greek War of Independence, the mountainous strip of land between the Black and Caspian Seas had become a sprawling military encampment; Kafkaz was a critical center of influence in the East for Russia in her endless search for a warm water port. For this reason, whenever any of the inhabitants of the region interferred with the movements of Russian troops, they were severely punished.

During the 1830's there were local rebellions, and many Georgian villages were attacked and burned in retaliation. In the meantime, Nicholas I, who had issued even more restrictive legislation against the Jews in the territory acquired from Poland, decided to limit still further the areas in which Jews could live and do business. In 1835, the Jews of the northern Caucasus region were expelled, while those in the area south of the mountains were forced to flee when the gentile villages were attacked. This upheaval in their lives was complicated by the fact that they were not permitted to own land inside the Russian Empire, and were now being forced to live in a relatively small portion of the country, later known as the Pale of Settlement.

Zalman Yitzchok's vineyards had been confiscated by soldiers carrying out the orders of the highest military command. He had been forced, along with most of the other Jews of Tiflis and the surrounding area, to depart at once for the north. When he inquired as to whether or not he would be reimbursed for the loss of his property, he was told by the officer in charge that he would have to file a claim in St. Petersburg – an enormous distance to travel in the days when the railroad was a novelty reserved for the amusement of the nobility.

Zalman Yitzchok was a man broken by grief long before he

arrived at his destination. Since Jews were not allowed in St. Petersburg without an official permit, he decided to settle in Vilna, a relatively short distance from the Imperial capitol. Here his family could remain in relative safety while he filed the claim for his confiscated lands. But by the time he arrived in Vilna, only his seven year old daughter Bayla survived, of his once thriving family. His two oldest sons had been taken from their parents and forced into military service, while the two younger boys had mysteriously disappeared. His grief stricken wife, Zipporah, had not been able to withstand the rigors of the long march north, and had died of exhaustion and a broken heart.

In the years that followed, Zalman mourned not only for his wife, but for his sons, whom he would never see again. It was not difficult to predict their fate. Should they survive the twenty-five years of compulsory military service, they would be completely alienated from family and religion, and would have been converted to Russian Orthodoxy, the all pervading state religion. Thus, Imperial Russia under Nicholas I enforced its policy of "Russification."

The great majority of the Jews of Kafkaz had gone into exile, bearing with them the memory of their suffering at the hands of the military. Relatives and friends disappeared without a trace, and children were snatched from their parents during the night. No one would ever forget the gallows that had been erected for the resisters, whose bodies had been allowed to remain until they rotted, as foetid reminders of the penalties meted out to the enemies of the Czar. Many had perished during the long march to the northwest under the rifles of the accompanying gendarmes and the murderous whips of the mounted Cossacks.

Zalman Yitzchok never forgot that the Turks had valued their Jewish citizens, who were respected as productive elements of their society. Many of the Sephardim, who had lived there for centuries, had become prominent in affairs of state, finance and the professions. They had produced fine poets, men of letters and musicians. Even Zalman himself, in his youth, had been awarded a special permit to study the violin at the conservatory in St. Petersburg.

In a community where the average citizen could play an instrument, Zalman Yitzchok had been recognized as a gifted musician. He had been an extremely handsome youth – tall, slender, with masses of wavy dark hair. The inhabitants of the Georgian countryside had idolized him, and his abilities were always in great demand, especially during the harvest festivals. As arranged years before, he had returned to Kafkaz and married Zipporah at the age of eighteen. His parents had never expected that he would ever become a professional musician, since they took it for granted that he would inherit his father's vineyards in due time. The peaceful life of a vintner had always been Zalman's primary goal in life. In those days of comfort and affluence, no one had forseen that a time would come when Zalman Yitzchok would be forced to earn a living with his violin, as a member of a roving troupe of musicians, in order to support his young daughter and himself.

Soon after his arrival, he had already begun to achieve quite a reputation in Vilna and the surrounding area. His growing circle of admirers nicknamed him "Itzele Metter;" "Itzele" was the diminutive of Yitzchok, and a term of endearment, while "Metter," they said, referred to his virtuosity as a performer.

Despite his success as a violinist, it had not been easy for him to adjust to his new situation. He was sustained only by the hope that someday he would be reunited with his sons, and they would be allowed to return to their homeland. More than once he had recalled the warnings of Isaac Ashkenazi, his banker in Tiflis, who had told him that the East European Jews, who had only recently settled in Kafkaz, were leaving the area en masse and returning to their families in the old Polish provinces. As for himself and his family, they were leaving immediately for Zurich, where their money had already been transferred. Zalman Yitzchok could contact him there in the event that he wished to dispose of his property while there was still time, and transfer the proceeds to the safety of the Ashkenazi bank.

But Zalman had refused to worry. Of course, he had heard of disastrous sea battles, and the fall of the great fortress Valadi Kafkaz to the Russian Army. He was sure, though, that by the time the grape harvest was over, things would settle down.

More than a decade had passed before Zalman had met and married Dvera in St. Petersburg, where he was finally permitted to file his claim. His daughter Bayla had, by that time, married a young Jew from Tiflis who was a printer by trade. Shortly after Zalman's remarriage, his son-in-law, Meiron, received a special dispensation from the Czar to return to his native land, since printers were needed for the growing number of military installations. It was rumored that Russia's restrictions against the Jews were loosening, and those with highly-valued skills were slowly being allowed to return to Kafkaz. Bayla's husband had purchased a printing press with funds from an undisclosed source, and had also paid an enormous sum for his permit to leave the Pale of Settlement. Bayla had said farewell to her father and his new wife, and departed for Tiflis with her husband and baby daughter. Zalman Yitzchok hoped to join them with Dvera once his case was settled.

Dvera had suspected all along that her husband had given Bayla and Meiron money to purchase the drucke, or printing press, although he would never admit it. Zalman forbade her to ever mention the matter to anyone, and told her only that the purchase price had come from a secret source.

Before the birth of their two daughters, Dvera would often accompany her husband when he traveled with his troupe of musicians, her presence had stirred great curiosity and interest.

"Is it true," they would ask when she appeared at a wedding, "that your husband once owned an estate as large as a Russian province? It is said that Itzele Metter knows the language of the birds."

Though Zalman had been among the first of the Jews to file a claim for his confiscated land, it had been years before he was actually summoned for a hearing. By the time his name was placed on the court calendar in St. Petersburg, their older daughter, Channa was five. Unfortunately, his permit to reside in St. Petersburg did not include his family, and Dvera was forced to remain in Vilna with their small daughter. In the years that followed, she seldom saw her husband, since travel was such a costly undertaking, and she gave birth to Tziril Miriam, her second daughter, alone.

When Zalman Yitzchok died in the seventh year of the suit,

his friends summoned Dvera to St. Petersburg, arranging for
her permits and papers. She departed immediately, leaving her
children with Rosa Grodnick, a close friend in whose home
they had been boarding. Three years had gone by since she
had been home, and she owed Rosa a considerable sum of money for her daughters' board. But now Dvera was ill and without
funds, and after such a long absence, she wouldn't even be
bringing them good news.

Vilna

Huddled in her threadbare cloak, Dvera staggered from the train carrying her meager possessions. The journey to Vilna had completely exhausted her. The train had been delayed for several hours, and the confusion and bustle of the station in St. Petersburg had been extremely unnerving. She was a somber, unsmiling figure – tall and frail, and haunted by the years of litigation that had ended in disaster.

Dvera Gordon was a woman facing problems far beyond her powers of solution, magnified by the desolation of the uprooted, at the mercy of a host country that showed no compassion. Before his death, her father had predicted that the scars of their expulsion would remain unhealed for generations. Their ordeal, he had said, would be preserved in legends that would one day gnaw at the conscience of humanity. "But in the meantime," he had mourned, "we suffer."

The dimly-lighted streets of Vilna were crowded, despite the lateness of the hour. As her hired carriage rumbled over the uneven cobblestones of streets no wider than alleys, Dvera told herself that nothing had changed in the three years she had been in St. Petersburg. The aged, bearded men were still strolling sedately in their flapping caftans and wide-brimmed streimels on their way to and from the house of study. Even the smells in the open drains and the odors of the market stalls were just as she remembered.

Zalman had been so happy to leave Vilna. Never for a moment had he believed that the claim for compensation would be rejected by Russia's highest tribunal. Yet there were other things which preyed on her mind. He had never told her the full extent of his role in his daughter's purchase of the printing press. Zalman had been exultant at the thought that his daughter had been able to return to the land of her birth, and the printing business had been highly profitable from the beginning. "One day we will all benefit from it, especially our children," he would say. "Never forget that, Dvera."

As the carriage rumbled over the cobblestones, it occurred to Dvera that letters from Bayla had been quite infrequent since her father's death. Why hadn't she written? In her last letter she had announced the betrothal and forthcoming marriage of her only daughter. Her joy, she had written, was mixed with sorrow, for her father had not lived to share in her great simcha, the marriage of her daughter and his only grandchild.

At last the carriage came to a halt before a shabby tenement in a narrow street. The driver helped her climb to the top floor where Rosa Grodnick lived. Dvera planned to write to Bayla that very night; she would not be able to rest until she had done so. Bayla, prosperous and rejoicing over the marriage of her only child, would respond generously once she learned of their dire need. Dvera had no one else to turn to.

Gasping for breath, she knocked on Rosa Grodnick's door. Dvera's return to Vilna unannounced in the middle of the night was a shock, and Rosa could not hide her dismay. As she welcomed Dvera, she tried to conceal her distress, and wondered where Dvera would sleep that night. The room Dvera's daughters shared was tiny and cramped. She herself had been sleeping on a cot in the kitchen. The spare room that had once been Dvera's was now occupied by a couple of students.

"You should have written! You should have let us know you were coming! But we'll manage. Let me take your bags – you look so tired."

And then the bedroom door opened, and Dvera suddenly found herself in tears. She saw at a glance that her daughter Channa was now strikingly beautiful – slender and as tall as herself. She had become a dark-haired beauty with large sparkling eyes. As though in a state of shock at her mother's unheralded return, Channa passively submitted to her mother's embrace. But Tziril Miriam, the younger daughter, was almost hysterical with happiness, and clung to her mother kissing her again and again. She was simultaneously laughing and crying with an abandon only a child could display.

Tziril Miriam appeared younger than her eight years. She was pale and thin, with a face so like her father's that Dvera was overwhelmed. She remembered at once that Tziril Miriam had always been known for her quick temper and tantrums.

"Mama! Mama! You've come back to us! I knew you'd come back." Tziril's voice was shrill. "Every morning and every evening I prayed to Ha Shem, blessed be His Name, to send you back to us!"

"That's enough, Tziril," Rosa Grodnick snapped. She was still disturbed by the shock of Dvera's return after such a long absence. She'd have to get rid of the boarders in the morning, no doubt.

"Your mother is very tired. She had a long ride. Let her sit down and rest. Channa! Don't stand there like an ornament! Put on the kettle!"

As she gave orders to the girls, Rosa helped Dvera remove her cloak. She was stunned by her friend's great loss of weight, and her emaciated look. To her experienced eyes, Dvera was a very sick woman.

"You're so pale," she said in a voice now softened by pity. "Don't try to talk. There will be plenty of time later for that. Right now just rest."

Dvera moved toward her bag which lay on the table. Rosa and the girls watched in frightened silence as Dvera opened the bag and found her vial of pills, her hands trembling. After a few minutes the color returned to her cheeks. At that moment, Rosa knew for certain that Dvera did not have good news to impart. But the latter was not going to speak of such troubles in the presence of her children.

Rosa Grodnick, a middle-aged widow of limited means, held a dim view of what had transpired in St. Petersburg. She sensed that Dvera had lost the case. What else could have brought her back to Vilna in such a state of despair? She no longer felt any guilt about renting the spare room which Dvera had not occupied since Zalman's death had summoned her to St. Petersburg. Besides, Dvera was many months in arrears for the children's board.

After the girls were sent to bed, Rosa made up a bed for

Dvera in the kitchen on a cot borrowed from a neighbor.
Through the closed door, Rosa and Dvera could hear the voices
of Channa and Tziril Miriam raised in unison as they recited
the Krishmeh, their bedtime prayer. Tonight Tziril Miriam recited her prayers with heightened fervor. She was thanking
Ha Shem who had finally answered her prayer; her mother had
at last returned. But the child now had another request to make
of the Almighty; her mother's return to health.

As she prayed, Tziril remembered that Reb Isaac, the half-
blind Torah scribe who lived in the basement, had told her that
Ha Shem answered prayers that came from the heart.

"He has an Eye that sees and an Ear that hears," he had told
her. Tziril couldn't wait for morning. Before she left for the
girls' cheder, she would visit the holy man and tell him that he
had been right.

Though she and her sister had a rule that neither of them
could speak after their bedtime prayers, Tziril could not sleep.
On the Sabbath she would be going to the Synagogue as usual,
but this time she would have her mother with her. Usually she
went with Rosa Grodnick. She had the greatest respect for her
mother's friend, and found it inspiring to sit with the older
woman as she pored over her Siddur and davened, swaying
like a man.

Very few of the women who attended the services could
read a Siddur. They would listen to Rosa and weep in unison,
although they could not understand a word of the chanted
prayers.

More than anything else, Tziril wanted to grow up and be
able to read a Siddur like Rosa. She knew also that her own
mother was considered to be very learned, as well as beautiful.

Reb Isaac the Scribe had said with admiration that Dvera's
was a most beautiful script. Whenever a letter had arrived from
her mother, Tziril would run to his basement room and show
it to him. As he studied Dvera's letters with his eyes that had
grown dim, Reb Isaac had always said that even he could not
have done better.

The Letter

Dvera and Rosa talked late into the night, in spite of the former's great fatigue. Though the bedroom door was closed, Channa could hear their muffled voices, and broke the bedtime rule of silence.

"Tziril," she whispered, but Tziril had fallen asleep at last.

Channa wondered what they were discussing in such hushed voices. She crept from her bed and crouched by the door for a few minutes, but understood little of what she could hear. Shivering from the cold, she returned to the warmth of her featherbed. Ever since her father's death, she and her sister had boarded with Rosa Grodnick, and Channa could recall that even before her sister's birth, she and her mother never stayed in one house for very long.

Channa could not remember a time in her fifteen years when her father had spent much time with them. He was forever traveling about the countryside or attending to his business in St. Petersburg. Often, she remembered angrily, her mother would be summoned to meet him and would drop everything at his command. Channa would be left alone with strangers, although after Tziril Miriam was born this did not happen quite as frequently. Channa also remembered other babies who had been born in the years intervening between Tziril and herself – babies who had died almost as soon as they had arrived. She was not quite sure how many years there were between Tziril and herself, but believed that she would be sixteen on her next birthday.

Her mother had been home only once since her father's death, and could not possibly be aware of the other side of Rosa Grodnick's personality. In any event, Channa would refuse to live there any longer under any circumstances. In the morning she would tell her mother the truth. Besides, Channa didn't think that Dvera would consider remaining there for more than a few days at the most.

The way that woman spied on her, watching her every move, the way Rosa criticized everything she did – these things made living with Rosa Grodnick unendurable. Rosa didn't approve of the jewelry she wore. Why shouldn't she wear the jewelry if she wanted to? It belonged to her own mother. The jewelry was kept in the trunk in their bedroom for safekeeping. What business of Rosa's was it if she also liked to try on her mother's clothes that were stored in the trunk? It was nearly daybreak before Channa fell asleep, exhausted by her own silent resentment, as Tziril slept soundly beside her with a smile on her lips.

❧

Rosa Grodnick was deeply concerned about Dvera's predicament and had no faith in her hope for help from her stepdaughter in Kafkaz. She had to admit, of course, that Dvera had nothing to lose by writing and informing Bayla of their great need. Yet, Rosa had argued, was it not a fact that during the past few years, at a time when Dvera's problems had been most acute, Bayla had shown little interest or concern?

It was apparent to Rosa that Bayla was living her own life and was obviously far too involved in her own affairs to have time for others, even such close relatives as her half-sisters and her own father's second wife. She sighed. How could she point this out to Dvera without offending her? All she could bring herself to say was, " try and get some sleep."

Yet Dvera could not rest. "I must write Bayla; I can't wait. I know I won't be able to sleep until I write. Tomorrow – after I have written the letter – then I'll see a doctor. I'll do anything you tell me. You've been a true friend, Rosa, and even if I get no help from Bayla, I still have some valuable jewelry. Most of it belonged to my mother, and it should be worth something. I promise I'll pay you every cent that I owe."

It was a carefully composed but impassioned letter which Dvera wrote to her stepdaughter. She began with a formal statement in which she expressed the hope that all was well with her and her family, and that the drucke was prospering. Dvera then outlined the events that had followed Zalman's death, particularly the manner in which their carefully prepared case had been disposed of.

Her own health, she wrote, had been shattered. At present, she and her children were living with her dear friend Rosa Grodnick in Vilna. Rosa was most generous and had proved to be a devoted friend in a time of tragedy and hardship, but she, Dvera, was deeply in debt, and had no one else to turn to.

"It was most unfortunate," she wrote, "After all these years, that our petition for reparations was denied. Your father, dearest Bayla, was spared that terrible blow."

Dvera concluded with a plea that Bayla would respond most generously and not fail them in their desperate need. As for herself, she was a very sick woman and was worried about what the fate of her daughters would be if she were to die – an event that was not unlikely.

"I know that you will prove to be a worthy daughter of a most illustrious and generous father, whose devotion to you in his last years I am sure you cannot forget. He did not hesitate to help you and your husband so that you could live in comfort and dignity as the proprietor of a drucke, rich vineyards, and a name which is the envy of all who know you."

Dvera read and reread what she had written, and signed her full name, Dvera Esther Gordon. The envelope sealed, she finally lay down to rest.

But she was far too troubled to sleep. It seemed to her as though she had fallen into a bottomless pit, from which there was no escape. Memories of the trial haunted her, but above all, she could not forget her frantic attempt to procure a permit for the children to accompany her to St. Petersburg for their father's funeral, and the anguished realization that his body had been removed from St. Petersburg even before her arrival. She had been told by the authorities that his remains had been transported to some remote village where the interment of a Jew was permissible in accordance with Russian law and Jewish ritual.

Bitter sobs wracked Dvera's wasted frame. She no longer

had any illusions that someday it would be possible to visit Zalman's grave with her children. She had hoped at least to be able to erect a tombstone to mark her husband's final resting place.

That was a night Rosa Grodnick would never forget. Before daylight, before the sound of men's footsteps on the narrow stairways as they left for the morning prayers at the synagogue, the doctor had been summoned. Dvera had suffered an attack from which she never recovered consciousness. Before nightfall she was dead.

The Orphans

The women of the Vilna Chevra Kadisha, the Burial Society, were summoned immediately. As was the custom, they were responsible for attending to all funeral arrangements for Dvera, widow of Zalman Yitzchok Gordon. The society that ministered to Jewish widows and orphans would assume all of Dvera's financial obligations, and after the end of the required period of mourning, Haknoses Kalah, the "Society to Dower the Bride," would take personal charge of the young orphans. A husband would be found for the older girl, and with her safely married, the younger one would be assured of a home. Such was the defensive solidarity of the Vilna Jewish community.

Yet even before the first week of intensive mourning had ended, plans for the girls' future were being openly discussed in their presence. The matter was one of extreme urgency, and there was no alternative.

Channa pretended not to hear the kind ladies who asked her how old she was. When pressed, she would run from the room in tears. By the hour she would sit in her room, stony-faced and withdrawn. The worst times were when Rosa attempted to explain that the good folk, strangers all of them, who crowded into their cramped quarters, were pious, God-fearing people, concerned only with her welfare.

"Remember, you are no longer a child," Rosa would chide. "They ask only to be allowed to help you and your sister. For your own sake and for Tziril's you should at least treat them with respect."

All of Rosa's pity, though, was for Tziril Miriam. The child would constantly cling to Channa, unable to be consoled.

Rosa sighed. Why shouldn't the little one weep? What worse
fate could befall a child? She was going to have a hard life,
especially if she had to depend on Channa who cared only a-
bout herself. Channa was luckier than she deserved. Before
long the matchmakers would find her a husband. But the little
Tziril Miriam. . .

The matchmakers all agreed that Channa Gordon had great
beauty, and possessed yichus, or family prestige. But though
things were in her favor, she lacked a dowry. It was not going
to be easy to arrange a prestigious marriage for her, or even an
ordinary one, for that matter. Moreover, she had a sister who
would also have to be supported. But Channa was the daughter
of Itzele Metter, and that meant something in shtetl society.
Her yichus might possibly outweigh material considerations,
they decided, even the lack of a dowry.

Of course, the younger sister was going to present a problem. In comparison with Channa's dark beauty, Tziril's appearance was colorless. Her face was small and pinched-looking,
and her nose was disproportionately large. Tziril was thin and
undersized and was known to have a sharp tongue and a quick
temper. Though she was wise beyond her years in many ways,
when crossed she would fly into a tantrum.

On the other hand, Tziril Miriam was a great favorite with
the tenants in their building. She was friendly, obliging and
willing to run errands for the elderly and the sick. The child
had a good heart and was a good student, they all said. She was
the opposite of her sister who could not even be bothered with
responding to a civil greeting.

One day, the shadchen, or matchmaker, Reb Tevya Gedalya, told the Haknoses Kalah that he knew of a recent widower with two young sons in Kovno. He had heard that the
widower was anxious to remarry as soon as his gravestone was
unveiled. The wife had died in childbirth, and at this point he
was not adverse to an introduction. Gedalya the shadchen was
eager to arrange a meeting, since he believed the period of
mourning for the dead wife would soon be over, and told the
Society to Dower the Bride that he was planning to speak to
the man, one Reb Yosef Rosenblum, who was a prosperous
trader in grain.

When Gedalya made his report to Haknoses Kalah the next week, it seemed to be nothing short of miraculous. The shadchen had interviewed Yosef Rosenblum, who had made it quite clear that he did not place much credence in the matchmaker's flowery description of Channa's beauty and youth. But the important thing was that Rosenblum had actually agreed to come to Vilna to see Channa for himself.

"A clever man," Reb Tevya Gedalya had observed. The widower had been well aware that the matchmaker had avoided any mention of the dowry. However, he had only told Gedalya that the matter of the dowry, and the other details, such as the existence of a younger sister, would be discussed after the introduction.

There was great jubilation after Reb Yosef's anxiously awaited meeting with Channa. He told Gedalya that the girl was everything he had been looking for; the matter of the dowry was of no consequence to him. His business was flourishing and he owned his own home. Even Tziril Miriam would not present a problem.

"She will be company for my sons – like a sister," he said. "The house is large; there is plenty of room for everyone. Besides, the boys are in school most of the time. Tziril Miriam will also go to school."

As he spoke, Reb Yosef fixed his eyes on Channa, who sat there in silence with her face flushed. The girl could only stare at the floor. But the Society congratulated themselves, for they were pleased that Reb Yosef, a kindly but humorless man in his mid thirties, was so obviously taken with Channa. He was just the sort of husband the girl needed. He would be a good provider. All would be well with little Tziril Miriam, and Channa would live like a queen.

It did not seem to matter in the least to anyone that Channa sat scowling and showed little interest in this stocky man who barely reached her shoulder. Channa was quite tall, and though she was barely sixteen, her figure was well developed. It was obvious to everyone that Reb Yosef could not take his eyes off her; he had his heart set on possessing her.

They all complained that she sat there like the proverbial block of ice, but Channa, not one to show her feelings, had actually suffered a tremendous shock when her mother died. Since then, every moment held its measure of fear. Although Channa had always resented her mother's long absences, Dvera had represented at least a dream of security to her daughter.

And now that dream was gone. To whom could Channa turn? She had a vague recollection of a letter her mother had written to a relative just before her death. She knew it had been posted, but nobody seemed to expect a response. Now that her mother was dead, Channa realized she had no real choice but to allow these outsiders, whom she despised, to arrange a marriage for her. Rosa Grodnick did not have to tell her that there was nothing to be gained by opposing marriage to this "little old man," an elderly stranger who was prepared to provide a home for her and Tziril. Actually, it would be a relief just to get away from Vilna and Rosa Grodnick.

❦

There were times when Rosa could barely restrain her urge to give Channa a thorough shaking until the teeth began to rattle in her head. Such a fool! Why couldn't the girl be more reasonable? She was always so hostile. Forcing herself to smile, Rosa congratulated Channa.

"You're a lucky girl! He's such a fine man. He's willing to marry you." Rosa's voice became loud and strident. Marriage to this solid, mature widower would be far better, she added, than to be homeless and dependent on the goodwill of strangers.

"What a lucky girl you are that such a fine man is willing to marry you," she repeated. "He could have had his pick a-mong the daughters of wealthy men who would come to him with a handsome dowry, and not a younger sister he'd have to support. Why do you turn away when I'm talking to you? You act as though you are going to marry a common beggar, a thief!"

"Who said I was marrying him!" Channa retorted. She was livid with resentment as she confronted Rosa Grodnick.

"Oh? And what will happen to you, my lady? If you throw away this chance you will regret it for the rest of your life!"

Channa ran from the room and locked herself in her bedroom. From behind the closed door she wailed at last, "All right. Only shut up!"

Tziril Miriam pounded on the door, begging her sister to let her in.

"Go away!" cried Channa. "Leave me alone! All of you!" She'd marry that old man just to get away from these hateful people.

She was sick to death of them with their false smiles and their endless whisperings. Above all, she found the way in which Rosa Grodnick continually told everyone how much she had done for her dead friend – for Dvera and the orphans – unbearable. She never stopped reminding them that Dvera had owed her a considerable sum of money when she died. Dvera had promised to repay her, with interest, when her case was settled.

Channa writhed at the memory. She was certain that her mother had more than repaid her debt. What about her mother's jewelry and the beautiful clothes bought when times were good, that had disappeared piece by piece from the trunk? What about her wedding ring and the gold watch that had once belonged to Dvera's father. Channa had never even had the chance to tell her mother. Everything had disappeared. The trunk was empty.

Channa's Wedding

Haknoses Kalah took full credit for Channa's betrothal, for
the tenauim which followed — the signing of the marriage
contract which was as binding as the ceremony which was to
take place a week later. On the eve of the wedding, a committee of women escorted Channa to the mikvah, or ritual bath.
Before the immersion, her head was closely shaved and her
finger and toe nails were cut to the quick. Channa already
hated the traditional wig which she was expected to wear for
the rest of her days and had wept piteously when her long dark
hair had been cut.

The Society to Dower the Bride had invited the entire congregation to the wedding, which was held in the synagogue
where Rosa Grodnick worshipped. At last Channa stood under the bridal canopy with Reb Yosef, in a white gown and
veil borrowed from the Society. Beneath the veil, her face was
pale and drawn, her eyes red rimmed and swollen, but she
forced herself to keep remembering that she had been told
there were things in life far worse than marriage to a stranger,
and she managed to maintain her composure.

After the ceremony there was feasting and merriment. Such
a marriage was something special. Haknoses Kalah received the
congratulations of all who were present; they had saved two
young lives. Because of their good deeds, two penniless orphans had been spared untold hardships. No mitzvah could
have been greater!

"Mazel Tov! Mazel Tov!" was the cry on all sides.

By the time the wedding party had departed the following
morning, the marriage had already been consumated. Channa
and her husband had spent the night in a small room adjoin-

ing a chapel that was part of the huge synagogue complex, with its study rooms and accommodations for mendicants and travelers in need of a night's lodging.

The women of the Society had led Channa to this room where a marriage bed had been prepared. A table set with food and wine for the couple reminded the girl that she had been fasting all day. Just then she heard Tziril Miriam's voice. A very determined Rosa Grodnick restrained the younger sister, who was trying to follow Channa into the bridal chamber.

Reb Yosef was waiting for her. The man, whom she considered old enough to be her father, was radiant with happiness. What followed was something for which, unlike the Mikveh, she found herself totally unprepared. At Reb Yosef's touch, her heart suddenly began to pound. Sensing her fright, he gently lifted her veil.

"My bride, my beloved," he kept whispering over and over again. Never had she seen a man so overcome by emotion.

As though it were a dream, Channa could hear the loud merriment of the wedding guests. The distant fiddles played the familiar tunes of wedding dances, but the music seemed so far away.

"It's time we broke the fast," Reb Yosef finally said. He filled the wine glasses. "Drink," he ordered. "It will soon be morning – see it is already getting light. L'Chayim!"

But before he drank a generous glassful, Yosef remembered the old blessing, "Blessed art thou, O Lord, our God, King of the Universe, who creates the fruit of the vine."

When they left for Kovno the following morning it was snowing, but Reb Yosef's sleigh was sturdy and piled high with fur robes.

"My team is young and fleet of foot," he assured the frightened Channa, who had never traveled in a sleigh before. Although the icy winter winds were nothing new to her, she shivered beneath the mounds of fur. Tziril Miriam wept softly at her side, as though shaken by the uncertainty of it all. Her sobs were audible as she huddled under the fur robes.

"I can hear them! They are following us," Tziril Miriam

cried, convinced that they were being pursued by wolves. Channa was too unnerved to be much of a comfort to her sister, and it was Reb Yosef who calmed Tziril.

"It's the wind," he said gently. "There are no wolves in this part of the country. I've driven in worse storms; this is nothing." Yosef laughed. "Before long we'll be home."

There was reassurance for the frightened girls in the confidence and warmth of Reb Yosef, as he guided the team of horses through the blinding snow. Channa took heart in the strength of his fur gloved hands as he masterfully held the reins. This quiet, soft-spoken man was her husband now. He was taking her away from what might have been a terrible fate. She would be spending the rest of her life with him.

Nothing that had happened since her mother's death had any semblance of reality other than the fact that she and her sister were alone in the world. And yet, this change in her life was also like a dream – the signing of the marriage contract, her resigned horror at the mikveh when her long, beautiful hair was cut. She remembered that at that moment she had wanted to die. That feeling had never left her, even while she stood with Reb Yosef under the marriage canopy. It was all fading into a half remembered nightmare as Rosa Grodnick's words kept ringing in her head: "The worst of all fates is to be a homeless orphan without a roof over your head."

As Yosef's sleigh flew through the snow, Channa's tears at last flowed freely. But she found some comfort in the thought that no future could possibly be worse than what she and Tziril Miriam had lived through in the past few weeks.

By the time they reached the outskirts of Kovno the snow had stopped. The tree-lined streets glistened in the winter sunshine. Tziril Miriam still slept at her sister's side. In spite of the weather, Reb Yosef had made the trip in record time, although they had made a few stops at wayside inns.

"This is Kovno; we're almost home," Reb Yosef told Channa. This was her first trip to Kovno. The houses they passed were nothing like the old, multi-family dwellings of Vilna, and Kovno's broad, tree-lined avenues bore no resemblance at all to Vilna's congested alleys. It occurred to Channa that by comparison, the buildings of Vilna were no better than hovels. But she would soon find out that Kovno too had its crowded ghetto. They were now in a section where Kovno's wealthier Jewish residents had settled, and here Reb Yosef lived.

Channa was overwhelmed when her husband drew to a halt in front of a two-story frame house. Was this to be her new home? To her it seemed like a palace.

Tanya the housekeeper greeted them at the door. She was a muscular woman of Polish peasant stock with a full bosom and wide hips. Her high cheekboned face was pockmarked, and her starched white apron rustled as she walked. Tanya bowed respectfully as she greeted her new mistress in Polish, which neither Channa nor Tziril understood. She swore that she would serve her new mistress as faithfully as she had served the old, although she had never expected that the bride would be so young.

Reb Yosef inquired about his sons, but without waiting for a reply, he grabbed Channa possessively by the arm and ushered her into the adjoining room. Tanya, as though obeying an unspoken order from her master, prevented Tziril from following. Instinctively, Tziril felt threatened by the huge bulk of Tanya's presence. To the child's amazement, in fluent Yiddish, Tanya ordered her to wait in the kitchen. It was the master's wish.

"The children are never permitted into the best parlor except on special occasions," she instructed. "The carpet shows every footprint. It leaves a disfiguring mark. And remember, none of the ornaments are to be touched. One may look, but never touch."

The housekeeper went on to explain that the family ate in the dining room only on the Sabbath or on the Jewish festivals when they used the fine silver and china stored in the elaborately carved cabinets. Most of the time, they had their meals in the family room adjoining her spotless kitchen, which was lined with shining utensils of copper and brass.

Tziril Miriam was numb with fear; she had never felt more trapped. Where was Channa? She only wanted to return to Vilna. She was too terrified to move with Tanya looking down at her so menacingly. Trembling, she listened as the housekeeper warned her that she was never to intrude on the master. His privacy was to be respected. She was never to forget that her sister was now mistress of the house, and more importantly, his wife.

With a great display of pride, Reb Yosef escorted his bride from room to room. He had bought the house just before the death of his first wife. With a sigh, he told Channa that he had had it completely renovated, although the furniture and carpeting had been purchased from the former owner, a highborn Pole. He directed Channa's attention to the intricately carved cabinets in the dining room, which reached almost to the ceiling, and to the sparkling china, crystal and silver behind the doors of polished glass.

There were no pictures on the walls, except for the ornately framed Ketuba, the wedding certificate of Reb Yosef and Yetta, his first wife. The Ketuba was designed after the artist's highly stylized conception of Solomon's Temple in Jerusalem.

"My Yetta, may her soul rest in everlasting peace, never lived to enjoy this beautiful home. My poor Yetta. She died in childbirth."

Channa averted her eyes. She didn't want to think about Yetta's awful death. Equally distasteful to her were Yosef's constant allusions to his motherless sons. Reb Yosef had told her that he expected her to be a real mother to them. What she really wanted to tell her husband was that she was very hungry. They had hardly eaten at all since the wedding, and she had had little appetite when they had stopped at roadside inns for refreshments and rest. She had heard that Tanya was an excellent cook.

Channa was wondering what Tanya had prepared for dinner, as they paused in the dining room which was already set for the evening meal as though it were the Sabbath. They would dine here tonight, in honor of Reb Yosef's marriage, and would be served on the beautiful china. They were only waiting until his sons returned from cheder .

Reb Yosef led Channa to the red velvet couch and spoke to her earnestly of his motherless sons. They were good boys and diligent students.

"They won't be much trouble. Besides, they are in school

most of the day. Poor boys. They still miss their mother very much. Now Channa. I want you to listen to Tanya. Let her teach you – she is a most competent housekeeper." In addition to Tanya, there was Katya the kitchen maid who helped with the heavy chores.

"Come, I hear the boys," he finally said. "They are home; now we will eat."

Early the next day, many of Reb Yosef's relatives and friends came to pay their respects to his new wife. They had all heard of Channa's beauty and the high social position of her family. Though they had not been invited, Yetta's bereaved parents were among the guests. The couple wept without restraint. To think, they mumbled, that this stranger was now settled in the home of their beloved daughter, so soon after her death. They fondled their grandsons and bemoaned their lot – to be left motherless at so early an age. They hadn't forgotten that their daughter had brought Reb Yosef a handsome dowry that had enabled him to establish a profitable business and purchase this handsome dwelling. And now another woman was to enjoy the good things that their Yetta had been deprived of by her untimely death.

The bitterness of it made life unbearable for them. Their life had lost every trace of its beauty and joy. "Poor Yetta," they moaned over and over again. "To be forgotten so soon!"

Kovno

Life under Reb Yosef's roof was difficult for Tziril Miriam from the beginning. It seemed to her that a great wall had been erected between her and Channa, and she saw very little of her sister. Her loneliness was increased by the fact that Reb Yosef's sons, who were her own age, were at school or busy with their lessons most of the day. In the evenings, the boys followed their father into his study where he quizzed them on the day's schoolwork.

They were pale faced city boys who spent much of their time indoors poring over their books. There were no girls at their school, and they seemed much younger than their years. Their shyness made getting to know Tziril extremely difficult for them. Yet, Tziril and the boys slowly began to understand each other, for all of them had known the orphan's loneliness.

It was not long before they all became close friends, and Tziril Miriam would await their return from school with eagerness. Bendit, the older boy who was her own age, and Shaul, the younger, who was afflicted with a leg deformity, finally admitted to her that she was the first girl they had ever spoken to. Bendit and Shaul also confided to her that they felt ill at ease with their father's new wife, and were beginning to feel an increasing distance between Reb Yosef and themselves as well.

After Channa and Tziril's first week in Kovno, the seamstress began her daily visits to their home, and most of Channa's time was taken up with fittings and conferences. She was getting a new wardrobe which would be in keeping with her station as mistress of a prosperous household and Reb Yosef's wife.

Tziril Miriam, though, did not know what to do with herself. Her unhappiness seemed unbearable at times. Reb Yosef had promised her that she could go to school, but she had been told that it would be necessary to wait for the start of the new term. She was homesick for her friends in Vilna, and Channa seemed to have no time at all for her. Her sister was always annoyed when Tziril Miriam spoke of Vilna, her former schoolmates, and her disappointment about her education.

"School is for boys, anyway," Channa would tell her sharply. Tziril was already more advanced than most girls her age. Why, she could read a prayer book and she knew all the blessings for bread and wine. What more was there for a girl to learn?

Yet these things would have been endurable if it hadn't been for Tanya. Wherever Tziril turned, the housekeeper was at her heels chasing her from one place to another. She kept the girl under constant surveillance, and it seemed to Tziril that she was being spied upon as though she were an intruder.

Reb Yosef had given Tziril permission to browse among the books in his study. Every day she would dust them lovingly, and spent hours leafing through whatever caught her eye. They reminded her of Reb Isaac's rooms in Vilna, which had been filled with the yellowed manuscripts he had been working over for a lifetime, and stacks of dusty books from floor to ceiling. How she longed to see him again, and how she missed Rosa Grodnick who had never told her that schooling was only for boys!

Reb Yosef left Kovno at least once a week on business, and often remained away from home overnight. On these occasions, Channa would take Tziril Miriam for long strolls along the broad avenues of Kovno. Sometimes they would wander through the park on the banks of the River Niemen. Frequently, there were trips to the marketplace in the center of town – a congested area teeming with pushcarts and open stalls. One could scarcely hear oneself talk above the tumult, as the vendors hawked their wares. This was the heart of the old ghetto, so reminiscent of Vilna, where the majority of Kovno's Jews lived and worked.

Jews, Poles, Lithuanians and Russians mingled freely here,

and bought and sold from each other such items as farm animals, vegetables, and live fish and poultry. The bargaining was loud and raucous, as each side fought to win a victory of a few kopecks. It was not long before Tziril and Channa began to acquire a respectable Polish vocabulary.

But occasionally, Tanya would accompany them. She would help Channa select fruits and vegetables at the open stalls, and taught both girls to bargain with the vendors over the prices of fish and poultry. Invariably, though, Tziril Miriam would grow sulky when Tanya came along, for she felt that her sister completely ignored her in the housekeeper's presence.

The daily visit of the seamstress was a welcome diversion in the routine of the household. She would arrive early in the morning, often accompanied by an assistant. Channa's new clothes were nearing completion, and as the seamstress gloated over the piles of velvet, silk and fine wool, she told Tziril that as soon as the mistress's wardrobe was finished, she would be busy outfitting her as well. Such was Reb Yosef's wish. With every word she uttered, the woman stressed the good fortune of the orphaned sisters.

By this time Channa was quite aware that her husband was a man of some importance in the community. People had great respect for his sharp business acumen and his innate love of humanity. He was charitable and always ready to help anyone in need; to the Jewish community of Kovno, Yosef Rosenblum was simply a man who loved people, despite his somewhat gruff exterior.

Channa's rotund, bearded husband was the first security she had known since the death of her parents. She was quite awestruck by the luxuries with which Reb Yosef surrounded her. Nothing was too good for her. His patience with her young sister, who irked Channa beyond endurance with her whining and complaints, was beyond Channa's comprehension.

❧

Tziril Miriam had been a problem ever since their arrival in Kovno. Nothing pleased her and she acted as though she hated her new home. She complained incessantly of Tanya, who was her "mortal enemy," and would weep for hours that,"Nobody loved her, not even her own sister."

She pleaded almost daily to be sent home to Vilna. Channa, she claimed, was busy with her clothes and jewelry and spent all of her time in front of her mirror. She had no friends. Bendit and Shaul cared only for their books.

"What am I ever going to do with my sister?" Channa would wail. She could no longer hide her impatience and resentment from her husband. Reb Yosef would have to take charge of Tziril Miriam, for Channa told him that she was no longer capable of dealing with her.

"You promised she'd be sent to school," Channa complained. "But when? When? I can't stand having her around me all day, weeping for Vilna. She will drive me to an early grave!"

Reb Yosef said that he understood. He had the deepest pity for the Little Tziril Miriam.

"Remember Channa," he said. "She is homesick, lonely. She is an orphan. My own sons were no different. The boys still haven't recovered from their mother's death. Give her a little more time."

Actually, Reb Yosef was quite distressed. He realized that Tziril was a difficult child, and that his wife, scarcely more than a child herself, was incapable of handling the situation. At first he had, indeed, been willing to be patient, and had indulged Tziril's every whim in the hope that she would realize that the move to Kovno had been arranged with her own welfare in mind. School? Maybe next year if the child settled down.

In the four months since his marriage, though, she had shown no sign of improvement. Channa was becoming increasingly nervous and distraught, and to add to all this, she was expecting a baby. Since he could think of no other alternative, Reb Yosef decided to consult Tanya.

He confided to the housekeeper that his wife was pregnant and was not having an easy time. Channa tired very easily and he didn't want her to be disturbed with her sister's constant demands. There were the fittings with the seamstress, which his wife was beginning to find most fatiguing. With the utmost discretion, he suggested that Tanya could be of great assistance if she could manage to keep Tziril Miriam occupied so that she wouldn't have so much time to brood and complain.

Tanya was most cooperative. She would allow Tziril to help her with the cooking. There were many light chores that would keep a child busy, and she would take her along on her daily marketing excursions.

Despite her initial dislike of the housekeeper, Tziril Miriam grew to admire her skill in bargaining with the dealers in the marketplace. No one could fool Tanya! She was gradually becoming an industrious and careful child, and was learning many things that would prove useful in later years – the baking of bread and communicating with the gentiles of the area.

☙

The servant girl Katya was always busy in the kitchen with the heavy chores. As she scoured the pots and pans under Tanya's relentless supervision, she would often mutter angrily to herself. She resented Tziril's presence in the kitchen, feeling that the child was a threat to her interests. Both Tziril and Tanya sensed this, and on one occasion Tanya had administered a severe beating to Katya in Tziril's presence. It was a surprise to Tziril when one day Bendit whispered to her that Katya was Tanya's own daughter – an illegitimate one, of course – that the housekeeper had never acknowledged.

A few days later, Tziril Miriam burst into her sister's room and flatly demanded to be sent back to Vilna. She had overheard Tanya telling her "daughter" that as soon as the master's wife had given birth – as yet Channa showed no signs of pregnancy – there would be a great change made in the household.

Suddenly the two of them had become aware of Tziril's presence. Katya had burst into coarse laughter.

"I can't wait," she had taunted. "The mistress will dress me in a fine nurse's uniform and I'll be given charge of the infant. What a time I'll have pushing the perambulator in the park! And you, Tziril Miriam, you'll be down here with Tanya all day scouring the pots and pans!"

Channa had been completely unnerved by the unexpectedness of her sister's outburst. She hadn't even told her yet about her pregnancy. After all, she had been married for less than six months. And wasn't it unseemly to discuss such matters with a child of nine?

"Oh that ugly Katya!" Channa had fumed. She had been feeling unusually ill that morning. "Don't worry, Tziril. She'll never come near my baby. Yes, it's true; you're going to be an aunt. You – and only you – will take care of my baby. I told Reb Yosef that I didn't want a nursemaid while you were here to help me. I only want you. I trust you. That filthy, ugly Katya. She isn't fit to scrub my floors. I told Reb Yosef I couldn't bear the thought of having her in my kitchen. But she's some sort of relative of Tanya's. He thinks that Katya is her own daughter, though she will never admit it. I get sick to my stomach when I look at her with those horrible pockmarks and that harelip!"

Channa shuddered. "They say that a harelip is bad luck, and the mark of the evil eye. I'll never let Katya even look at my baby!"

Aunt Tziril

Ten months after her marriage, Channa gave birth to her
first child, a sturdy boy with dark, curly hair. They called him
Nathan. Tziril Miriam had no idea for whom the baby had
been named, but knew only that it had been Reb Yosef's decision. She would never forget how for the entire week following his birth, their home was the scene of every kind of lavish
festivity. In honor of the birth of their son, Reb Yosef presented Channa with a string of fine, lustrous seed pearls, so
long that it could encircle her slender throat three times.

Channa couldn't bear to have Tziril leave her for a moment,
and she would entrust Nathan to her sister alone. As for Tziril
Miriam, from the moment she first held the baby in her arms,
her happiness was as intense as if he had, indeed, belonged to
her. At times she would even imagine that he was her own son.
She cuddled him; she changed him; she fed him. Nathan was
her sole charge and her devotion to the child began to fill the
emotional void of her girlhood.

By the time Nathan was three years old, his mother gave
birth to a second child, a girl whom they named Feigele.
Already Nathan was old enough to begin his formal education.
Tziril was as hysterical as Channa the morning Reb Yosef
bundled the squalling toddler into his voluminous prayer
shawl and carried him in his arms to the cheder. Before they
had left for Nathan's first day of school, Reb Yosef had poured
honey over the pages of his old prayer book, and ordered
Nathan to lick it clean, so that all his life he would find learning sweet. Such was the tradition.

Channa had bitterly opposed her husband's decision to start
their son's religious training at so early an age. With Feigele at

her breast, she began to wail as they departed, "He's only a baby, he can wait another year! It's monstrous! Such a cruel thing to do." But her pleas were to no avail. When Nathan returned it was already dark; he had been in the classroom for eight hours. Channa nearly fainted when she saw him. His knuckles were bruised from the rebbe's pointer, which had not been spared. The child's face was streaked and grimy with tears.

Nathan began to weep the moment his mother gathered him into her arms. Channa swore to her husband that she would never permit her son to return to that cheder. If Reb Yosef was so determined to start his son's education while he was still an infant, he would have to hire a private tutor, even if it meant an addition to their already growing household.

Within a few days, Reb Yosef had engaged a melamed to come to their home to instruct Nathan. Since he was an extremely active child who found it hard to sit still, Reb Yosef decided that Tziril Miriam should sit with him during his study periods to keep him quiet. Tziril was overjoyed at the idea; this was her chance to continue her own education which had been interrupted when she left Vilna. She would learn to read and write as well as Rosa Grodnick!

Though the meaning of the prayer book was still something of a mystery to her when she began, she improved rapidly under the guidance of Nathan's melamed, who found his charge's young aunt to be an intelligent and serious student. Tziril began to realize that Channa's reluctance to let her study stemmed from the fact that her sister had forgotten almost everything she had ever learned. Channa, after all, was the mistress of the house, and was not to be outdone. Tziril, however, could not understand that her sister had no desire to begin again, although she had every opportunity. But Tziril's progress was so rapid that within a year the melamed asked her to assist him in teaching Nathan elementary Hebrew grammar.

Channa gave birth to three sons and three daughters during the ten years after her marriage. As her family grew, she became increasingly inaccessible to her sister. Her life revolved around her children and their education, adornments for her home and person, and her many social obligations. She had little time to spare for Tziril Miriam.

But Tziril had grown accustomed to this state of affairs. Soon after Nathan's birth, Katya had been dismissed and Tanya too, soon gave her notice. Tziril, of course, realized that much of the responsibility of managing her sister's home had been placed on her shoulders. Although there was hired help most of the time, Channa was never too busy to find all sorts of work for her which "Only Tziril could do."

Bendit and Shaul also felt like strangers in their father's home. It seemed to them that they were there on sufferance, living on the periphery of Channa's charmed family circle. They looked on in envy. Yet Tziril envied them. They spent most of their time at the yeshiva, and life wasn't all that difficult for them. At least they still had a father.

But Tziril's envy turned quickly to pity when she learned that they were going to be sent to America. There the boys would be expected to make a life of their own and find some gainful occupation. Most important of all, they would in this way escape compulsory military service in the army of the Czar.

Tziril never forgot how Bendit and Shaul wept on the eve of their departure. They promised to send for her as soon as they had saved enough money for her passage. Bendit even offered to marry her. Tziril Miriam wept too, and promised to write.

Everyone had always agreed that Tziril's handwriting was excellent. The melamed, who had stayed on to instruct Channa's other children, was extremely proud of his eldest pupil, and had often boasted that few women could read a prayer book so well, or write as legible a letter as Tziril Miriam.

Yussel The Red

During the years she lived with her sister, it had been most deeply impressed upon Tziril Miriam's mind that she must always refrain from bringing up the subject of their parents. She had to be on her guard against this if she wished to live in peace with Channa. Tziril, however, brooded over the matter. It seemed ridiculous to her that she did not even know their names, and it saddened her to think that, as far as she knew, none of Channa's children were named for their maternal grandparents. Where they had been born, where they had been buried — such questions were always in the forefront of her thoughts, although time and experience had taught her to keep silent.

Once, when Tziril persisted with her questions, Channa angrily replied, "They are both dead. Our father was an old, old man. Our mother was his second wife and she was much younger, I can't even remember what he looked like. He was never home with us. Where was he? I never knew. Our mother left us for months and years at a time. And then she died. You should at least remember that. We were always left with strangers."

Channa's voice rose, harsh and bitter.

"They died and I got married. You have a home. What else was there for me to do but get married? The shadchen found me a widower with two children. They all said I was so lucky — I was a girl without parents and I didn't even have a dowry. If I hadn't married him, you and I, if we managed to stay alive, would be beggars wandering from town to town. That's what the good people of Vilna told me. So now you have a home. What more do you want, I ask you? What could you have to complain about?"

40

With difficulty, Tziril held back a flood of bitter answers. She had plenty to complain about, but she would be silent for the present. What disturbed her the most was that she was already well past her eighteenth birthday, an age when most girls in Kovno were married. An unmarried woman who had passed a certain age was not to be envied. Tziril Miriam was sure that her sister would feel no guilt at all if she were to remain unmarried – an *alte moid* – forever. To Channa she was no more than a maid of all work.

Whenever Tziril tried to bring up the subject of her future, Channa would remind her, not too subtly, that even in the best of times, life in Imperial Russia was always precarious for the Jews. Their money was not endless, and her own children would have to come first. Channa made it quite plain that she had already begun to plan for her daughters' marriages. Although they were still children, it wouldn't be long before the shadchen came to call. Channa's three daughters, pampered and dressed like exquisite dolls, would have no trouble finding suitable husbands. They had to have generous dowries, and then there were Channa's sons, who would soon have to be ransomed from military service.

"You're treated no worse than Reb Yosef's sons," was Channa's usual excuse. "They were sent away to America, and are now toiling long hours in New York making men's clothing."

In fact, Tziril Miriam had not been lacking for suitors. But without a dowry, she knew she could not aspire to anything better than a common worker without much education. The butchers and teamsters who sought her attention were all under the impression that the prosperous Reb Yosef Rosenblum would provide a handsome dowry for his sister-in-law. Tziril's obvious disdain for these fortune-hunting young men angered the matchmakers. Who was she to act as though she were a member of the nobility? Indignantly they warned Reb Yosef that Tziril would never find a husband, and would shame them all before the community. Besides, they would point out, she was no longer so young and was far from beautiful. Already she had a reputation as a shrew.

❧

It was not unusual for Reb Yosef to bring a guest home to share their meal on the eve of the Sabbath. He was known throughout Kovno for his hospitality to wandering scholars and mendicants whom he would meet at the synagogue. One Friday evening, he was accompanied home by a young man whom he had met at the late afternoon service.

He was a distant cousin from the town of Wilki. Without the slightest hesitation he told Reb Yosef that he had heard of the latter's unmarried sister-in-law, and had come to Kovno to meet her. Reb Yosef took a liking to the young man, especially when he learned that both of them were named for a common great grandfather. The guest was nicknamed "Yussel," "Yussel the Red," he added with a smile. He had thick, wavy red hair and a carefully clipped beard that was a shade darker.

Tziril Miriam lost her usual reserve when she was told that their dinner guest was a relative. She studied the young man with speculative interest and decided that she liked his red hair and easy laugh.

He told them to call him Yussel. He was a full head taller than Reb Yosef, and was muscular and lean with the healthy appearance of a man who spent much of his time outdoors. He had been apprenticed to Frumkin the building contractor after his mother died when he was eleven, but had completed his training and had found work with a local baker.

Suddenly Tziril remembered that she had seen him before. So, he was the young man who had helped her with the Sabbath dough at the bakery, just a few weeks before! He had been attentive and had offered to carry the fresh loaves home for her.

Yussel focused his eyes on her. He had been waiting all evening for her to recognize him, he remarked with a laugh. As they watched and listened, Reb Yosef and Channa could not be blind to the young man's interest and to Tziril's unusual responsiveness.

Yussel told Tziril that his childhood had not been much different from her own, and she was filled with sympathy for him as he spoke of the lonely years that had followed the death of his mother.

Tevya, his father, had immediately remarried, and the second wife had had two children of her own. There were now seven children to provide for, and soon new babies began to arrive. His stepmother began to complain bitterly that there were just too many mouths to feed.

"In desperation," he told her, "my father apprenticed me and my younger brother Schmuel to Frumkin the building contractor."

"Hm, Frumkin." Reb Yosef grew attentive. He knew this Frumkin quite well; he was one of Yosef's own circle of business acquaintances. It was common knowledge that Frumkin's young apprentices were usually exempted from military service, since the builder was awarded many government contracts.

"But my oldest brother, Herschel, was not so fortunate," Yussel continued. "The year my mother died, Herschel was seized one day on his way home from cheder. He was taken into the army and we haven't heard from him in years."

Yussel then reminded them, as though they weren't already aware of the fact, that in the Czar's army, the term of service was twenty-five years.

"Herschel was just thirteen when they took him. It was as though the earth had opened and swallowed him forever."

From that day, Yussel became a frequent guest at the home of Channa and Reb Yosef. It was no surprise to anyone that within a short time Tziril Miriam announced that she and Yussel planned to be married. Tziril was triumphant, but her greatest satisfaction was in knowing that no shadchen had been involved.

An End
to Searching

Soon after their formal betrothal, Tziril Miriam Gordon and Yosef Yacov Wilkimirsky were married. The Jewish community of Kovno was taken by surprise, to think that such a rebellious and independent thinking woman, no longer very young, would find a handsome husband with good prospects for the future. And she hadn't even consulted a matchmaker!

Reb Tevya Wilkimirsky, Yussel's father, who worked as a night watchman for Frumkin, came to Kovno for the wedding, accompanied by his wife, numerous children and all his friends and relatives.

Reb Yosef and Channa were surprisingly generous, and Tziril Miriam would begin her married life in comfort, despite her earlier misgivings. She was provided with a more-than-adequate new wardrobe and household furnishings of which she could be proud. Yussel's critical female relatives were duly impressed as they inspected the array of gifts: linens, heavy copper cooking utensils, china and bedding of pure down. In addition, Reb Yosef gave them a generous gift of money with which to begin their new life. It was a small token, he told Tziril on her wedding day, of his appreciation for her devotion to him and to his children during the years she had been a member of his household. Tziril Miriam, for once at a loss for words, found it difficult to express her gratitude. But it was a proud and happy moment for her, and she knew she would not be put to shame before her new husband's family.

Their first home was a small thatched cottage near Wilki. Because of the many advantages offered to former apprentices, Yussel decided to return to work for Frumkin the contractor. Their home was one of a group which the builder had

erected to accommodate his employees when they married.
The unmarried men and apprentices occupied a group of buildings nearby, constructed in barracks fashion. The "village" was
referred to as "Frumkin's" by the people of Wilki.

Theirs was a simple but comfortable dwelling, and Tziril was
beginning to be content at last. She knew also that Yussel had
begun to feel a happiness and peace of a kind he had not known
since his mother's death. He told her he felt like "one reborn,"
and Tziril knew that nothing she would ever do or say would
change what Yussel felt for her.

But the calm of the first year was broken when Tziril unexpectedly discovered that she had an older sister — a half-sister
to be exact — who had been searching for Channa and herself
for years. She learned that her newly discovered sister's name
was Bayla, and that she lived in Kafkaz, where she and her husband were winemakers and operators of a drucke, or printing
establishment.

Channa had been notified of their sister's whereabouts by
an emissary from the great Yitzchok El Channon Yeshiva in
Kovno. This academy was famous, not only for its level of
scholarship, but also for its success in locating and reuniting
families that had been separated by the shifting boundaries of
the Pale of Settlement, and in tracing the Jews who had disappeared at the time of the exile from the Caucasus region.

Without warning, Tziril and Yussel were summoned from
Frumkin's for a conference with the emissary. As they sipped
tea in Channa's parlor, they learned that they had been the
subjects of one of the most extensive and difficult searches
undertaken by the Yeshiva.

"Your sister Bayla in Kafkaz has been trying to locate you
ever since you were small children," they were told. He showed
them the voluminous correspondence between Bayla and the
Yeshiva, which he had brought with him in order to establish
without a doubt that Channa and Tziril Miriam were the
daughters of Dvera Esther and Zalman Yitzchok Gordon.

Channa couldn't hide her skepticism; it was preposterous.
After all these years such a thing couldn't possibly be true.

"It's all a mistake!   she told the emissary. "We have no living relatives — not in Kafkaz or anywhere else. " And yet, there

was something in the back of her mind, something about a letter, which made her uneasy. But the thought was too unsettling, and she dismissed it from her mind.

But Tziril Miriam hung on the distinguished rabbi's every word. She was so overcome with joy and astonishment that she later told her husband that had it been possible, she would have departed that instant for Kafkaz. Channa had a closed mind, but she, Tziril, was convinced of the emissary's sincerity. In her heart, she knew that every word of his story was true, as though the information had emanated from a divine source. At last there would be answers to the questions that had haunted her for as long as she could remember.

The sheaves of correspondence that had accumulated in the files of the Yeshiva contained the entire history of Dvera and Zalman Yitzchok. It told of the confiscation of his vineyards, the loss of his first wife and sons, and his marriage to Dvera. The guest handed Tziril the last letter Bayla had received from their mother, written before her death.

"The letter." Channa's voice was barely a whisper. Tziril saw through her sister's attempt to hide her feelings. How could Channa have forgotten that letter? Tziril distinctly recalled that their mother had written such a letter the night before her death, and that Rosa Grodnick had once told her that in her mother's last moments of lucidity she had inquired whether there had been an answer. Poor Dvera! She had died before the letter was posted.

"Read the correspondence," the emissary told Channa. "Your sister Bayla was rejoicing in her daughter's engagement when the letter arrived. You will learn that shortly after their marriage, the young couple lost their lives in a horrible accident."

Everyone else was silent as he spoke. "At the height of her grief, Bayla remembered the unanswered letter from Dvera and its appeal for help. She was tormented by remorse as she realized that several months had gone by since its arrival. She wrote in all her letters to us that she had been punished for her neglect, and she pleaded with us to make every effort to locate Dvera and her daughters. Bayla saw the loss of her only child as divine retribution. She had written letter after letter, but received no reply. Finally she turned to us."

"But how did you ever find us?" asked Tziril.

"It took time," the emissary shrugged. "Bayla suffered and she wanted more than anything else to make amends and be forgiven. In one letter she wrote us that every day of her life she would beat her breast and cry out that she had sinned, just as though it were Yom Kippur. There would be no peace for her."

With trembling hands, Tziril Miriam gathered up the bundle of letters the emissary had left behind. Channa refused to even look at them.

"It's too late for Bayla to seek our forgiveness," she said. "You're welcome to the letters, Tziril."

Tziril found her mother's last letter and read it aloud. Tears fell down her cheeks, and even Yussel and Reb Yosef were moved as they listened, but Channa ran from the room with a snort of anger. "Who needs Bayla now? Where was she when we needed her!"

There began a correspondence between Tziril and her sister in Kafkaz. Channa would have no part of it, and ridiculed Tziril who regarded the knowledge of the existence of another sister as miraculous. Channa declared that the rabbinical emissary was an imposter, hadn't he mentioned something about a fee for all the expenses incurred by the Yeshiva? Reb Yosef had been too generous!

In every letter, Bayla urged them to visit her; she would pay for their expenses. She herself was confined to her bed much of the time and could not undertake such a long journey. She wrote to Tziril that she suffered from severe arthritis and that her body was swollen with fluid. The wealth she and her husband had accumulated over the years was of little comfort, and who but her beloved sisters would inherit it? Her only child was dead.

Channa accused Tziril of being interested in Bayla's money, and refused to read the letters which Bayla addressed to both of them. There were times when Tziril had the notion that her sister was unable to read or write, and realized she had never seen her open a book.

But Reb Yosef was different. He was always interested in a

letter from Bayla, and would ask Tziril to send her his good wishes. Yosef was actually a scholar by temperament, although his business took up most of his time, and he possessed a respectable collection of books. Once, he had purchased an expensively bound volume of a special prayer book for women, hoping his wife would appreciate such an elegant gift, but Channa and her daughters had yet to open it. Tziril was the only one who used it during Sabbath services.

❧

Tziril was now impatiently awaiting the birth of her first child. Her joy and anticipation were increased by the long sought knowledge of her parents' names, for her heart was set on naming her child after one of them. If she gave birth to a girl, she would name her Dvera Esther. Yussel, however, insisted that the first daughter be named Hinda for his mother. Yussel, who was usually so generous and accommodating, possessed a streak of stubborness that Tziril was only beginning to discover.

In due time a daughter was born, and for the sake of peace between them they called her Hinda Dvera. Yussel was sure that there would be other children. The next child, he promised, if it was a girl, would be called Esther.

Yussel Escapes

The first months after the birth of Hinda Dvera were among the happiest of Tziril Miriam's life. Yussel's future seemed hopeful, she had given birth to a healthy baby, and for the first time she had discovered an identity of her own. She was the daughter of Dvera Esther and Zalman Yitchok Gordon; no longer was she the "little orphan" or Channa's unmarried sister — the nameless aunt. She was the wife of Yussel Wilkimirsky, and the mother of their child, but most importantly, she was Tziril Miriam, an individual with a knowledge of her past and great hopes for her future.

Her happiness was marred only by Channa's refusal to acknowledge Bayla's pleas for forgiveness. Soon after Hinda Dvera's first birthday, Channa announced that she never wanted to hear Bayla's name again. She had had time to think about it; could Tziril deny that Bayla had ignored the prayers of their dying mother and their dire need?

"Only when Bayla was struck down and lost her child did she remember her duty, her responsibility. Can you deny that, Tziril? Answer me. God meant for her to be punished," Channa declared. "We don't need her now anyway. Providence watched over us, not that one who dares to call herself our sister!"

"Does she take us for fools?" Channa continued. "Who does she think she is to be able to arrange travel permits, just like that? No Jew in Russia has that kind of influence, and these days, no Jew can afford it. We'll be the laughing stock of the city!"

Yussel knew that Tziril would never let Channa override her feelings for Bayla, and his wife's obsession with her newly discovered sister worried him. He knew that had it been at all possible, Tziril would have gone to Kafkaz at once, despite her pregnancy. At first Tziril's delight in Bayla's letters had amused him, and he had been indulgent since she was in the later stages of pregnancy. But after their daughter's birth, he began to lose patience with his wife's constant chatter about her sister Bayla in Kafkaz.

"That was all so long ago. Think of what you have here. You have an infant to take care of; you have me — certainly I should mean more to you than a half-sister you have never met. There are plans to be made, plans for us to make together."

And again, Tziril was pregnant. Besides, they would soon be moving back to Kovno. Yussel had been offered a better job with one of Frumkin's competitors, and he was anxious to begin work.

Tziril was glad that they were returning to Kovno. She had missed the synagogues, yeshivas and the tree lined avenues; Kovno was home. She had also missed her sister, Reb Yosef and her young nieces and nephews. They were the only family she knew, and more than anything, she wanted her children to feel close to them.

Hinda Dvera was barely two when Tziril gave birth to her second daughter; as Yussel had promised, they called her Esther. At last Tziril had two children named for her mother. She had always felt uncomfortable that none of Channa's children had been named for their parents, and she never believed that Channa had forgotten their names.

Their new home in Kovno was located in the heart of the Jewish ghetto with its old buildings and winding streets, so reminiscent of Vilna. In order to visit Channa, it was necessary to cross a drawbridge which separated the older part of the city from the new residential area that had sprung up on the other side of the Niemen. But Tziril and Yussel were content, despite their awareness of the economic gulf that separated them from Channa's family. Yussel would tell his wife that he was still young, and by the time he had reached Reb Yosef's age, she would also be surrounded by luxuries of every description.

But their lives were not to proceed as smoothly as Yussel envisioned. Esther was only a month old when Yussel was

forced to flee Kovno for America. He left furtively in the stillness of the night when even the street lamps had been extin-
guished.

He was not the only one; many young men, married and unmarried had suddenly disappeared and it was no coincidence
that all the fugitives were Jews. In Yussel's group were his
brother Schmuel and two of his cousins. They had all been
notified that they were being drafted immediately. Suddenly,
Tziril Miriam was left alone with two infants to manage as well
as she could.

On the morning before their departure, the men awoke to
find Kovno swarming with gendarmes patrolling every street
and alley. Military posters were plastered on every available
inch of wall and lamppost. The billboards read that all men
whose names were listed were to report for immediate military
duty. All who attempted to evade the summons would be
caught and arrested.

Induction meant twenty-five years of military service, often
without leave. Nicholas the First had been responsible for this
curse of young men and boys which had suddenly caught up
with the Jews of Kovno, who had been enjoying one of the
first periods of tranquility in years. There were to be no excep-
tions; no one would be permitted to hire a substitute.

That night, Yussel, Schmuel and their cousins planned their
escape. After midnight, they met on the road leading to the
nearby Prussian border, dressed in work clothes, and without
baggage. They had barely managed in a few hours to beg and
borrow enough money to get them to the Jewish Immigration
Agency in Bremen, where they would be provided with steerage tickets for one of the steamers of the German-American
line.

They hastened along the dark roads until dawn, when they
hid in the forest and slept. After another night's journey, they
arrived at the appointed place where a farm wagon was waiting. Climbing aboard, they buried themselves under huge sacks
of grain, only to discover at least a dozen other footsore and
famished travelers like themselves.

The driver lost no time, and as the wagon sped past the border, the stillness of the night was shattered by the bullets of

the guards on both sides. The driver later told them that there really had been no danger, rifles had been fired into the air, the guards had all been bribed.

Smuggling emigrants out of Russia was a lucrative undertaking which could never have been so successful without the tacit approval of both Russia and Prussia. The owners of the German ocean liners had become enriched by the revenues provided by the wholesale emigration of Russian Jews to the American continent. Smuggling Jews across the border was actually in accordance with Russian policy. It was no secret. In this way, one third of Russia's Jews were encouraged to emigrate, while another third were converted to Russian Orthodoxy through military service and schools. The rest of them? They were left to the mercies of the *Pogromishkes* – Russia's solution to the "Jewish Problem."

11

Yussel Returns

For Tziril Miriam and her children, loneliness intensified the misery of their situation. Six months passed before Tziril received the first money-order from America. But after that, Yussel began to send money regularly. He wrote that he had become a peddler in the farmlands of New Jersey, and traveled from farmhouse to farmhouse with a pack on his back. At the close of each letter he wrote that he was saving every penny he could spare and was counting the days until he would have enough to send steerage fare for Tziril and the children.

Shortly after Esther's second birthday, without notice, Yussel came home. To Tziril's great joy and astonishment he returned along with his brother and cousins. No one had been notified of their plans, for they feared that news of their arrival would be reported to the authorities, or that informers among their own people would notify the police.

Once again, the border guards had been bribed. The men had been smuggled back into Russia in the same manner in which they had left two years earlier. Between the embraces and tears of their families, they told the story of their perilous re-entry. To the Jews of Kovno, the accounts of their escape and home-coming represented the victory of good over evil. They had been nearly penniless when they left and had returned after only two years as prosperous looking "Americans." Yussel's huge silver pocketwatch was regarded with astonishment. Gone were their long beards and payoth and they had discarded their caftans and high boots in favor of American ready-to-wear. They were almost unrecognizable even to their wives! They brought beautiful gifts, as though words alone could not tell of the good life awaiting all who were industrious and

53

unafraid of hard work. They had all taken out their first citizenship papers, for they had found America to be the *goldene medina* of their fantasies.

"It's such a big country," Yussel declared earnestly, "and desperately in need of willing hands to help it grow."

Yussel's younger brother Schmuel, was not so enthusiastic, and spoke of the difficulty of living up to the many mitzvoth, or religious commandments.

"A *treife* land," was his was of describing it. America was irreligious and not ritually fit for the Orthodox. It's good for the goyim, no doubt, but for the Jews?"

Their visit was brief, for they knew it would be impossible to keep their presence secret for very long. Besides, there was work to be done! The main purpose of their return was to make arrangements for the departure of their families.

Tziril found the idea of leaving Kovno for good disturbing, despite her loneliness in her husband's absence. Schmuel's words had alarmed her almost as much as the idea of undertaking such a hazardous journey with two small children.

"But Tziril, you'll be traveling in a group, all together," Yussel explained. "And don't pay too much attention to what Schmuel says. In America one just has to try a little harder to keep the commandments. You'll be happy there, and... the schools are free! It's no good for us to be apart. In America we'll have a good life. Finally we can be together again."

All that week, friends and relatives poured into Tziril's small dwelling. The day after Yussel's return, his father, Tevya, came from Wilki, bringing his new wife, whom his sons had yet to meet, and most of his still increasing family. The old man greeted his sons and nephews with affection, anxious to hear about the new lives they had made for themselves. Yussel was glad to see that his father was still vigorous and healthy despite his age, and noticed, with pride, that his new wife was conspicuously pregnant.

But most important, Yussel was glad to be with his wife and their two small daughters. When he had left for America, Esther had been a tiny infant sleeping in her cradle. Now she was an energetic, curly haired two year old who was beginning to talk.

Hinda Dvera never forgot how her father had played and
romped with them. How many times had he tossed them up
into the air! How she and Esther had clung to him and followed him from room to room! He would take both of them
in his arms and whirl merrily around the floor. It was almost
as though Yussel were discovering his children for the first
time, and even the four year old Hinda could sense his amazement and wonder at their growth and intelligence.

Above all, Hinda remembered her mother's happiness. Tziril,
usually so solemn and intense, was full of gaiety and mirth. It
seemed as though she never stopped laughing while, in fact,
her laughter was mingled with tears of joy. The Master of the
Universe had been good to her!

Despite the danger inherent in shouting to all their joy at
the return of their menfolk, it was impossible for Tziril and
her family to hide their good fortune from their neighbors and
friends. It was impossible to suppress the excitement they felt
at their now imminent departure for America. And more than
impossible, it was unthinkable not to have a celebration in
honor of the occasion and a large family gathering was arranged
to be held shortly before the men were to leave Kovno.

The highlight of the feast was the distribution of the gifts
they had brought – clothing and gold brooches for their wives,
each item identical so as not to arouse jealousy, and toys,
clothing and sweets for the children. The women were in a
state of rapture. Never in their lives had they expected to pos-
sess such treasures.

After the last gift had been opened and exclaimed over,
Yussel pretended to be surprised by the discovery that a very
elaborate nightgown remained to be disposed of.

"Who is it for?" demanded the women, as one by one they
were permitted to inspect the filmy garment. Who was the
lucky one? Each longed to have this amazing confection of
lace and embroidery that dangled so temptingly in front of
their eyes.

The men withdrew for a conference, as if they were decid-
ing a most weighty and solemn issue. Finally, Schmuel returned
with a verdict.

"This beautiful nightgown," he told the eager women, "is

reserved for the lucky wife who will be the first to give birth
to a son after our departure. It will be given to her to be worn
at the Bris."

Before the party broke up, Tevya made a speech. He was
proud of his sons, and only wished that his brother were alive
to share in the good fortune of his sons, Velvel and Yudel. He
spoke eloquently, but he had no words to express what was
really on his mind — that he knew for certain that once they
left Kovno this time, he would never see his sons again.

The few short days Yussel and the others could spend with
their families were soon over — someone had reported them to
the police and a warrant had been issued for their arrest. Everyone was aware of the penalty for desertion: exile for life in
Siberia, or worse. They believed, however, they were not saying goodbye for long, and though they left reluctantly, they
believed that soon their wives and children would be joining
them.

Hinda never forgot that farewell. She had been awakened
from a child's deep slumber, and had opened her sleepy eyes
to see her parents hovering above her. Her mother wept, shad-
ing the lamp she held from her tears with a cupped hand. Her
father bent over her frightened face and kissed her, all the
while mumuring endearments. "Goodbye, Hindele, my child.
Look after Mama and little Esther. You'll come to me soon, in
America, with Mama and the baby. You will come soon..."

But before she was fully awake, the light had been extin-
guished, and Hinda could hear only their footsteps retreating
in the darkness. Alone, and too frightened to cry out, she lay
in her bed, her heart pounding, while Esther slept soundly in
the crib close by. Hinda knew that her father was leaving them
again. There would be no more laughter and fun, no more
rowdy games and fond caresses. Soon her mother's solemn expression would return. Her father was leaving them; he was on
his way back to America, once again they would be alone.

Yussel's departure left Tziril unnerved and despondent.
Only after word arrived that he had escaped the net of the military police, did she relax and settle down to the daily humdrum
of her existence.

The Jews of Kovno were in an uproar — there was a traitor in their midst. Who was the enemy who had informed the police? How could anyone be so depraved that he would betray a fellow Jew for a few rubles? Yet they were certain that it was one of their own people.

Few men of military age remained in the Jewish quarters of Kovno, and those who were still there moved with extreme caution. Many were making secret plans for an immediate departure for America or other places. People began to complain that their lives were becoming more and more difficult every day, what with curfews, police surveillance, taxation and restrictive legislation of every description.

Even the devoutly orthodox were preparing to leave, although they were well aware that America was a *treife* land, where it was too easy and convenient to shed their traditions and religious observances along with their old world clothing. It was said that in America it was the rare Jew who clung to his old customs. But hopes and spirits were high, for their goal was survival, and despite its reputation for materialism and impiety, America would fill this need. It was the *goldene medina*.

Tziril, too, was busy with preparations for her departure. Although she was excited at the prospect of being with Yussel again, she had reservations about leaving, conscious of a deep disappointment and a sense of impending great loss. More than anything else, she wished it were possible to visit Bayla before she left. The longing to meet her half sister was intensified by every letter she received from Kafkaz.

Alone with her children, Tziril read and reread Bayla's letters in the weeks that followed Yussel's departure. Once she was in America, she knew that Yussel would never permit her to make the long journey to Kafkaz. Even before he had emigrated, he brushed aside her desire to see Bayla as something unattainable and even ridiculous.

"Oh, Kafkaz," he said derisively, "why, that's at the end of the earth. It would cost a fortune for you to get there and back, even if you could manage to get the necessary papers. Some misfortune would be sure to befall you. Whatever it is that you have to know, you can find out by writing a letter."

According to Yussel's instructions, they were to leave Kovno as early in the spring as possible. Tziril would travel with her sister-in-law Soreh, Velvel and Yudel's wives, and their children. All together, they would be a large group. Yussel had written that they would settle in Jersey City, just across the Hudson River from New York, a city which he said already had one of the largest Jewish populations in the world. He would meet them at Castle Garden in New York Harbor.

And now the snows were disappearing, and their preparations were near completion. Household goods, bedding, clothing had all been packed — everything that could be taken with them on the journey to their new home. Anything that would have to be left behind was sold or given to the needy.

Before their departure, Tziril and Soreh decided to take their children to bid farewell to their grandfather, Tevya in Wilki.

Reb Tevya Wilkimirsky, bearded and dressed in his long, black caftan and wide-brimmed streimel, was the town patriarch, greatly respected and loved for his compassion, geniality and wit. His house was crowded with the children and stepchildren of his three marriages, as well as the guests who were summoned when the word spread that unexpected visitors from Kovno had arrived.

With tears in his eyes, Tevya blessed his daughters-in-law and grandchildren. Tziril's heart ached to think that she might never see this old man again. He had been like the father she had never known.

On their last Sabbath in Kovno, Tziril attended services at the synagogue where she had worshipped since she had moved to Kovno at the age of eight. America, for all its wealth and greatness, had nothing to compare with the synagogues and yeshivoth of this town. Tziril was sure that there were no famed scholars and learned rabbis in Jersey City

She would miss the rabbi of her old schul; she would never forget all he had done for her in the years she had known him. When she had been a lonely orphan he had given her solace. Once, during the weeks before the Days of Awe, when everyone flocked to the cemeteries to visit the graves of their parents and grandparents, she had come to him in despair because she did not know where her parents were buried.

"What does one do?" she had demanded. "What can one do when one cannot pray at a parent's grave?"

He had looked at her with eyes that shared her suffering. Such a solemn child! What could he say that would ease her heartache, that would satisfy her longings?

"Take your troubles, little daughter," he had said, "to the tomb of the Tzaddik of Lodz. He is buried here in Kovno. You will find peace and consolation there. People from all over the world make pilgrimages to the grave of the martyred holy man — they come from everywhere. Alas, in these times you are not the only one who does not know where a parent is buried."

On the day before she was to leave, Tziril visited the grave of the Tzaddik of Lodz once more, this time with her children. But she could find no peace. She should be the happiest woman on earth, she admonished herself. She would soon be reunited with her husband, who waited for her with open arms. But instead, she was filled with a melancholy that was almost overwhelming.

With a small daughter clinging to each hand, she left the cemetery, aching with emptiness.

Departure Deferred

In the final hours before Tziril's scheduled departure, a throng of friends and neighbors gathered in front of her house. Channa and Reb Yosef arrived bringing farewell gifts and candy for the children. Channa embraced her sister, and in a voice husky with emotion, assured her that she would miss her tremendously.

Her sister's warmth surprised Tziril. She could hardly believe that Channa would really miss her — Channa with her lively household and all the obligations of a rich man's wife. But she was deeply touched, and returned Channa's embrace with feeling.

One by one, Tziril kissed her nieces and nephews. They wished their aunt a safe journey, and Nathan and Feigele especially, remembered all she had done for them when they were small. Hadn't she tended to their needs, fed, bathed and comforted them during their early years? Nathan still remembered those long afternoons when Tziril patiently tutored him, until even the critical melamed had been satisfied with his progress.

Tziril was in tears as she looked at their young faces for what might be the last time. The sight of her nephews was almost more than she could bear. They were such tall and handsome young men, with their broad shoulders and dark hair. With more than a touch of pride, she imagined that in his youth, her father must have resembled these handsome grandsons whom he had never lived to see. They certainly looked nothing like their own father.

After weeks of frenzied activity, everything was in readiness for the journey. Barrels and bundles of Tziril's treasured possessions were heaped in the narrow street — her bedding, her dishes, clothing and portraits, and her prayer books, thumb-worn and stained with tears. Her Siddur and Yiddish Bible commentary had been her faithful companions for years and had brought her courage in unhappy hours; she would not be without them during the long voyage ahead. She had packed enough black bread and salt herring to sustain herself and the children in the steerage of a Hamburg-American Line steamer.

She piled her belongings on the wagon that would convey the party to the border, and at last they were ready to depart; she climbed aboard with her daughters. The wagon was filled to more than capacity with people and baggage, and there was literally not a fraction of an inch to spare. Hinda, Esther and their young cousins squirmed with excitement; even the tearful Channa was caught up in the event.

But something was wrong. One look at the panic-stricken faces of the women and children jumbled in the wagon, and the crowd began to whisper among themselves. What had happened? How? In seconds, Tziril Miriam had collapsed into a crumpled heap before their eyes.

"Oh my God! She's bleeding!" cried her sister-in-law, Soreh. Tziril began to moan with pain.

"A miscarriage! Tziril is having a miscarriage!" one told the other — she was in no condition to travel.

"But us — what about us?" demanded Velvel's wife, Soreh Ruchel. "We've waited long enough, and now this has to happen! Why didn't she tell us before? My God!"

Channa ordered Nathan to run for the midwife. Tziril was carried into her empty house with her wailing children close behind. The huddle of women at her bedside were sure this was the result of the excitement and strain of the weeks of packing and preparation. Not even Channa had suspected that Tziril was pregnant. Tziril Miriam, everyone whispered, had always been secretive. Nobody dared venture a guess about what she was thinking.

The midwife arrived as Tziril's belongings were carried back into the house. One by one those who were about to leave wished her a speedy recovery and hastened back to the wagon. Soreh was the last to go. Sympathetically she wiped away the great beads of perspiration that shone on Tziril's forehead.

The midwife began her ministrations, while Hinda and little Esther watched at her side. They finally had stopped crying, at least.

Soreh murmured words of comfort. Tziril was not to worry. What had happened was the Divine Will – this she knew in her heart. And more than anything else, she knew that Tziril was no more eager to go to America, the treife land, than she was. Clearly, the Rabbono Shel Olom had intervened; the way of the Master of the Universe was inscrutable, and Tziril must accept His will.

"Poor Yussel in America," she whispered to Channa, as she left the room. "That poor man! What will he do when he finds out that everybody has arrived safely except his own wife and children."

Until Tziril recovered, Channa came every day to care for her and the children, and if she was too busy, she sent one of her daughters. Channa's eldest daughter, Feigele, was Tziril's favorite niece. Feigele was tall, with her mother's dark beauty, but had the gentle voice and manner reminiscent of her father. Tziril was not very fond of her other nieces, whom she considered frivolous and spoiled. But Feigele, she noted, had not inherited her mother's obsession with finery and adornment.

She grieved for her unborn child, but continued to insist that she had been unaware that she was pregnant. She had been worn out, what with her husband's hasty departure with the military police one step behind him, and in the weeks that followed, with the hectic preparations for the journey.

No wonder she had miscarried! No one had helped her in the packing, and she had two small, active children to care for, besides. The only one who had shown any concern for her plight was her neighbor, the Shabbos goy, a gentile woman who assisted her on the Sabbath with the tasks she was forbidden to perform on the day of rest.

She was grudgingly grateful for Channa's help, but to Hinda and Esther, their aunt's presence was a delight. The Muma Channa, as they called her, never came empty handed, but always brought them gifts and delicacies. They adored her, which gave Channa immense pleasure, for she reveled in admiration of any kind, even that of her young nieces. No matter what hour of the day she arrived, she was a figure of elegance. Hinda would finger the heavy silk fringe of her paisley shawl, while Esther would play with her gold watch chain, as though in a trance.

But within a week or two, Tziril was on her feet, though she was still a bit weak and had grown considerably thinner. She was actually relieved when Channa's visits ended. She didn't need her sister who made such a show of her concern, when she had such a kind neighbor.

In the first letter which she wrote to Yussel after her miscarriage, Tziril told him she had no plans for the present. She was too exhausted to make any major decisions, and any effort at all was beyond her strength. She had unpacked all her belongings and some of her furniture had been returned. The thought of beginning again with packing and arrangements was staggering. She begged Yussel to be patient with her.

She couldn't forget Soreh's parting words, and like her sister-in-law, Tziril had a deep seated belief in signs and portents. Had her miscarriage been an omen? Could it be that the Master of the Universe hadn't intended for her to go to America after all? It was a land so far from the center of Yiddishkeit, so distant from the teachings of the Torah. She would have to think about it. Perhaps it was the Divine Will that she and her children would remain in Kovno.

The spring and summer passed quickly. Yussel sent money regularly, and each draft was accompanied by a long letter. He wrote of his loneliness and his love, but that he would be patient. He knew that she would do what was right for her, in any event. But she did have to know that their landsleit and the entire family could not understand why she procrastinated so long. They were all critical, he wrote, especially Velvel's wife, Soreh Ruchel, and his cousin Etta Teresa.

That summer she saw Channa infrequently, and the times they did visit were not pleasant. To Tziril's annoyance, Channa pried, and insisted that Tziril was keeping something from her. There had to be a motive for her irrational reluctance to leave Kovno, Channa said. Although she never accused Tziril in so many words, her implication was clear. She was alluding to Bayla, and to the correspondence that continued between the two sisters. Channa suspected that Bayla had influenced Tziril's decision to put off her departure for America indefinitely.

"But there's nothing to keep you here!" Channa charged. "How can you live in this hovel?" She glanced scornfully at the bare and carpetless room.

"Yussel writes that he is doing well and could provide a fine home for you. Why don't you pack and go? Besides, how long do you think a man is going to wait? Admit it — you're a fool!"

Despite her nagging, Channa was worried about Tziril, who was pale and tired and listless. Even the children had changed. They had always been alert and mischievous, now they seemed wan and neglected, as though their mother was too preoccupied with her own troubles to notice their lassitude and loss of appetite.

One night, Channa told Reb Yosef there was nothing more she could do for Tziril, who was as stubborn as ever and would not listen to anyone's advice.

Once again, it was winter. The snow seemed to fall endlessly. The windows rattled with the pounding of the Arctic winds. It would be days, thought Tziril, before a path could be cleared to her door.

Her thoughts wandered frequently to Channa, warm and comfortable, with servants to attend to her needs. Of course, Channa had no thoughts to spare for her, alone with her children on the opposite bank of the frozen Nieman. Channa had given her a roof over her head, but she, Tziril, had worked for her like a slave. The truth was that she owed her sister nothing. Hadn't she cared for Channa's children, and even assisted them with their studies? She recalled the hours she had labored in Channa's kitchen, no better than a maid. There had been times when Channa had been without any other household help, and who but the orphan sister had to do all the heavy work?

The Shabbos Goy, her neighbor was kinder to her than her own sister. What would she have done without Katerina?

Bundled in her heavy shawl and high boots, Katerina went to the marketplace for provisions. She never left their house without asking Tziril, "Panya, what can I bring you?" If it hadn't been for Katerina, they would have been hungry and cold on more than one occasion. She would bring in the firewood and start the stove when the flames had died down. With the kitchen warm, she would sit with them; she would tell stories and knit, for her hands were never idle.

She taught Hinda to knit. "A girl is never too young to learn," she would say. "Your hands should never be idle." Hinda was a good pupil. One afternoon, she asked Katerina to teach her how to knit stockings.

"Stockings? Already?" Katerina was surprised. "For the Papa in America?"

Hinda dropped her knitting needles and ran to the window. She began to scratch the frost away until she uncovered a small peephole.

"Look!" she cried. "They're still out there. Mama, come and see! The ketzelach! Look at the poor baby kittens; they're so cold."

Tziril and Katerina exchanged an amused glance. Through the small aperture in the frosted glass they saw a pair of half frozen kittens, nearly buried in the snow. They were scrambling about frantically as they scrounged for the food which was usually left for them beneath the windowsill. Their piteous meows were heard above the rattle of the windowpane.

"I want to knit stockings for the ketzelach," Hinda said, as she came back to the stove.

Tziril looked at her daughter fondly and laughed. What has happened to me, she thought. This is the first time in weeks that I've laughed or even smiled.

"Tonight I'll write the *Tateh*," she said. "I'll tell him that his Hindele, God should reward her for her good heart, has learned to knit. I'll write him that she is knitting stockings for the ketzelach outside in the snow." She laughed as she imagined Yussel's reaction.

That winter, Hinda also learned to read and write, and her mother proved to be an exacting and patient teacher. Tziril began to drill her children in the morning and evening prayers which they recited together daily. Hinda learned rapidly, and her memory was faultless. Tziril wrote Yussel that before long he would be receiving letters from his daughter. As time passed, Hinda studied eagerly, and would try to teach Esther everything she had learned.

❧

Before that winter ended, Tziril received an urgent summons from her father-in-law in Wilki. Yussel's brother Herschel, who had been conscripted as a boy of thirteen, had been discharged from the army and was coming home after an absence of nearly twenty years. Due to his poor health, he had been exempted from serving the full term of twenty-five years. There was to be a family reunion in honor of his homecoming. Tziril was urged to come to Wilki at once, since the guest of honor was not planning to remain there long, but would soon be joining his brothers in America. This would probably be Tziril's only chance to meet him.

She read and reread the letter. She sensed something strange about the way it was written, and knew that Tevya was hiding something. Herschel, she believed, was dying, if not already dead, and she was being summoned so that her father-in-law could tell her the story himself, since it was dangerous to mention such things in a letter. Herschel's death was not going to be reported to the authorities.

She knew that deaths, like births, were never registered, if at all possible. Tziril was certain that one of Yussel's brothers was going to assume the identity of the dying soldier and would then be able to live in Russia without fear of conscription.

Her intuition proved correct. When she visited Reb Tevya in the spring, she was told, in strictest confidence, that there had, indeed, been a death in the family. Herschel Wilkimirsky had returned a broken man, whose physical and emotional health had been shattered by the years he had served in the army of Imperial Russia. He had been sent home to die in despair among his people.

It was no surprise when she learned that Schmuel and Soreh planned to return to Wilki with their children, and that Schmuel would assume the name and identity of his dead brother. Soreh had been extremely unhappy in America, for she had found it impossible to live there as an Orthodox Jew. The idea of trying to adjust to her new life was abhorrent to her, and she had sworn to her husband that she would rather die than live and raise her children in such an irreligious atmosphere.

13

A Visit to Vilna

Despite Yussel's continued pleas, Tziril was still in Kovno, even though more than a year had lapsed since her miscarriage. Her husband wrote that he was prospering, that he no longer peddled among the farmers with a pack on his back, but was employed by a building contractor in Jersey City, and was earning a good wage installing plate-glass windows. Yussel could see no reason why she shouldn't join him immediately, and even he had to admit his patience was wearing thin.

Tziril knew that she could no longer put off telling him that her heart was set on visiting Bayla before she finally left for America. She would have to be frank with him, and her honesty would be the proof of her love. They had already been separated for so long that if he really loved her, it would make no difference.

Never again would she have such an opportunity, she wrote, to visit the land where her father was born. Bayla was getting old and was in poor health — this might be the only chance she would ever have to meet her. True, it would be a costly undertaking, but Bayla promised to defray all the expenses for the children and herself. They would travel in the kind of comfort which only people of means were accustomed to enjoy. All that Bayla desired was that they be her guests, even if only for a few days. At the close of her letter, Tziril added that as yet she had not informed Channa of her plans, since she knew that her sister would voice her usual objections.

Bayla's letters had also revived the suppressed memories of her childhood in Vilna. Of late, she had been haunted by voices and images she had thought were long since buried in the past. Tziril began to wonder whether any of the people who had

known her as a child were still alive. She could vividly recall
Rosa Grodnick and Reb Isaac the Scribe. She could still picture Rosa with her prayer book, and the aged scholar in his
dim basement room piled with books and yellowed manuscripts. If only she could tell them everything that had happened to her in the years that had slipped by; if only she could
show them her two bright and well brought up daughters!

What a miracle it would be if someone could locate her
mother's grave in one of Vilna's old cemeteries. She knew for
certain that her mother was buried somewhere in the city, and
the Chevra Kadisha, or Burial Society, ought to have the records. More than anything else, she wished to visit her mother's
grave, The final resting place of her father was another story.
Not even Bayla herself could tell her that.

Bayla had recently sent her the names and addresses of some
old family friends in Vilna. It was possible that some of them,
or perhaps their children, still made their homes in the old
Jewish quarter. Surely she could find someone there who could
help her.

It was due to no sudden impulse, then, that Tziril finally decided to spend a day in Vilna. She arranged to leave Esther
with her neighbor Katerina, and take Hinda along for the train
ride. It would have to be an overnight journey, since the train
schedule made it impossible to return to Kovno the same day.

Anticipating what Channa's reaction would be, Tziril made
no mention of her plans. Her sister would disapprove, as always.
Also, Channa had endlessly expressed her conviction that a
mother's place was with her children, and under no circumstances were they to be entrusted to strangers, even for a day.

In later years, Tziril and her daughter Hinda would often
relive that visit to Vilna and brood over its significance, as
though fate had decreed that they would leave Kovno on that
particular day.

From the start, the excursion was a disappointment, as
they wandered from house to house inquiring about the old
friends and acquaintances whom Tziril sought. At last they
reached the narrow street in the old Jewish quarter where
Tziril had lived as a child. But not one person they encountered
had ever heard of Rosa Grodnick or old Reb Isaac. And as for

Dvera Gordon and her husband Zalman Yitzchok, the only responses Tziril received were blank stares and the deep sighs of women who told her that they themselves had no idea of the whereabouts of many of their own relatives, and all had resigned themselves to the dislocation and separation of their families.

In years to come, Tziril could never satisfactorily explain to her daughter Hinda what the real object of her visit had been, for had it been old friends she had been seeking, she would have returned to Vilna years before. To Tziril's way of thinking, a day's journey by train was an inconsequential detail.

After they had made the rounds of all the synagogues in the area, Hinda began to complain that her feet were sore and that she was tired and thirsty. Tziril realized that the child was exhausted and that she could probably cover more ground alone. Returning to the railway station, she settled Hinda on a bench with a bag of food they had brought, and warned her not to wander. She would return before long, and they would spend the night together in the station before their return to Kovno in the morning. There were many things her mother still had to do — Tziril had wanted to visit some more cemeteries and speak to the caretakers, and Hinda was already worn out.

But soon after her mother's departure, she became frightened. It seemed as though hours had passed, and she became certain that her mother would never return. It grew dark, and the waiting room was chilly. What would she do? She had no money, and no idea which train would take her back to Kovno. People came and went; they were all in such a hurry and didn't even notice her. Trains pulled into the station, picked up and discharged passengers. She was surrounded by bustle and confusion. And still there was no sign of her mother. Finally, she began to weep, the loud, frightened sobs of a child filled with the dread of uncertainty.

Heads began to turn. Until now, nobody had been aware of the small child seated on the bench clutching a bag of bread and butter. Suddenly, she was surrounded by a curious and sympathetic throng. Who could not notice a little girl who wept so piteously, who was so alone?

"Little girl, what's wrong? Why are you crying? Who are you? Where is your mother? Where do you live?" The questions came in rapid Yiddish.

Between sobs, Hinda explained that she was waiting for her mother. She was out looking for the mishpocha. She, Hinda, had been waiting for hours and hours, and she knew that her mother was dead and would never return.

The crowd shook their heads, certain that here was an orphan or an abandoned child.

"But you must have a name? A family? A grandfather?"

"Yes, a grandfather," Hinda repeated, nodding her head. "He was a great man." She suddenly remembered that her mother had often told her that if she ever found herself alone in a strange city where there were Jews, all she had to do was to announce that she was the granddaughter of the celebrated musician Itzele Metter, and people would rush to her aid. It was no small matter to be his grandchild. Tziril had assured her that everyone would know who she was and would treat her accordingly.

"My grandfather — he was Itzele Metter," she announced. Her sobs quieted, and she wiped her nose on her sleeve.

"Itzele Metter?" repeated a beshawled, wrinkled old woman to the elderly man beside her. "It just couldn't be. Itzele Metter's grandchild?"

Itzele Metter had been dead for years, though no one quite knew the circumstances of his death. And hadn't there been a pretty young wife? But of course they had heard of him, even those too young to have heard him play the violin. After all, who wouldn't remember such a man?

Hinda turned to see her mother approaching, looking tired and disappointed, even at a distance. Tziril didn't notice her daughter until Hinda called out to her. She had had no success at all, and one disappointment had followed another. The sexton of the last cemetery had had two funerals that day, and had had no time for her. She hadn't even been able to discover which cemetery her mother had been buried in. There was nothing in the records, the Burial Society had told her.

But who were these people? She had warned her daughter not to talk to strangers. One never knew the sort of people a little girl could encounter in a train station.

As she approached Hinda, there was no time for scolding. The crowd pounced on her, plying her with innumerable questions. They extended offers of assistance, and the elderly couple, learning that Tziril was planning to return to Kovno the following day, offered her the hospitality of their home. It was unthinkable that she and her daughter should spend the night on a bench in the station.

The crowd began to disperse. A gray bearded man told her that Itzele Metter had played at his wedding.

"There'll never be another like him," he said. "He came to Vilna at a time of great sorrow and distress for the Jews and he relieved our suffering, if only for an hour. People will never forget him."

"You see, my child, people still remember your grandfather," she told Hinda as they boarded the train the next morning. The trip had been a success after all. She couldn't wait to tell Channa; after all these years it would be a pleasure to prove that her sister had been mistaken all along.

Mother and daughter sat in silence on the trip home. Tziril had too much to think about. All the blank stares she had met with! Nobody had shown any concern at all; they had brushed her aside as though she were a fool. And then that incredible incident at the station! She gloated as she remembered the amazement of the crowd when they learned that she was Itzele Metter's daughter.

But from the moment she and Hinda reached their home, the events of the two days were forgotten. Katerina was waiting for them at the doorstep. Even from a distance they could see that she was wringing her hands in distress. As they approached, they could see that her hair was disheveled, her face was flushed with anxiety.

"Panya! Oh Panya Tziril!" the woman shrieked. "Esther! Little Esther is sick. I swear to you, by the Holy Virgin, yesterday she was fine. She laughed and played. She went with me to the market. She went with me to church. She was happy as a bird. But then last night..."

Tziril's heart began to pound.

"Esther wouldn't stop crying. She couldn't sleep. What could I do? Thank God you are home!"

Ignoring Katerina's attempts to explain, Tziril ran into the bedroom. The curtains were drawn, and in the dimness her eyes could barely focus on the inert form of her child. Esther lay there motionless, her face swollen and covered with ugly red blotches. The child was burning with fever.

"Estherel. Little one. It's me. Mama. Esther, look at me!" Tziril's whisper became a frightened sob. There was no response from the sick child.

Katerina approached cautiously. At the sound of her footsteps, Tziril lost her composure.

"What happened to my child — I left a healthy little girl!" she wailed. "What did you do to her? How could you let this happen? What kind of curse struck her down?"

Tziril grabbed Katerina by the shoulders and shook her violently.

"Why didn't you send for the doctor? Imbecile that you are! Ignorant peasant! How can you stand there doing nothing? Go! Get the doctor! Run!"

She pushed her to the door.

"I'm going, Panya! I'm going!" Katerina ran from the house, forgetting her cloak in her haste and fright. Hinda tore after her, shouting that she was going to fetch the Muma Channa. The Muma Channa would help them; she always knew what to do.

Later, Katerina reported to her friends that the Panya Tziril had been like one struck mad.

"I almost fainted in terror," she told them. "I even feared for my life."

Hinda ran breathlessly toward her aunt's home on the opposite side of the Niemen. In her haste she failed to notice that the drawbridge was open to permit the passage of a large steamer.

"Little girl! Get back!" the crowd on the dock called after her. Hinda was stunned by her narrow escape. "The bridge is open — what's the matter with you anyway?" they hooted.

Channa came at once, while her husband stopped to summon their physician. But their efforts were in vain. That night, the four year old child was seized with violent convulsions, and despite the ministrations of the physician who remained at her side, her condition grew steadily more serious.

In a last desperate attempt to save Esther's life, Tziril went to the synagogue with Reb Yosef. Though it was well after midnight, the rabbi was summoned. They opened the ark containing the holy scrolls, and special prayers were recited for the child's recovery. But there was to be no mercy, and by daybreak Esther was dead.

Tziril was beyond consolation. All during Shiva, the week of intensive mourning, she could only question why the Master of the Universe had seen fit to mete out such a terrible punishment. What had she done that had offended Him?

She could not forget her sister's reproaches the night they had watched over the dying child. Channa had been right! She should never have left her daughter with a stranger, no matter who it was.

Of course, the insensitivity of the well meaning visitors did not help matters. All sorts of rumors spread about Esther's sudden illness and death. The well dressed matrons of the synagogue told her that Katerina had taken her daughter to church, and that she had had the audacity to boast to all the neighbors that the priest had sprinkled the Jewish child with holy water. He had even allowed her to swallow the Host.

Tziril apologized to Katerina as soon as she realized the enormity of her accusations. If guilt were to be charged, she, the mother, would be the one to be judged. Worst of all, she must write to Yussel and tell him of their loss.

Yet, in a sense, the week of Shiva was a diversion. Tziril's small home was crowded with people from early morning to late at night. The well meaning guests brought delicacies to tempt her palate, and expressed their endless clucking sympathy, as though that were sufficient to assuage her grief.

The moment she was left alone, her thoughts wandered from her dead daughter to her husband, whom she had not seen for almost two years. Things might have been different, she thought bitterly, if Yussel had not been forced to flee to America. If one thought about it long enough, it might have been the Czar himself who had been the cause of Esther's death. The inhumane ruler who separated parents from children, husbands from wives...

There were moments when she actually believed that the Angel of Death, the dreaded Moloch Hamoves she had feared since childhood, had always been hovering over her healthy and innocent children. And the minute her back was turned, this malevolent ruler of the Underworld had snatched her Esther and made her his own.

How else could she understand her child's mysterious death? How else could she accept its finality?

Rabbinic law prohibited mourning after thirty days. The old rabbi who had officiated at Tziril's wedding, reminded her that life was for the living. She had another child to think of. Sternly, but with compassion, he told her that it was her duty as a mother to shake off her depression.

"To continue to mourn is the road to madness. It leads to the pit from which there is no returning. So taught our sages, men versed in the holy law."

She took his admonition to heart. She tried to believe that the Almighty One had a reason for everything. There was no course other than to accept His judgment.

Reb Yosef wrote to Yussel the day after the funeral. On the first day after the end of Shiva, Tziril determined to write to him also. She would omit nothing. It was not an easy letter to write, and as she wrote it she couldn't forget that Channa had warned her that Yussel would never forgive her if the child failed to recover. Channa had said many cruel things that night, and each word had gone like a knife stab to Tziril's heart.

There were other thoughts, too, that terrified her. What if Yussel, on an impulse, decided to return to comfort her? Surely he would be arrested, and perhaps even shot as a deserter. She warned him that their house was under constant watch, since the police expected him to return to his family as soon as he learned of Esther's death. She pleaded with him not to take undue risks. The police had boasted that though he had escaped their net twice, the third time they were certain to succeed. And finally, as though it were only an afterthought, she reminded him that he had yet to answer the last letter she had written, in which she sought his permission to visit Bayla.

It seemed as though years had elapsed since that letter.

14

Yussel's Reply

Just when it was beginning to seem to Tziril that years had gone by since she had written to her husband, a letter arrived. Under the circumstances, she had not expected that he could write anything so full of compassion and understanding. Though he grieved deeply at the loss of their child, he held her blameless, and felt no bitterness toward her.

"Why couldn't I have been there," he wrote, "to comfort you, my dearest Tziril?"

As for her earlier plea for permission to visit Bayla, he wrote that he neither approved nor disapproved. Until now, he had never believed that a trip to Kafkaz was possible, but since Bayla had offered to bear the cost, Tziril would have to make her own decision.

"For all I know," he wrote, "by this time you have received all your travel permits and bought your ticket. If it will make you happy, and if your heart is set on it, all I can do is tell you to try and make your visit as brief as possible. Did you ever think I could dissuade you from accomplishing anything you thought was right? All I ask is that you remember that you are my wife and that your place is with me. We have been apart too long." Even after the long months of separation, he still signed his letters, "Your Yussel."

Tziril's first impulse was to show this letter to Channa. She would prove to her sister that Yussel still loved her, and did not hold her responsible for Esther's death. Yet the memory of Channa's reproaches on that terrible night was enough to restrain her, and she could not bring herself to announce her impending journey.

Channa never seemed to understand the forces behind her

sister's curiosity about her parents and family. Tziril's trip to Vilna had aroused all sorts of suspicions, and after Esther's death, Tziril had not been able to face Channa's interrogation. In truth, the only one who had ever been sympathetic was Yussel. He had finally realized that there would never be peace in her heart until she visited Bayla and learned all there was to know about her family. Yussel understood how she yearned to find her roots.

⁂

Lately, meal time with Hinda became an ordeal. The child refused to eat, or sat for hours toying with her food and fidgeting in her chair. One evening Tziril noticed how pale and thin Hinda had become and could suppress her anxiety no longer.

"Eat!" she demanded, her voice sharp, despite her concern. "It's a sin to waste food!"

Hinda began to weep. "I'm not hungry, Mama." Hinda missed little Esther, and mealtimes reminded her of the fun they had had together. Later, at bedtime, she began to cry again. She and her little sister had always said their prayers together and whispered in the darkness until they fell asleep.

"Now I've got nobody." Hinda's eyes were red. "Only you, Mama, and you're always crying and writing letters to the Muma in Kafkaz. The Tateh is far away in America. I'm all alone."

Tziril tried to comfort her, but her sobs could not be stilled.

"But Mama, the thirty days are over, and still we're mourning. And we don't visit Muma Channa anymore. We used to go to her house every Friday night for Shabbos. I miss my cousins."

There was no simple way for Tziril to explain her estrangement from her sister. Of course the child missed the close companionship of the only relatives she knew, and the warmth and luxury of the Muma Channa's Sabbath table. On Friday nights, the Vetter Yosef chanted the Kiddush over the wine and would refill the silver goblet and pass it around the table. Each of the children would repeat the blessing, take a sip and pass the cup along. This ceremony had been the highlight of Hinda's week. After dinner, she played with her cousins, while sweets and delicacies were served to the family and guests.

"It's so lonely here," she repeated. "With only the two of us, what kind of Shabbos is it? Please, Mama. Let's go to the Muma Channa's this week."

"All right. We'll go. Now stop crying. Yes, I promise."

The next morning there was a sharp rap on Tziril's door. Expecting to meet the stern face of a policeman inquiring about her husband, she was not only relieved, but overjoyed to see a young messenger from the local post district. The boy handed her a notice bearing an official-looking stamp, which requested her immediate appearance at the post office. Her papers had arrived! There was registered mail from Bayla waiting for her which could not be delivered without the proper signatures and notarization. She would have to bring along several documents to establish her identity, and would also have to bring a reputable witness to guarantee her signature. As she dispatched Hinda to summon Reb Yosef, Tziril could hardly contain her excitement. Early that afternoon, her brother-in-law returned with Hinda, and he accompanied her to the post office where he witnessed her signature and made sure all was in order.

She was speechless with happiness and surprise as she left the post office with a bulky paper parcel under her arm. She could not believe that she actually possessed the documents and credentials that would permit her to make the long journey to Kafkaz — her travel permit, itinerary, transport vouchers, visas for both Hinda and herself. Each document bore a conspicuous government seal. And in addition to these official papers, Bayla had sent a draft on a Kovno bank for "incidental expenses," in an amount exceeding Tziril's wildest hopes. She had not seen such a large money-order since her girlhood in the house of Reb Yosef!

Before evening, the news had spread that Tziril Miriam Wilkimirsky, a Jewess and the wife of a "deserter" had managed to procure a visa and a permit to travel beyond the Jewish Pale of Settlement.

To the inhabitants of the old Jewish Quarter, this was a startling turn of affairs. The law was strict; there were stringent prohibitions against Jews traveling outside the restricted area without official sanction. Were times getting better? Could it be that regulations were loosening? Perhaps a better day was approaching.

Now they recalled the rumors that had spread about the Wilkimirskys before Hinda's birth. Hadn't Tziril and her sister Channa, wife of the wealthy Yosef Rosenblum, met with the representatives of the Yitzchok El Channon Yeshiva? Some remembered talk of another sister who had been searching for them for years.

And Tziril was actually going to Kafkaz for a visit. Friends and neighbors had only to look at her face to discover her good fortune. She'd travel in style to the land of the Tartars and Cossacks, a mysterious fairy tale kingdom from which the Jews had once been expelled. Yet there were few who envied her. It would be far better, they thought, if she were to take the money and join her husband in America.

As Reb Yosef left Tziril's house after he had escorted her home, he chided her for her long absence from his home.

"You are part of our family," he said. "Never forget that." He made her promise to spend next Sabbath with them, as she had done in the past. Tziril could only make excuses for her reluctance to face her sister.

"I know. I know. Nathan came to see me last week. I told him my heart was too heavy, and that my sad face would spoil your Sabbath. I thought it better not to come. But I promise. This week. Give my greetings to Channa." There was a trace of uneasiness in her voice.

As he departed, Tziril almost regretted the fact that he had witnessed her signature. Of course, that had been unavoidable, but she would have liked to have kept Bayla's generosity a secret. One of the many things Channa had accused her of being "secretive" about was the state of her finances.

Since her marriage to Yussel, frugality had become a way of life. She had even managed to save a small sum out of the modest allowance her husband sent her each month. She did not begrudge the money-order that went to his father with the same regularity. But now there was money for everything she needed, and more. She and Hinda would travel first class, and Bayla had itemized all their other needs: gratuities for officials, tips for porters, and even a new wardrobe for the journey. There was a generous sum allotted for emergencies, which Tziril found especially reassuring.

As they sat at the long table in Channa's dining room that Sabbath Eve, Tziril realized how long it had been since she had seen her daughter so happy. She had to admit that it was a pleasant change to sit at a table sparkling with crystal goblets and fine china. Nor could she remember a time when she had been the center of as much attention as she received that night. The questions came from all sides. Surprisingly, Channa's children were very curious about their previously unheard-of aunt, although it did not seem strange to Tziril that Channa had never mentioned Bayla to them. But Channa finally put an end to their exclamations and eager inquiries; she had too many questions to ask Tziril herself, none of which really pertained to her sister's approaching journey.

Channa's disapproval was obvious, as she asked how Yussel was doing in America. It couldn't have been more plain, and more than once Reb Yosef felt obliged to cough in embarrassment.

"But Tziril," came her customary reply, " your duty is not to Bayla and her bad conscience, but to your neglected husband." She smiled virtuously.

After the Sabbath, Tziril began her final preparations for her journey. She felt certain that she would never again return to Kovno; she would go directly to America as soon as she left Kafkaz. So bitter were her feelings toward Channa, that she contemplated leaving without bidding her farewell.

Once again, she disposed of her household goods, giving even her personal belongings to the poor. A few especially cherished items were to be stored in a trunk which Channa would keep for her. After her visit with Bayla, she would go directly to America, and Channa could have the trunk sent there. As her final step, she decided to have new traveling outfits made for Hinda and herself.

For once, she would have the best that money could buy. More than anything else, she wanted to introduce herself to Bayla looking well dressed and prosperous, and not like the proverbial "poor relation." It seemed to her that for as long as she could remember, everything she and Hinda had worn had belonged to Channa or her daughters. Now she would show her sister! Never again would she wear Channa's cast-offs, no matter how good and serviceable they were.

Mutual acquaintances brought word of Tziril's activities to Channa. They told her that her sister had bought a velvet bonnet with an ostrich plume – Tziril, who never in her life had worn a bonnet. Rostow, the most fashionable ladies' dressmaker in Kovno, was making her a cloak of bright blue wool.

Channa listened impassively. "Why shouldn't she?" was her only response.

"My sister, you know, can't go on a journey like that looking like a pauper. She's had her share of troubles, and if her luck has changed for the better, we shouldn't begrudge her that much." Actually, Channa was quite annoyed that Tziril had become the center of so much attention, especially from the prosperous matrons of her own circle.

Hinda was eager to show her new clothes to her aunt and cousins, but Tziril told her that they had no more time for visits. Ever since her last visit to Channa, she had been brooding about their relationship, and if anything, her resentment had grown more intense. She was obsessed by the belief that Channa resented any good fortune that came her way. Tziril believed Channa wanted her to be indebted to her for everything, even her own husband and child. For this reason, she had always suspected that Channa was jealous of her relationship with Bayla and their long correspondence.

But in her heart, Tziril knew that she could never leave Kovno without saying goodbye. Despite their frequent quarrels, she would miss Channa, and Reb Yosef had always treated her kindly. She felt especially close to Channa's children, whom she had helped raise. She loved them almost as though they were her own.

Channa was not surprised at their unheralded appearance on the day before their departure. Her welcome, however, was not cordial. Even Hinda could sense that her aunt was angry.

Channa pointed out that it was Tuesday, as if to remind Tziril that Tuesday was especially inconvenient for her; it was the day the seamstress came. She never received visitors on

Tuesday. Channa quickly appraised their new outfits but made no compliments.

The smile of expectancy left Hinda's face. She had been expecting her aunt to admire her new coat and hat. Channa didn't even seem to notice her new red kid shoes, and the cousins just stared. Reizel, Channa's second daughter, remarked that the Muma Tziril's bonnet was very stylish and must have been expensive, but her sisters Feigele and Sheindel remained silent.

"We've come to say goodbye," Tziril remarked flatly. "We leave tomorrow. I'm sending over a trunk for you to keep for me. The droshky will call for us and take us to the railroad station."

Channa's expression had never been more stolid. "Have a good trip," she said. "Go in good health. I hope you know what you are doing. I hope you are not going to regret..."

"Regret!" Tziril was livid. "Regret? It's you who should regret! Just remember this, Channa. It is because of you that I am going to Kafkaz. It's like making a final visit to the graves of my parents! That is why I must go!"

And then there was much more. Hinda had never imagined that her mother and aunt could say such terrible things to each other. Never before had she seen either of them so angry. She would never forget how her mother, usually so decorous and grave, and her aunt, always so elegant and ladylike, had screamed at each other, behaving in a manner which Hinda had associated with the peasant women in the marketplace.

She tried to pull her mother toward the door, but Tziril brushed her aside. She wasn't finished yet.

"Mama, let's go home," Hinda pleaded. Tziril shook with indignation, and the Muma Channa's rage was frightening. Finally, Channa's daughters intervened, and shouted that Tziril and Hinda should leave at once, before anything terrible happened.

Still furious, Tziril grabbed Hinda by the arm and stormed out the door. That visit was the final straw. Even Hinda was depressed; nobody had even noticed her new clothes. There had been no gifts for her. The Muma Channa had not even offered them the customary refreshments. And now they were leaving Kovno forever. She would never see any of them again.

Her cousins had always lavished gifts upon her, and she had many toys and trinkets that had once belonged to them. Hinda had always treasured anything they gave her. Reizel had given her ribbons for her long, fair hair. Moshe had given her books that he had outgrown, some of them with beautiful illustrations. She wore the dresses Channa's dressmaker had made for Reizel and Sheindel.

Her boy-cousins were tall, strapping fellows, even Feivel, who was almost her own age. Hinda adored them. They would carry her on their shoulders, and Nathan, the eldest, who was already grown to manhood, would throw her up in the air. Every time she saw him, he would tell her that she had hair "like sunshine."

But now the marked contrast between her aunt's well appointed home and her own sparsely furnished dwelling only made Hinda unhappy. Never before had the differences been so strikingly obvious to the seven year old, although her mother had always kept everything spotlessly clean. Hinda felt only pity for her mother, who had always worked so hard. She had no jewels, not even a strand of pearls for the Sabbath. She didn't even own a single crystal bowl.

By comparison, every meal at the Muma Channa's was a sumptuous feast. Though Hinda could never recall going hungry, her mother never served her costly fruits and delicate pastries, even during the best of times.

With anguish, Hinda, for the first time, began to ponder over the inequities and injustices of life. She began to wonder why Channa and her mother, children of the same parents, were not equally blessed. How could the Muma Channa and her children have so many good things in life, while she and her mother had so little? And strangest of all, the adults she knew never seemed to question why this should be. Hinda thought she would never be able to take such injustices for granted.

A Journey to Kafkaz

By train, by boat and by horsedrawn coach, Tziril and Hinda made their way toward Odessa, their port of embarkation on the Black Sea. In later years, Hinda would often remark that no other experience had ever equalled the adventure and excitement of that childhood odyssey. Even as a grandmother, Hinda recalled the names of the towns and villages she had passed through with her mother.

Tziril never failed to be astonished by her young daughter's perceptiveness and memory, and though she was as grave and serious minded as ever, her daughter's fascination with the strange world that engulfed their senses quickly became contagious. Odessa was more than a cosmopolitan port city; it was a true crossroads of the world.

In years to come, both Tziril and Hinda would vividly describe the colorful panorama of the waterfront where, for the first time in their lives, they encountered peoples of all races and nationalities who spoke every language imaginable. There were wealthy European merchants, and traders in exotic oriental goods. There were veiled women swathed in layers of silk, accompanied by turbaned men and fierce looking bodyguards. Everywhere the bleating and braying of animals could be heard, even above the din of churchbells and the mournful calls to prayer from the tall minarets. Slavers and monks mingled with British diplomats and young girls en route to the harems of the East. It was a carnival of princes and Cossacks, of which their children and grandchildren never grew tired of hearing.

All too soon, the signal was given, and Tziril and her daughter boarded the steamer that would carry them across the

Black Sea. As she approached the gangplank, she became the object of intense interest and speculation — a young matron traveling alone with a slight, fair-haired daughter. The other female passengers had hurried below deck as soon as they boarded the ship, while Tziril and Hinda stood at the rail until Odessa was only a thin line on the horizon.

Each day, the curiosity of their fellow passengers increased, especially when it became known that they were Jews. Tziril was a dignified and attractive woman, though unsmiling and aloof. Her wig proclaimed her an Orthodox Jewess, and she never appeared without her ostrich tipped bonnet tied securely under her square chin. Both the sailors and male passengers observed that both mother and daughter were well dressed and traveling first class; they were judged to be people in at least comfortable circumstances, since they could afford the trip from Kovno to Tiflis. The men noted with approval that she never permitted the beautiful, dark eyed child with the long blonde braids out of her sight for a moment.

Tziril's fearless manner, her air of independence and her biting wit stirred the men with seemingly honest admiration, and discouraged familiarity, even though no other women were seen on board, even at mealtimes. Among themselves they could only conjecture over the business that was taking her so far from home, and ventured doubtful guesses of all kinds. But they were very proper and respectful whenever they encountered her, as though it were necessary to continually assure her of their honorable intentions.

Yet, one evening the captain summoned Tziril from her stateroom. He had an important message for her — a business proposition, to be more exact. Bluntly, and with extreme frankness, he informed her that certain of the men on board were very interested in purchasing her small, blond daughter. Hinda, she was told, would bring quite a fair price in gold.

Tziril was stunned. She could hardly believe that she heard him correctly, and the shock was so great that for a moment she thought she was about to faint. But the captain's message was clear. Despite their blandishments and show of respect, these strangers, men with bold smiles and cruel expressions, were greedy for her child. They actually coveted Hinda! Tziril's fear was quite plain. She swore to the captain that she had distrusted those men from the moment she first noticed how their eyes had followed Hinda's every move. Their polished manners and honeyed speech had been devices to entrap her!

With a great display of indignation, the captain declared that her fears were groundless. She had no reason to be alarmed. He had personally guaranteed her safety and that of her daughter, and she had his word that in any event, her decision as a mother would be respected. On the other hand, if she changed her mind, a most advantageous marriage could be arranged for her daughter when she reached the proper age.

"Madam," he began, "you are traveling to a part of the world where marriages between Jew and non-Jew, especially among the well-born, is not uncommon. Invariably, brides are pur - chased from their parents. This is a fact of life. If the truth were known, the blood of Jew and non-Jew have intermingled for centuries in the East." How else could he explain it?

"Other mothers would have been flattered by such an offer," he concluded.

From that moment, Tziril felt threatened, in spite of the captain's assurances. For the remainder of the voyage, she avoided all contact with the other passengers, and kept the door to her small stateroom securely bolted. Hinda, an energetic and fun-loving child, could not understand her mother's determination to keep her isolated. But finally, Tziril succeeded in thoroughly communicating her distrust of everyone on board to Hinda. Though she did not say so in so many words, she made it clear that even the captain was plotting against them, and that if Hinda was not for sale, she could very easily be stolen.

Tziril lay awake all through their last night on the boat. All her confidence in her own judgment had disappeared, and she found herself worrying about the strained relations between Channa and herself. She began to doubt even her decision to make the journey at all.

Not for one moment had Channa believed that Yussel had given her his approval. Her sister had warned her in no uncertain terms that if she persisted in such a wild venture, it would ruin her marriage forever. Throughout the night, Channa's warnings kept ringing in her ears. And then, there was the fear that Hinda would be snatched from her, kidnapped and sold to a trader in young girls. She remembered the throngs of closely guarded young slaves and concubines on the docks of Odessa; only this time, her beloved Hinda's face was among them. How would she ever explain that to Yussel? She could picture her husband alone and embittered, his love for her turned to hatred. She had not cared for their children; she had abandoned him. Channa had warned her endlessly that this was something a man could not forgive, and she had been right after all.

Tziril was acutely depressed by the time the final stage of their journey had begun. Their baggage was transferred to a mail-coach that traveled along ancient caravan routes, carrying passengers and mail through the rugged mountains of the southern Caucasus Range. Hinda, on the other hand, showed no signs of stress, even after such a long journey, but was still wide eyed and alert. Tziril was thankful that they had seen the last of the captain and his passengers, but the uneasy thoughts of the voyage were still with her. It seemed to her the farther they traveled from Kovno, the greater was the distance between Yussel and herself. Her husband began to dominate her thoughts almost completely. Now that she was actually doing what she had been yearning to do for years, her sense of guilt was enormous.

Unaware of her mother's dark mood, Hinda was enthralled by the landscapes that sped past the carriage window. "This must be the top of the world," she was thinking, as the coach rumbled over the rocky gorges. They crossed innumerable narrow bridges spanning clear mountain streams that sparkled in the sunlight. Hinda cried out with excitement and happiness every time she pointed out a wild goat or a dark-skinned man on horseback, clad in white sheepskins.

It was spring, and the roads they were traveling were lined with flowers of every variety and hue. The air was sweet with the scent of orchards in bloom, as they now passed through thriving villages and farms, and countless houses covered with grape arbors and roses. And in the distance, always dominating every vista, were the snow-capped peaks of the great mountain chain, reflecting the sky of deep cobalt color.

Lost in her thoughts, Tziril did not even notice the vineyards for which Kafkaz was famous, until Hinda pointed them
out to her.

Suddenly, Tziril was awestruck. The vineyards seemed to
stretch for miles! She could hardly control her emotions. It
was all as Bayla had described. There was a lump in her throat,
if only Yussel were here to share her joy! Who could know?
Perhaps these were the very vineyards that had once belonged
to her father, the fruit of his ancestors' labor after their exile
from Spain so long ago. She felt as though she had come home
at last. Suddenly, her guilt and self-hatred vanished, and her
thought was that she never wanted to leave this beautiful
country.

The coach with its double team of horses came to a final
halt at a small bustling town just outside the city of Tiflis,
where Bayla had planned to meet them. Tziril and Hinda were
the only passengers, since the coach also carried the mail. As
she glanced around the small combination station and post office, it seemed as though the whole town had come to greet
them.

The noise and confusion filled Tziril with panic. Exhausted
by the journey and her own emotions, she thought for a moment that no one had come to meet her. Then she saw the
elderly couple that left the noisy throng and rushed toward her
with outstretched arms. Suddenly she could not restrain her
tears of thankfulness and relief.

Both women wept as they embraced. There was an immediate rapport between them, although neither Bayla, nor her
husband, Meiron, were in any way as Tziril had expected. They
were much older than Reb Yosef. Tziril was amazed, though,
at the strong resemblance between Bayla and Channa, although
Bayla was old and extremely obese. She was completely gray,
and her dark olive skin was creased with innumerable deep
lines, the result of long hours under the sun in the vineyards.
She did not wear the traditional matrons' wig, Tziril noticed,
and when she asked about that she was told that none of the
Jewish women in that area followed that custom. Bayla

expected that Tziril would soon be discarding hers. But Bayla's long, elaborately embroidered shawl could not hide her great bulk, and her ankles were so swollen that Tziril wondered how she could walk.

Reb Meiron was a frail, stooped figure, with a scholarly manner. Tziril was overwhelmed by the warmth of his welcome, and Hinda took a great liking to him immediately. She clung to his hand as he directed them to his wagon where the driver had already loaded their baggage. During the short ride to Bayla's home, Tziril decided that despite his delicate appearance, Meiron was a man of great vitality, who was still in excellent health. Unfortunately, she couldn't say the same about Bayla.

Their home, which everyone referred to as the drucke, was a solid, two-story structure of whitewashed stone. A balcony with a railing of ornately wrought iron extended the entire length of the second floor. The house was surrounded by trees and flowering shrubs, and was set back far from the dusty road. Here they lived and conducted their business, Bayla explained. For the large building contained both the printing press and the cellars where they made their wine.

Immediately, their guests began to learn the routine of the household. Both Bayla and her husband spent the better part of their days in the drucke and the large anteroom where patrons were received. The elegant anteroom contained half a dozen marble tables, and chairs upholstered in red velvet for the comfort of their customers. No patron ever left without enjoying the hospitality of the house.

With the help of an assistant, Reb Meiron operated the printing press, which was housed in a special wing of their home. Even Bayla knew all there was to know about the business, and during particularly busy weeks she would help her husband. Tziril was amazed at the size of the machine, as Reb Meiron described the various procedures involved in his work and in the maintenance of the drucke. The printing press was one of the finest in Kafkaz, he told her proudly, and with proper care it would last a hundred years or more. Still, it was weeks before Tziril finally grew accustomed to the noise.

Reb Meiron had been fortunate enough to have been awarded a government contract, and the drucke did most of the print-

ing for the nearby military garrison, while occasionally being
commissioned by the great fortress of Valadi Kafkaz. Each day,
without fail, huge stacks of military manuals, reports, maps
and other documents were turned out. In addition, the drucke
enjoyed the patronage of a large circus whose winter encampment was nearby. Reb Meiron and Bayla boasted that their
circus posters were works of great art, and were distributed
throughout Imperial Russia and even in Western Europe.

Soon after their arrival, Bayla showed Tziril the wine cellars.

"We're expecting a vintage harvest this year," she added.
"This may be the last year for me, but I will teach you everything I know. When you leave my house you will be ready to
start your own business. 'Tziril the Winemaker' — that's what
they'll call you!"

She continued after a brief pause. "We will even teach you
to operate the drucke, which will be your inheritance. Promise
me you'll never forget that, Tziril. Someday it will be yours."

Tziril could not believe that she ever would be able to handle
such an intricate machine. But what really captured her imagination was Bayla's wine-press — huge wooden tubs set on a
heavy platform — and she tried to imagine Yussel and herself
working together to fill them with ripe fruit.

"Hinda! Come and see!" she called to her daughter, who was
exploring the dark recesses of the cellar. Bayla's assistant, a
"hired man" nearly as old as she was, lifted the wide-eyed Hinda so that she could peer into the deep tubs, which were
stained a vivid purple with the grapes of many harvests.

The first Sabbath which Tziril and Hinda spent under Bayla's
roof was a memorable occasion. The drucke was closed for the
day, and the house and garden were crowded with friends who
had come to pay their respects to Bayla's guests. In her first
letter to Yussel since she left Kovno, Tziril wrote that Bayla
had spent an entire day in her kitchen supervising the preparations for the Sabbath meal. Enough challah had been baked
to last an ordinary family all week, she wrote, and there was
enough spiced gefilte fish to feed a regiment. Bayla's honey
cake was almost too big for her huge outdoor oven.

But the most amazing occurrence was the weekly visit by the
officers of the local garrison. Just before closing time on Friday

afternoon, they had come swarming into the drucke with their clanking spurs and swords. Yet, their manner was genial and their greetings warm, and as Tziril wrote to her husband, they were nothing like the often brutal soldiers they had encountered in Kovno. They were the elite of the Imperial Army — the officer class. In their polished boots and elegant uniforms they towered over Reb Meiron, as he rushed to bid them welcome. Hinda, especially, had been impressed by their pomp and splendor.

The soldiers were graciously ushered into the anteroom and seated at the marble topped tables. Bayla's elderly housekeeper smiled toothlessly as she served the officers huge portions of fish swimming in rich aspic and thick slices of warm challah.

Tziril and Hinda watched them eat in utter amazement; never before had they seen such appetites. Tziril noted the frequency with which they asked to have their goblets refilled. The wine had been carried up the narrow stairs in an enormous copper pail, the likes of which Tziril had never seen. By the time the soldiers departed with their week's worth of printing, the huge vessel had been emptied.

"Every week at this time they come to pick up the printing; they always receive the hospitality of our home, and it has almost become a ritual," Reb Meiron explained.

In her letter to Yussel, Tziril also wrote that never before had she received such love and tenderness from a relative. Bayla and Meiron made her feel as though she were a beloved daughter who had returned to the home of her parents after a long separation, and they treated Hinda as though she were the grandchild they never had. In the short time since she had arrived, she had learned many things, and when she arrived in America, she intended to establish a winery of her own. Like Bayla and her father, she would become a master winemaker. They would all prosper as a result of this journey. Bayla had promised to teach her everything she knew and would give her the formula which had been a family secret for generations.

People traveled long distances to buy Bayla's wine, since she only made it when the crop was good. Every barrel was marked with its vintage year, and her customers trusted her judgment without reservation.

A bright future was beginning for all of them. Tziril's one regret was that her husband was not with her to share in her joy and excitement. She knew now why her father had so longed to return to this bountiful land of his birth; such a life was not to be given up without a struggle. If only Channa knew what she was missing, Tziril mused. How could her sister ignore such a rich heritage?

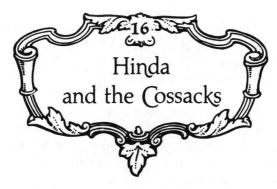

16

Hinda
and the Cossacks

The unused, high ceilinged rooms of her aunt's house held a strange fascination for Hinda. Every piece of furniture was always covered, and the musty smell of camphor and ancient grandeur clung to the faded damask curtains and the thick oriental rugs. Except for the huge kitchen and the bedrooms, which were furnished in heavy, dark woods, the other rooms were rarely entered. But it was a splendid place for a child to play, and Hinda told her aunt that her home was even more elegant than the Muma Channa's.

Bayla could only sigh. Most of the rooms had been shut after her daughter's death, and she and her husband preferred to use the rooms adjoining the drucke. Here they spent most of their days, since these rooms were close to the kitchen and Bayla found it difficult to climb stairs.

Bayla and Tziril would sit in the kitchen for hours on end, as they talked of their father and their family's reverses of fortune. Tziril could not get enough of Bayla's accounts of her parents and the stories about their ancestors Bayla had been told as a child. Bayla retold the story of her return to Kafkaz many times over. Zalman Yitzchok's generous gift which had enabled them to purchase the drucke had been the beginning.

"Did you know," remarked Bayla one afternoon. "that your mother bore stillborn children between you and Channa?"

Of course this was something Tziril had never heard before, but there were many things she had yet to discover. She had often wondered about the age difference between Channa and herself, though she wasn't exactly sure of her sister's age, or her own, for that matter.

Bayla recounted the joy and pride with which she and Meiron had furnished their home. After all, she had had a young and beautiful daughter who was already betrothed to a most worthy young man. Just when she had been busy with arrangements for her daughter's wedding, Dvera's last letter had arrived. Bayla's eyes were wet with tears as she told Tziril how she had put the letter aside until after the wedding. Only a short month after they were married, her daughter and son-in-law and several others had been killed when a bridge collapsed during a storm.

It was during Shiva, the seven days of mourning, that she had suddenly remembered Dvera's letter which lay unanswered. She had written to Dvera immediately, and had promised to do all she could for her father's second wife and their children. No one informed her of Dvera's death, and because her letter had never been returned, she continued to write, imploring Dvera to contact her so that she could make amends. But none of her letters were answered, and after a time they were only returned. In desperation, she had turned to the Yeshiva in Kovno, and after several years the search for Dvera and her daughters began in earnest.

Bayla's voice was choked with emotion. "When I look at you, Tziril, I keep seeing my father's face. You have his wonderful eyes — all his features. Once, I had brothers and sisters, but now I'm the last of my mother's children. So much has happened to us — so much grief. If it weren't for my husband, my life would have ended when my daughter died. Oh, Tziril! Stay with us for a while. Please don't leave us. The drucke will be yours; I promise you. It is written in my will that this will be your inheritance.

"Write to Yussel — you must! Please. Tell him that we will help him to settle here with us. You will never regret it — both of you!"

❧

Hinda spent very little time indoors. So long a city child, she delighted in exploring the vineyards and fields in the vicinity, and spent many hours picking flowers and wild berries. It was unfortunate that she had not yet found any playmates, but the child had never seemed happier. From the kitchen windows, Tziril could watch as she ran through the garden, her long braids flying in the breeze. Tziril and Bayla would smile as they listened to her laughter, and sometimes she would even play games with the trees and flowers.

It was obvious that Hinda was playing some sort of game that she found exceedingly amusing. Now and then she would pause, as though conversing with an imaginary companion, and would then throw back her head with a merry laugh.

One day, their curiosity got the better of them, and the two women questioned her. For a moment she seemed embarrassed, but then replied that she was only playing "make believe."

"But what are you 'making believe'?" asked Tziril, fondly. "First you stop running, then you talk and laugh, and then you begin all over again, only this time you run in circles. What kind of a game is that?"

Hinda hung her head. Finally she answered in an unusually solemn voice.

"I am making believe little Esther is here and that we are chasing butterflies. I even let her catch them sometimes. Esther would have loved it here! All the flowers and the beautiful butterflies..." Hinda could not bring herself to continue.

"My poor child. I understand." Tziril turned away so that Hinda would not see her tears.

Bayla's friends soon welcomed Tziril into their circle, for they had rejoiced for Bayla when she had been reunited with her half-sister. Most of them were from the northwestern part of the Russian Empire, and all spoke fluent Yiddish. Like Bayla and her husband, they all had received permits which enabled them to establish their homes and businesses outside the Pale of Settlement. They too were "Privileged Jews," most of them highly educated and prosperous.

In the years since their arrival, they had built an Ashkenazic synagogue and a school where the instruction was mostly in Yiddish. As soon as the new term had begun, Hinda began to attend, and had less time for games of "make-believe." The Sephardic Jews of the area were also beginning to send their children to that school, since it was considered the finest in the vicinity. Hinda began to meet a number of children who were of Turkish extraction, as well as some who spoke Ladino, which was a hebraicized Spanish, and several of the local dialects.

Still, Hinda's favorite companion was her pet goat, which Bayla had given her. The elderly couple doted on the child, and more than once, Tziril had good-naturedly accused them of spoiling her with their gifts and surprises.

Bayla had told Hinda that the goat was to be entirely her responsibility. It was the perfect present for a small child living alone with busy adults. Hinda's goat was very young, and had a will of its own. Often it would resist her attempts to make it follow her home. Bayla soon advised her to find a switch and to apply it with a will whenever her pet began to balk.

"Teach your pet a lesson on its hind quarters," she would say. "This is the only language that a goat will understand. Always carry the switch with you and don't be afraid to use it."

Hinda had been warned many times to avoid the broad highway where the Cossacks had the right of way. They never stopped for anyone, as they came galloping, often twelve a-breast, not even for a little girl. If one did not move fast, he or she would be trampled to death beneath the hooves of their powerful steeds. When in formation, the Cossacks would rush headlong looking straight ahead, and would disappear in seconds as unexpectedly as they had arrived, leaving nothing behind but clouds of dust. Such was the Cossacks' "code."

One sunny afternoon, Hinda ventured onto this forbidden roadway, leading her goat by its rope. Suddenly and without warning, she heard the clatter of approaching horsemen in the distance. She panicked as she remembered her aunt's warnings, and began to run, attempting to drag her goat behind her. But her pet had chosen the wrong time to be stubborn, and refused to budge.

She was terrified. How could she run and leave her pet to be trampled? Almost instinctively, she began to beat the animal, striking it again and again in desperate fury. Suddenly the little goat took a great leap forward, dragging Hinda behind.

As they crouched by the side of the road, the Cossacks galloped past like a whirlwind.

Hinda was positive that they had seen her, for as they sped past she had caught a glimpse of flashing teeth under their bristling mustaches. Evidently, they had thoroughly enjoyed her predicament, but she was certain that they had also appreciated her quick wit that had saved both her goat and herself.

Not long after this experience, she encountered a small, dark-skinned boy one day while she was gathering blackberries. Intrigued by his round cheeks and slanting eyes, she tried to make his acquaintance, but he spoke only a strange tongue that, to her dismay, she could not understand. Somehow, though, they managed to communicate, and he followed her back to the drucke, sensing that she wanted a friend to play with.

To Hinda's surprise, Bayla introduced him as Abdul, the young son of a local nobleman's gardener. She greeted him warmly in his own language, and told Hinda how pleased she was that she had made friends with him, since the estate where his father worked was within walking distance of their home.

The next day, Hinda set out to visit her new friend, following the careful instructions Bayla had given her. It was not long before she reached the high brick wall that surrounded the estate; her pet goat followed behind her.

Abdul was expecting her. The boy sat crosslegged on top of the wall, eating a huge, golden peach, his hands and face stained with the juice of the ripe fruit. He shouted a greeting to her and then disappeared from sight. A moment later, as if by magic, a door opened in the wall, and he beckoned her into the garden. As she stepped through the gate, she gasped in amazement. There were fruit trees of every description as far as she could see, and the air was fragrant with their ripeness. Abdul pointed out his father, the gardener, and then led Hinda and her pet through a wilderness of plenty. He helped her climb to the top of the wall where they feasted on luscious pears, pomegranates and peaches that had fallen to the ground.

Hinda would always remember the happy hours she had spent in the fruit orchard with Abdul and her goat, and the baskets overflowing with ripe apricots and plums she had carried back to the drucke. It was no wonder that her Aunt Bayla often told her that many people believed Kafkaz to have been the site of the Garden of Eden.

Soon she began to understand some of Abdul's language, especially the words that were similar to the language of her Sephardic schoolmates. One day, he announced that the circus would be arriving soon, and there was nothing more exciting than that. The performers were even more spellbinding than the galloping Cossacks whom he and Hinda often observed from their perch on top of the wall.

Hinda watched the arrival of the circus wagons as they moved into their winter encampment. The quarters were open to the public, and everyone flocked there to watch the clowns paint their faces and to marvel at the wild animals. The performers practiced all day, since they broke in their new acts during the winter season. Every day, Hinda and Abdul returned to the campground where, along with the other children, they would march in back of the band, imitating every kind of military maneuver. The children would march in near perfect rhythm, shouting and laughing as they imitated soldiers and bareback riders.

One day, while playing in the circus compound with a group of children, Hinda spied a jewel encrusted dagger glistening in the sunlight. She pounced upon the treasure, exclaiming over its beauty. Imagine — she had nearly stepped on it. The hilt was adorned with priceless sapphires, diamonds, and rubies.

"Look! See what I found!" she cried to the swarm of children who clustered around her. "Now it is mine!" Hinda had no idea of its value as she ran up and down the campground, twirling the dagger like a juggler with a baton.

She ran home to show her incredible find to her mother and aunt, certain that they would exclaim over its beauty. But Tziril and Bayla were almost incoherent with fright.

"Hinda — where on earth did you find that?"

"But Hinda, you must tell me. It could belong to a nobleman, or a high ranking officer. There could be trouble for us..."

Even as Tziril spoke, there was a pounding at the door, and

several officers pushed their way into the kitchen. Their swords clanged menacingly against their spurs and buckles.

"A jeweled dagger was stolen," shouted their leader in a threatening tone. "Witnesses say it is in the possession of the Jews!"

Tziril paled. Her hand shook as she handed him the missing object.

She gestured to Hinda. "The child found it at the circus. Nobody claimed it and she must have thought it was a colorful toy. Everyone saw her pick it up and play with it. How could she know its value? She brought it home to show me. What else could you expect a little girl to do?"

The soldiers burst into raucous laughter. Then, as if by habit, they sauntered into the adjoining anteroom. It was not the day they usually called for their printing, but there was wine, they were told, and fresh almond cake.

Bayla even promised them double portions of fish for their next visit.

Letters

The first year passed too swiftly, except for the long intervals when there was no mail from Yussel. It was not as though he didn't write, Tziril was told, but that mail from America took such a long time to reach them, and delivery was uncertain. She began to believe that many of her husband's letters had either been stolen or lost in transit. Bayla would tell her friends that Tziril was always so nervous and edgy until she had heard from him, but that the money-order he usually enclosed would reassure her of Yussel's devotion.

"I always read your letters to the mishpocha," wrote Yussel in one of his early letters. This troubled Tziril, who knew only too well the attitude of some of her in-laws. She sensed, even at a distance, their criticism and disapproval.

"They are only interested in knowing how long you are staying in Kafkaz," he wrote. As for himself, he wanted her to know that he was glad she had received such a warm welcome after her long journey, and had enjoyed her descriptions of the drucke, the winery and Hinda's adventure with the Cossacks. "But Tziril, enough is enough," he had concluded. "It's time for you to come to America."

These early letters had been a great joy and comfort to her. After her first year in Kafkaz, however, she gradually became aware of his deep hurt and displeasure at her protracted visit. Tziril realized that she had been writing at least three letters for every one she received. Lately, she had sensed a bitter note of resentment in his correspondence. He was not impressed, he had written, neither with the advantages he would have in Kafkaz, nor with the fact that she had learned to operate the printing press and make wine.

He was doing very well right where he was. The years of apprenticeship with Frumkin were paying off handsomely, and he was making a good living in the construction business. Furthermore, he resented the fact that she continued to refer to America as a *treife* land.

"How often do I have to remind you that we have built a schul and have a minyan twice each day? I'm not interested in Bayla's learned friends with their fine manners. My own friends and family are good enough. They were good enough for me in Wilki, and they are good enough here in New Jersey."

In America he was a free man. The inspector at the immigration center had advised him to change his name and he had never regretted it.

"Call yourself 'Freedman'," he had counseled. "Wilkimirsky? Who will be able to pronounce that? Joseph Friedman will look good on your citizenship papers."

Yussel was now an American citizen whose name had been legally changed. He had even voted in the last election, and he didn't want his wife to ever forget it.

Tziril was stunned when she read his concluding words.

"You needn't answer this unless you write that you are leaving Bayla immediately and are coming here where you belong. Otherwise, I don't care to hear from you again. My friends tell me that I'm a fool. If they had been in my place, they tell me, they'd have sent you a *get*, and we would have been divorced long ago!"

Bayla tried to comfort the distraught Tziril.

"Write your husband at once. Tell him we have influential friends who will get him a permit to come and see for himself how good it is here for the Jews. Write that we are giving you the drucke. Who else is there to inherit our possessions? You're like our own child! Until the day of his death, our father had expected you to return here someday. Explain this to that husband of yours."

"No." Tziril began to weep. Bayla's advice was useless. "I couldn't. He's such a proud man. I can't stay away any longer; I'll write and tell him I'm leaving."

"No — you can't," objected Bayla. "Not until after the harvest. Last year I was sick and we didn't make wine. But this year will be different. You have so much to learn—it takes years. Maybe in another year or so you'll be ready to try it alone. Yes. You need at least another year."

Late that night Tziril wrote to Yussel after Hinda had fallen asleep. She would be leaving immediately after the grape harvest. She agreed that she had been away from him too long, but the years had gone by so terribly quickly. Someday she would make it up to him, and meanwhile Bayla was teaching her everything she knew about winemaking.

The grape harvest was fast approaching, and Tziril didn't want to miss any of it, although she had forgotten how many harvests she had already enjoyed during the years in Kafkaz. She had been so busy most of the time learning and working in the winery, as well as helping her brother-in-law with the printing press. A frenzy seemed to have seized the entire community, even the school children. People were saying that it would be the finest crop in years, and excitement was high.

With Hinda in school, Tziril was free to accompany Bayla on an inspection tour of the vineyards. Each day, they drove many miles in the open carriage. Tziril gazed in awe at the huge clusters of ripening grapes ready for plucking. She had never seen anything like that in her entire life.

Early one morning, she and Bayla stopped at an ancient cemetery where the first Sephardic Jews exiled from Spain had been buried. Tziril was introduced to the caretakers who resided in a small stone cottage covered with ivy. Their language was strange to her, but Bayla conversed fluently in Ladino, their mixture of Spanish, Hebrew and Arabic. Bayla told Tziril that several of their ancestors had been buried here, and that their father had described the location of their graves to her long ago, when she left Vilna as a young bride.

Reb Meiron was worried that the daily excursions were too strenuous for his wife, but he could not restrain her. She had to be a part of the excitement and activity that was turning the entire community into a joyous carnival. People arrived daily in droves, some with large hampers that contained all their belongings balanced on their heads. Others came in horse-drawn carts and huge wagons that carried entire families with all their cooking utensils and bedding.

Tziril described the scene in a letter to Yussel. "They sleep in improvised shelters in the open fields, wrapped in blankets under the stars. They cook their meals outdoors, like Gypsies. They've brought with them every kind of musical instrument, which they play when their work in the vineyards is finished for the day. Nobody even sleeps. The young people sing and dance all night — you can't imagine what goes on here! If our Hinda were a little older, she'd be out there dancing with them, there'd be no holding her back!"

Bayla had told her many times how in his youth their father had always played at the harvest festivals. With his superb musicianship and his handsome appearance, he had captured the hearts of young and old.

And soon Bayla began to purchase grapes. Although their own harvest had been especially good, there were numerous other varieties which she bought for special types of wine. Bayla and Tziril went from vineyard to vineyard, inspecting and tasting at every step. It was like a triumphal tour for the older woman, and everyone seemed glad to see Bayla walking her rounds. She had been missed last year, they assured her. They remarked how well she looked, but above all, they were thankful that it was a good harvest and a vintage year. Everywhere, Bayla was received with respect and affection. But what impressed Tziril the most was the way in which Bayla selected the grapes she purchased, even before they were plucked from the vine.

Early in the morning, the grapes were delivered and carried down to the cellar. In an adjoining shed, the presses were in readiness for the first step of the operation.

Tziril soon lost track of the time as she helped clean, sort and separate the great clusters of fruit. It was a tiring and time-consuming procedure. Then came the measuring, the endless filtering and refiltering. Bayla claimed to follow the same formula which her family had adhered to since their winemaking days in Spain.

The women were assisted by two helpers who had been in Bayla's employ for many years. Barefoot, and stripped to the waist, they toiled for hours. Their heavy leather breeches were stained with purple juice. Tziril was amazed by the ease with which they manipulated the heavy presses.

Reb Meiron had often warned his wife that her zeal exceeded her strength. One afternoon, while supervising the work in the wine cellar, Bayla suddenly collapsed. Her legs and ankles had become so swollen from the long hours on her feet that they were unable to continue supporting her huge bulk. She was carried to her bedroom and the doctor was summoned. Anxiously he examined her swollen legs and listened to her heavy wheezing. He ordered Bayla to remain in bed, and decided to apply leeches.

Bayla, a woman of prodigious energy, found it very difficult to accept her forced inactivity. How could she remain in bed when there was so much to be done? Reb Meiron needed her to assist with the drucke, and there was still wine to be made. Her husband couldn't do everything by himself, and Tziril really hadn't had enough experience, no matter how willing she was to help.

But the fact remained that Bayla could not get out of bed without assistance. Her body was bloated with fluid and seemed twice its normal size, while her eyes were reduced to tiny slits in the mounds of fevered flesh that surrounded them. They reminded Hinda of black cherry pits. Just looking at the poor Muma Bayla frightened her, and she began to dread the visits to her aunt's room.

Despite her illness, Bayla gave orders from her bed. Her assistants and servants reported to her for daily instructions, and Tziril worked with them for long hours, making sure that everything met Bayla's specifications. The men had the highest praise for Tziril's diligence, and complimented Bayla and her husband for having such an apt pupil. Tziril was especially pleased by their approval, for she knew that before long she would be as good a winemaker as her sister, and would be capable of conducting her own business, even in America.

Finally the grapes were processed. The vintage was sampled, tested and poured into huge casks to age. After a few months it would be transferred to the barrels in the cellar.

The doctor began to visit Bayla daily. She showed no improvement, but on the other hand, her condition didn't seem to get any worse. The doctor told Tziril and Meiron that she could linger for years, and would probably outlive them all, despite her suffering. Such an idea was disheartening. How could Tziril forsake Bayla, whom she had grown to love like a mother?

Bayla's friends came every day, bringing delicacies to tempt her appetite. Everyone knew that she would never leave her bed, and her husband seemed almost as helpless. He kept mourning that he was now alone, and utterly overwhelmed without Bayla to work at his side. He would never be able to manage without her, and it seemed, even to Tziril, that the old man was already wallowing in self-pity.

Tziril was in despair. She did not have the words to tell Bayla that since the harvest and winemaking were over it was time for her to depart. She would never be able to leave Bayla bedridden and without other close relatives to bring her comfort. Despite the doctor's optimism, Bayla could be on the brink of death.

"Rabbono Shel Olom," she prayed as she went about the many duties that had been heaped upon her. "Master of the Universe, help me do the right thing. Help me find the right words to tell them I must leave and join my husband. Don't let Yussel hate me." Tziril shed bitter tears as she struggled with her conflict of loyalties.

Bayla slept much of the day, but her nights were restless. Reb Meiron had moved to another room where he could sleep undisturbed, and Tziril spent most of her nights at her sister's bedside. Despite her failing health, her mind was exceptionally clear and she would endlessly recount all that had befallen their family in years past. She spoke of Dvera, her father's young wife who had been only a few years older than she was, and she relived again the anguish she had felt when she had discovered Dvera's letter lying unanswered after her daughter's death.

"When my child died, I felt I had been punished. It was divine judgement. I vowed I would make amends, and I prayed to be given the chance. My prayers were answered when you came with your beautiful little daughter to bring me comfort in my last years. Oh, Tziril — every day was like the Day of Atonement for me. I would beat my breast and cry out that I had sinned, but it was no use." Bayla wept as she spoke.

She pleaded with Tziril continually to try to persuade her husband to join them.

"Tell him he can earn a fine living with the drucke. Why should you have to go to America and struggle? Besides, you know how to make wine. We still have empty barrels, and next year we can fill them if the crop is good. Between the wine and the drucke, you and Yussel will be people of means."

It was becoming painful for Tziril to sit endlessly at Bayla's bedside and listen to her pleas and ramblings. Meiron would only shake his head in despair; he could not bear to sit there and listen to his wife's plans for the future. He warned Tziril that it would be dangerous for her husband to settle in Kafkaz, even if a residence permit could be procured for him. Meiron could understand Yussel's unwillingness to return to a country that would have thought nothing of having him shot on sight for disregarding his summons to military duty. And why should any man risk his life for a country that denied him citizenship and the chance for a happy and peaceful life?

"Besides," he added, "Bayla must have forgotten that her permit for the drucke is non-transferable. It is in her name, and terminates when she dies. I'm sure her mind has been affected by her illness, and her age. Poor Bayla."

He also knew that it would be next to impossible for him to remain there after his wife's death.

"Everything is in her name," he told Tziril. "The drucke was purchased, anonymously, of course, with your father's money. He paid for it in gold through a third party and gave it to Bayla, even though I was to actually operate it. I'm sure you know by now that she intends for you to inherit it. There was an agreement with your father. But did you know that even our residence permit is in her name?"

Tziril burst into tears.

"It would be good to live here, but if my husband can't be with me, what good is it? Without him my life is empty — how I long to be with him again. But he doesn't even write. He doesn't answer my letters anymore."

"Listen to me, Tziril," Reb Meiron spoke soothingly. "Listen to what I'm telling you. I don't expect to live here alone without Bayla. Once she's gone I won't need the drucke or the winecellars. When you leave, I'm going to London where I have a brother and nephews I haven't seen in years. And I must tell you, the doctor told me last night — Bayla won't last the year. She is deteriorating fast and could die any day now." His eyes were moist, although he tried to maintain his composure.

"Please, Tziril. Stay with us until it is over, and then, when you leave I'll go with you."

"And the drucke?" asked Tziril.

Meiron shrugged. "It will be dismantled and shipped to Kovno. Then you can decide, you and your husband, either to sell it or go into business. It's worth quite a bit of money.

"I hear that the city of Telschi in Lithuania is a good place to live, with an excellent school for girls and a famous yeshiva. Many great scholars have settled there, and once we were thinking of moving there ourselves, before we received our permit to return to Kafkaz. You should do well there. The people are prosperous and cultured. Tell Yussel that."

Bayla's friends continued their daily calls. They sponged and bathed her; they combed her hair and made her as comfortable as possible. It took three of them to turn her. The doctor told them that he could not understand what was keeping her alive. Despite the leeches, her body was swollen with fluid, but her tenacious will to live and her keen interest in the affairs of her household amazed everyone. Every day she inquired whether there had been a letter for Tziril and how Hinda was doing in school. Her sense of smell was sharp, her appetite surprising, especially when it was stimulated by the fragrant cooking smells from the kitchen below.

"What is for dinner," she asked eagerly one day, long before the usual dinner hour. She looked at the clock on her bedside table.

"Why, it's not even noon," she announced, "but already I'm famished."

But Bayla could not even swallow the savory roast duck that was served her. The food stuck in her throat.

She could not bear to have Tziril out of her sight, and missed

Hinda's presence and the child's laughter. Tziril explained that
Hinda was in school.

"She's growing up very fast," she said. "Yussel won't even
know her when he sees her."

Bayla did not want Yussel's name mentioned in her presence.

"This is where you belong, Tziril," she said. "Your roots are
here, in Kafkaz."

Bayla's friends pitied the grieving Tziril. They were aware of
her troubled spirit and the anxiety which she was no longer
able to hide. As the weeks and months passed without a letter
from her husband, they tried to comfort her — without success. Tziril brooded continually over Yussel's blunt assertion
that everyone was advising him to divorce her. If Yussel decided to send her a get, no rabbi would contest it, since they
hadn't seen each other for almost seven years. Still she could
not bring herself to leave Bayla.

Tziril's red-rimmed eyes testified to her sleepless nights.
Bayla's friends wished they could help her, but she was as sensitive as ever. One day they told her that there was little anyone could do for Bayla, and that it would all be over soon.
Bayla probably wouldn't even know if she packed up and qui-
etly left to join her husband. She had been more than devoted,
and Meiron would understand.

"It breaks our hearts to see you suffer," they told her. "We
all know how devoted you've been, and what joy you've
brought to this lonely house — you and Hinda. You owe
something to yourself. You have to realize that your own happiness is important."

"But where will I go?" Tziril asked one day. "My husband
wants to divorce me and I can't face my sister Channa now."

Her mother's weeping and the excited voices of the guests
disturbed Hinda who was preparing her lessons for the next
day. Her mother was always crying, it seemed, and kept her a-
wake at night with her sobbing. The drucke was very depressing these days. Every day when she came home from school,
her mother wanted her to go into the Muma's room to cheer
her up, but as soon as she got there, Hinda couldn't wait to
leave. The odor in the sickroom was terrible, and she never
knew what to say to her aunt, whose breathing was so labored.

As Hinda entered the kitchen, the women suddenly pointed at her. They seemed quite excited. Hinda, they exclaimed, almost in unison, should write her father a letter.

"And why not?" asked one. "There is every reason for her to write. How could Yussel not answer a letter from his daughter?"

"He'll never answer, I'm sure," Tziril said. "He's sending me a *get*. It's been more than a year since I heard from him — why, it's been seven years since we were together."

"He might remain indifferent to you," was the shrewd reply, "but a letter from his only child might soften his anger. It's worth a try."

Though Tziril was skeptical, the women began to give Hinda orders.

"Put away your books and write a letter to your father in America." Hinda was handed a long sheet of lined paper, and someone thrust a sharpened quill into her hand. "A long, loving letter," she was told.

They all watched anxiously as she began to write. The girl's face was a picture of deep concentration.

Actually, Hinda was bewildered at this unusual request. Never before had she been formally requested to write to her father.

"But what should I write?" she asked.

"We told you. A long, loving letter." The women were all talking at the same time.

"Fill every line! Tell him that the Muma is dying. Tell him that you miss him. Go ahead — write!"

Tziril began to dictate. "My beloved, worthy, respected father, Yosef Yacov Wilkimirsky."

There was a moment's pause. Hinda wrote what was dictated, looking up every so often, a frown joining her delicate eyebrows. They all watched as she continued. She filled every line down to the bottom of the sheet, just as she had been instructed. Then they nudged each other in satisfaction.

What had she written? As she guided the pen across the page, Hinda was remembering that her father hadn't written or sent them money for over a year, and that he was the cause of her mother's sleepless nights and tears of anguish. She had been told to fill the page, but after the dictated salutation she did not know how to continue, and had signed her name. She still had to fill the page!

Almost automatically, she proceeded to sign her name again and again, until only two lines remained. Then, in her most careful penmanship, she added that she sent her love, and signed her name again at the bottom of the page, "Hinda Dvera Wilkimirsky."

"What a neat letter," the women noted approvingly at the first glance. "It's perfect, except for an occasional ink-blot."

Hinda's letter was handed around, and the women laughed good-naturedly.

"It's perfect! Perfect! Tziril, you must send this to your husband right away, just as it is. I'd like to be there when Yussel reads this!"

But Tziril was horrified.

"How can I send this to my husband? Yussel will think that his daughter is a half-wit, a girl without a brain! That I have raised a child without any intelligence. I can't send that! It's not even a letter."

But her friends persisted.

"The letter is perfect," they insisted. "Send it just the way it is; don't change a single word."

Hinda mailed the letter to her father that very day.

Days of Mourning

Though Bayla's long illness seemed to have prepared her family and friends to some degree, in the end her death came as a great shock. The household was plunged into the prescribed rituals of mourning. To Hinde, the drucke seemed haunted, with the printing press shut down and the mirrors draped in white sheets. Reb Meiron and her mother sat on the floor in their stocking feet and would sit thus, according to the custom, for the duration of Shiva, the seven days of mourning.

Friends of the family had made all the arrangements for the funeral and had taken complete charge of their home. The women came daily to comfort the mourners and attend to their needs, and the men joined them each morning and evening for prayers.

Bayla had been loved and respected by all who had known her, for she had been an active member of the Jewish community and a liberal contributor to every worthy cause. Tziril could not help but be aware that her sister's death was a personal loss to the many friends who had shared in the joys and sorrows of the long life she had lived among them.

After the funeral, there was ample time for loving reminiscences, as the mourners and friends sat and talked through the afternoons.

"On the day she dies," began one elderly woman, "she was so talkative — even more so than usual. She seemed for a few minutes to have recovered some of her old spirit. She asked again and again whether or not Hinda had heard from her father. I didn't know what to tell her."

"But you know it takes months for a letter to come from

such a distance," Tziril interrupted. The pitying stares of the women made her decidedly uncomfortable, and it seemed to her that they were all thinking that there would be no reply from Yussel after all. Their eyes seemed to repeat over and over again: "Your husband has washed his hands of you and has found consolation elsewhere."

But the women weren't even listening to her explanations, and Bayla's old friend continued.

"Two minutes later she had forgotten about Yussel and began to sniff at the air. 'What do I smell?' she kept asking. Poor Bayla — can you imagine — she was so hungry. 'I can tell,' she said. 'Roast lamb! How delicious it smells! I want to eat now; can't you see that I'm starving? Perhaps the lamb will restore my strength.'"

They remembered how Tziril had hastened to comply with what turned out to be Bayla's final request. They had all watched as the plate of succulent meat was placed before her. As a rule, during her final illness she was usually able to swallow only a few mouthfuls, though she had often complained of being "famished." This time had been a memorable exception. No one had ever seen Bayla eat with such a voracious appetite. The sick woman had declared that nothing she had ever eaten had tasted so delicious. Who could have known it was to be her final meal?

When they removed the empty plate, Bayla's smile had become almost beatific. Tziril and her friends recalled how they had settled her comfortably on the great mounds of pillows. Almost instantaneously, Bayla had fallen into a deep sleep from which she never recovered consciousness.

And now Tziril was inconsolable. She was pitied even more than Bayla's bereaved husband, since it was apparent to everyone that she was in mourning not only for the loss of her sister, but for the wreckage of her marriage. Though everyone sympathized with Reb Meiron, the general consensus was that he had lived a long and full life. How could they be too sorry for a man who had accumulated so much wealth and enjoyed such prestige in the community? There were those who even began to whisper that the elderly widower's life was "just beginning."

One day, the arrival of a letter from America diverted their attention from the future prospects of Reb Meiron. Without being told, everyone knew that it was Yussel's answer to his daughter's letter that had arrived by special post.

No one but Tziril ever saw that letter, not even Hinda, although her mother informed her of its contents, but overnight there had been a remarkable change in her which was quite obvious. Gone was her despondent expression, and she radiated a new confidence. In the privacy of her bedroom, she read and reread the letter, weeping and kissing its tear-stained pages. The Rabbono Shel Olom had not deserted her after all, but continued to watch over her, however unworthy she might have been.

There was no indication that Yussel had ever had any serious intention of divorcing her. Hinda's letter, he wrote, was a turning point in his life. Lonely and full of bitterness at his wife's seeming desertion, he had almost forgotten the beloved daughter who was dearer to him than his own life. Wherever he went he proudly displayed that letter, and before long, Hinda's letter had become the chief topic of conversation for his family in America. All Yussel could think of was that there actually was a Hinda Dvera Wilkimirsky. How could he have forgotten? As though to remind him, she had written her name on every line of the page.

His friends and relatives had begun to greet him with a boisterous " Hinda Dvera Wilkimirsky" when they would meet. Their salutation was always accompanied by a resounding slap on the back that nearly knocked him off his feet.

Still, soon Tziril began to wonder whether she was reading more into that letter than the situation could justify. Certainly Yussel was angry — he had a right to be, he had written. Of course, she hadn't exactly been a dutiful wife. Who could blame him, though? What other husband in his place would not be bitter? Only a man who was a fool. She knew that she could never have been so patient under the circumstances.

Tziril had known numerous deserted wives in Kovno, who had spent years waiting in vain for their husbands in America to send for them. These women had been abandoned forever, and Russia was full of innumerable agunahs, unable to even get a divorce and remarry, since it was impossible to determine whether their husbands were alive or dead. How those women had envied her! With the first money Yussel had been able to save, he had sent her a ticket for her voyage to America.

With his letter he reminded her how fortunate she was. But hadn't she deserted him! He upbraided her unmercifully, and did not spare his words this time. She had all but forgotten the duty she owed him, and he would never be able to forgive her. He was, however, demanding that she return to Kovno without further delay. He wanted to see his daughter. Yussel would meet them at Channa's house, and there, face to face, they would resolve what the future would hold for them.

Shloshim, the thirty days of less-intensive mourning, followed Shiva. According to Jewish law, it was now permissible for a mourner to attend to his everyday business and even remarry. To Tziril's horror, there were many close friends of Reb Meiron who began to whisper that such was the widower's intention. But in the meantime, Meiron was too preoccupied with settling his affairs to pay much attention to their gossip. He was liquidating everything and disposing of most of his possessions, so that he would be able to set out for London as soon as possible.

The news of his impending departure was more of a surprise to his associates than Bayla's death, although everyone knew that he had relatives in Western Europe and even in London. Over the years, he and Bayla had accumulated a considerable amount of money, and Meiron admitted to having an account in a Swiss bank.

"I don't have many years left," was his usual response to their inquiries. "I've decided to make the most of what is left. Bayla and I often discussed what I would do if she were to die first."

Everything was to be sold, except for the drucke, which Bayla had willed to Tziril. Meiron reminded everyone that it had been purchased in his wife's name. The entire printing press would be dismantled and shipped to Kovno, and Tziril could either sell it, or go into the printing business for herself.

At last, Tziril was preparing to return to Kovno. She had already written to Yussel, notifying him of her plans, and the fact that she was now owner of the drucke. Meiron had told her that if there was anything among the household furnishings that she desired, she had only to ask. Tziril decided to take Bayla's copper cooking utensils and her old brass samovar, and as the days passed, she also claimed the shallow pan in which the Sabbath Challah dough was left to rise, and the handsome copper pail. She couldn't help remembering how often she had filled these copper pails with wine and carried them upstairs for the refreshment of clients and officers to whom Bayla and Meiron had given freely of their hospitality.

Meiron also suggested that Bayla's best cashmere shawl, fringed and heavily embroidered in gold, would be the perfect gift for Channa. Bayla would have wanted her other sister to have it, he said.

As the day of departure approached, Tziril was aware that Reb Meiron was troubled. One day, almost timidly, he told her that if she had no objections, he would like to travel with her and Hinda as far as Kovno. From there he would proceed to London alone. He would, at least, have the opportunity to meet Bayla's other relatives, which was something he had wanted to do ever since Tziril's arrival.

Tziril hesitated, then replied thoughtfully.

"Channa has a big house. I'm sure you would be welcome for as long as you wish to stay. She'll be delighted to have this beautiful shawl — she has many fine shawls and dresses, but none so beautiful as Bayla's."

It was only then that Meiron confessed that the thought of being left alone depressed him. He simply could not bear the thought of remaining alone in the house he had once shared with his wife, even for a few weeks. Since his great loss, he had come to realize how empty life could be without love and companionship.

Tziril was stirred with pity for her elderly brother-in-law. Reb Meiron had no true friends, it seemed, and she was beginning to believe that everyone envied his wealth and never stopped whispering about the huge sums he was said to have put away in Swiss banks. It was rumored that not even Bayla had been unaware of the size of his fortune, and it suddenly occurred to Tziril that they probably had suspicions about her

relationship with her dead sister's husband as well. She began
to wish that she had not promised him that they would leave
Kafkaz together. Who could know for certain what they might
be saying about her that very moment?

With the same characteristic impatience that had marked
the days before her trip to Kafkaz, she began her final preparations for her return to Kovno. At last she was at peace, for
she had finally found what she had been seeking all those years.
Her mind was more at rest than it had ever been, and her only
remaining doubt was the kind of welcome she would receive
from her husband. Even the old bitterness toward Channa
eased. She was eager to embrace her sister, for she now knew
that she owed her very life to Channa, without whose concern
and sacrifice she might have perished.

And now Bayla was dead. Her memory, Tziril knew, would
survive as long as she lived herself. She would never forget
their long discussions of their father, Itzele Metter, whom
Bayla had loved and idolized.

Actually, they had hardly discussed Dvera, since Bayla had
admitted that she had not known her father's second wife very
well. She remembered her only as a young bride — a radiant
and accomplished woman who had been well educated and
greatly admired. Dvera Gordon had been known for her intel-
lect, but had also inspired respect and admiration for her devotion to her husband and his interests. After his death, Bayla
had reminded her, Tziril's mother had personally taken over
his lawsuit, using her own dwindling funds to pay the expenses.

But most of all, Tziril would never forget the pilgrimage she
and Bayla had made to the ancient cemetery where their Spanish ancestors lay buried. Whatever his feelings about her might
be, at least she could now approach Yussel with the knowledge
that she had found her roots at last. Even though no one knew
where her father was buried, Itzele Metter had not been
forgotten.

"While you live, Tziril," Bayla had said, "his memory will
survive. And even after you there is Hinda Dvera. I know she
will remember."

Home to Kovno

Tziril found the journey back to Kovno wearisome beyond belief. Of course, Reb Meiron's frailty and poor health did not help matters any. Soon after leaving his home, the old man lost his appetite completely, and he was extremely ill during the Black Sea crossing. There were times when Tziril didn't see how he would ever be able to survive the rigors of the journey ahead of them. What disturbed her more was the fact that Meiron seemed incapable of looking after his own needs. How would he ever manage once they had gone their separate ways? Could it be that she was to be saddled with his care? The thought was frightening.

Meiron himself admitted that if it hadn't been for Tziril, he wouldn't have wanted to live another day. He couldn't even for a moment forget all that he had lost, and was overwhelmed with grief and loneliness. But it seemed to Tziril that, in addition to his sorrow at losing Bayla, he was having second thoughts about the home and business he had so willingly left behind only a short time before.

Of the three of them, Hinda alone approached the journey with enthusiasm. As she eagerly took in the sights and sounds that surrounded her, she exclaimed excitedly over every familiar landmark she had first seen as a young child seven years earlier.

"Oh Mama — you see, nothing has changed," she said. "If anything, the mountains look higher and the sky bluer than they did when we first came. Why, the Black Sea is even wider than I remembered," and she declared that someday she'd return to show her own children this lovely land.

"I don't see how you could ever regret coming here. I know

I'll only have happy memories of these years as long as I live."

Tziril regarded her with great pride, for she had raised her almost single-handedly, and she took great comfort in the thought that if her attempt at reconciliation with her husband were to be a failure, she would still have her Hinda. But her daughter was no longer a child; the relatives in Kovno would never recognize her, and regardless of his feelings toward his wife, Yussel would be both overjoyed and overwhelmed when he saw his nearly grown daughter.

Hinda was taller than her mother, and her figure, though slight, was well developed and almost womanly. Her long fair hair contrasted with her dark eyes. She really was lovely, Tziril realized with a pang, and would have to be guarded and watched closely. She remembered too well the baser emotions behind the smiles of the men aboard the steamer during their first crossing of the Black Sea. As it was, Hinda was already very attractive to the opposite sex — the Master of the Universe should watch over her!

"Your guardian angel should watch over you and ward off any Evil Eye!" was Tziril's constant prayer. "Please keep my daughter safe with me, until the time comes when she finds a suitable husband."

What worried Tziril the most was that Hinda was light-hearted by nature, with a tendency toward frivolity. But she was still a young girl, and the fact that it took very little to keep her spirits high was almost a blessing under the circumstances. She even managed to cheer the ailing Meiron, Tziril observed with affection.

But as the time for their meeting drew near, Tziril became more and more preoccupied with the rift between Yussel and herself, but before she could decide what to do in the event that he rejected her, they were back in Kovno.

Tears were shed when Channa and Tziril embraced. Channa's voice quivered as she declared that she had no words to express how much Tziril and Hinda had been missed.

"We had a simcha, you know. Our Feigele became a bride. To think that you weren't here to share our joy — my own sister who helped raise her! How my Feigele missed her Muma Tziril at the wedding. And now she and her husband are already in America!

Reb Yosef proved to be a most gracious host, and extended a hearty welcome to Meiron whom, he said, they would be honored to have stay with them until he was ready to continue his journey. The house was big enough for everyone. After all, he was a member of their family, wasn't he?

Both Channa and Yosef were moved by Meiron's grief-stricken countenance. Here was a sad example of a good man left alone in the world with no children to comfort him in his declining years. They thanked him for his gifts — a tallith with an elaborately embroidered collar for Ren Yosef, in addition to Channa's shawl. Yosef and Channa were pleased by the thought that he remembered them in a time of sorrow.

"It's really nothing," Meiron shrugged. "But Bayla often remarked that she intended to send a gift to her sister in Kovno. Let your acceptance of these gifts be a token of your forgiveness. Bayla's conscience would never let her rest as long as she was alive."

Meiron responded to the friendly hospitality of the Rosenblums immediately. He admired Channa tremendously, and was quite impressed with his host's sons.

"One can tell right away that they are the grandsons of a noble man. I remember Zalman Yitzchok well. If only my Bayla, may her soul rest in peace, could have seen them, it would have gladdened her heart. The family resemblance is really remarkable! The same tall, slender build, the same fine features. Their eyes even have Itzele Metter's old fire!"

There was little sleep for Tziril that night as she and Channa sat until morning, talking and reminiscing. Time and separation had softened the bitterness between the two sisters, and for the first time Tziril genuinely appreciated her sister's closeness. She was able to discuss her worries about her marriage frankly, but at the same time was amazed to discover that Channa was having problems of her own.

"We've had nothing but troubles since you left," she admitted. In the intervening years they had lost much of their substance. The government had accused them of all sorts of violations and had levied fine after fine. But that wasn't the worst of it. They were being milked dry, according to Channa, to keep their sons out of the army; there was no end in sight to their woes.

Tears welled up in Channa's eyes, and Tziril noticed for the first time how much her sister had aged.

"As soon as it can be safely arranged, we will all be leaving for America," she said. "It's most important for my sons. There is no future for them here in Russia. We knew it when Feigele left — she didn't even want to wait until her child was born."

This was quite a turn of affairs, and Tziril was taken aback. It had never occurred to her that Channa, who had always seemed so protected and secure, might one day have to abandon her beautiful home and depart for America as a common emigrant with forged papers and bread-and-herring in her satchel.

❧

Whatever Tziril's doubts might have been, Hinda was excited and exhilarated at the approaching arrival of her father. She reveled in the attention she received from her cousins and their friends, who came every day to listen to her stories of life in Kafkaz. Though she was no longer a child, she still had only fond memories of her early years in Kovno when her cousins, Nathan and Moshe, had carried her on their shoulders. They often reminded her of those days, adding that now she was practically grown and a beauty, besides. The boys were lavish with their compliments, and made her repeat over and over again the tale of her encounter with the Cossacks the day she had ventured onto the highway with her pet goat.

They greeted everything she said with uproarious laughter, and more than once Channa felt obliged to tell them to lower their voices. But after a while, Hinda realized that her cousin Reizel was annoyed and skeptical, if not jealous, and that her accounts of those episodes Reizel's brothers found so amusing, were to her nothing more than fictitious bids for attention. Reizel began to refer to Hinda's anecdotes as "buba meissas," or "old-grandmother tales."

The news of their return spread rapidly throughout the community and old friends, eager to see Tziril and hear about her adventures, came to Channa's house at all hours of the

day. Many of them, notably the widows and divorcees, came
to meet Reb Meiron, for they had all heard that Tziril's wid-
owed brother-in-law, a man of substance, had accompanied
her on her return to Kovno and was a guest at the home of
Channa and Reb Yosef.

Ever since his arrival in Kovno, Meiron had accompanied
Yosef to the synagogue twice a day for morning and evening
services. Gossip had it that Rabinowitz the shadchen, had already arranged to introduce the widower to the wealthiest
widow in the gebarno, or province, and why not? Why should
not such a fine, wealthy man remarry? For a man to live out
his days alone would be to go against Talmudic teaching.

"Such an elegant figure of a man," people said of him.
"Such a fine sensitive face."

Fortunately, these references to Meiron were not as embarrassing to Tziril as the insinuations of his old friends in Kafkaz
had been about their personal relationship. Besides, it was obvious to her that her friends in Kovno began to regard her with
a new respect and no little envy. By now they had all heard
that she had inherited a printing press and had received many
valuable gifts from Bayla and Meiron. They approached her
constantly with questions about what she intended to do
with it, curious as to what, if anything, she knew about running a drucke, and whether or not she thought it would be
profitable.

It seemed to them beyond comprehension that she, a woman,
had learned to operate the drucke, and was planning to teach
her husband. It was simply unheard-of for a woman to understand the intricacies of such a complicated piece of machinery,
and they didn't mind telling her so. But the one thing they
could understand was that the printing press represented po-
tential wealth. Here was their neighbor Tziril Wilkimirsky, who
had left Kovno without a penny of her own, and returned as
a woman of importance. No longer did they refer to her as
Channa's poor sister!

❧

One day, not long after their return, Yussel's younger sister
Zlateh was among the visitors. Zlateh, a widow, arrived on the

mail coach from Wilki with her daughter Breina, bringing
greetings from old Reb Tevya, who was eagerly awaiting his
son Yussel's arrival.

Though she had not seen Zlateh for many years, Tziril still
knew she disliked her. She had always been a problem as far
as Yussel's family was concerned, even before her marriage.
Now she was a widow with a young daughter who was already
marriageable. Even when her husband was alive, Zlateh had
felt no compunction about calling her entire family for financial assistance and now, Tziril observed, her daughter would
soon need a dowry.

After Zlateh's departure, Channa confided that Tziril's sister-in-law was no stranger to Kovno, although she still lived in
Wilki, a fair distance away. She came to the marketplace at
least twice a week, getting a ride in a baker's wagon.

"Zlateh works in the bakery a few days a week and has another job plucking chickens. She kills herself trying to support
Breina and herself – poor woman. She does have a hard life."

"But she comes to Kovno not to buy, but to show off her
Breina." Channa shrugged her shoulders disparagingly. "Once
she finds a husband for Breina, she'll be out looking for one
herself, no doubt."

"She must have heard that Meiron was here," Tziril shrewdly
replied, and gave Channa a look that spoke volumes.

Channa nodded. "But of course she has heard. The last time
she was here, she asked a thousand questions. I could only tell
her what I knew from your letter – that he was old, ailing and
extremely wealthy."

Tziril was annoyed by the fact that Rabinowitz the matchmaker was becoming a frequent visitor, and what disturbed
her the most was how the old man was welcoming his attentions. By now it was quite obvious that Reb Meiron was eager
to remarry. Despite his age and infirmities, there was no deny-
ing that he was considered a highly eligible widower. But it
was amazing to see how much better he began to look after a
few days of rest, and how he seemed to thrive on all the attention he received. He had lost the awful pallor that so distressed
Tziril, and there was certainly nothing wrong with his appetite
these days.

The Wilkimirsky Family. Hinda in her green velvet dress,
Tziril in her copy of Queen Victoria's gown,
and Yussel in a Prince Albert.

Hinda Dvera at age fifteen.

Tevya Wilkimirsky, Yussel's father in Wilki.

Hinda: The photograph in her green velvet dress,
sent by Alte to his family in Vilna.

Alte Lipschutz

Reb Yeheschel and Rivka Lipschutz with their children:
Sonya and Mordechai (Motle) in the back,
Pasha the youngest in the foreground.

Wedding Reception,

— OF —

Mr. & Mrs. Abraham Lipschitz,

Sunday, Feb. 16th, '90,

TURN HALL

259 First St.

Jersey City. N. J.

MUSIC BY PROF. WOLLENBERG

Brooks & Goldstein, Print. 145 East Broadway, N. Y.

FLOOR MANAGER

Dr. D. Feigensohn.

Order of Dancing.

PART FIRST.

Grand March to Bride & Groom.

1. Quadrille.
2. Waltz.
3. Polka.
4. Lanciers Saratoga.
5. Schottische.
6. Quadrille Waltz
7. Spanish Waltz.
8. Polka,

MARCH TO SUPPER.

Order of Dancing.

PART SECOND.

Re-Entree to our Guests.

1. Lanciers.
2. Ladies Waltz.
3. Schottische.
4. Quadrille Waltz.
5. Polka.
6. Lanciers Saratoga.
7. Waltz.
8. All Sorts.

HOME SWEET HOME.

The Dance Program
for
The Wedding Reception

The author, in a picture taken at the beginning of her career.

It seemed to her that he had even put on weight and looked just as he had prior to Bayla's final illness. It was apparent that he was beginning to approach life with renewed interest. No one, however, enjoyed the shadchen's visits more than Reb Yosef, who made it known that he very much approved of Meiron's efforts to find a new wife.

And the old man's explanation was candidness itself. "It's hard to be alone, and every day it gets worse. Let me tell you something, Tziril — life without a companion is no kind of life for a man. But I told Rabinowitz I'm in no hurry. He seems to be getting impatient, because he's already introduced me to some very fine women. But to be truthful, none of them quite appeals to me."

Tziril was beginning to lose patience with him.

"Tell me the truth," she demanded. "The shadchen has introduced you to the finest women in Kovno, and nobody pleases you. Just what are you looking for?"

"All right," he said. "I'll tell you. After living so many years with Bayla, I can't be satisfied with just anybody. I want a woman I can talk to..."

"Meiron," Tziril replied, "the emes. Tell me the real reason!"

"The emes? You want the real truth, do you? All right then. These women — they are all so old! I can't marry an old woman! I want somebody young. A woman full of life. That's what I'm looking for. Somebody young — yes, that's it. She doesn't have to be beautiful or well off. Young is beautiful enough for me!"

Tziril repeated this conversation with Meiron to Channa who, in turn, told Reb Yosef, who chuckled through his gray beard.

"I knew Meiron was a smart man the minute I shook hands with him," he said. But beyond that, he refused to comment further on the subject.

Tziril assumed that Channa would repeat their conversation to her husband, but she was unprepared for the solution Channa proposed.

"Why not introduce him to Zlateh? She ought to be young enough. Of course, she hasn't the yichus of Rifka Gutschmidt, that banker's widow from Lodz. And she doesn't have Rifka's money. But she's still young and should make things lively for a man. At least Zlateh will know how to keep him busy — if nothing else, he'll know he's alive."

"Zlateh!" Tziril could not hide her dismay. Frankly, she was horrified.

"That slut? She can't even be trusted. Every time she came to see me, something was missing. You have to watch her every minute. Don't ever leave her alone when she comes here, Channa!"

"But Tziril, you know her need is great. It would be a mitzvah to introduce them. Life has not been good to Zlateh, and it's no wonder that she's anxious to get married. Besides, she is Yussel's sister. She is family, you know."

Tziril was convinced. Later that evening, she spoke to Meiron and invited him to visit Wilki with her. She told him that her husband had a younger sister who was a widow, and that she had decided the two should meet.

"Zlateh is young, good looking, even though it hasn't been easy for her. There is a daughter, though, but she'll probably be married before long. I'm not saying that Zlateh is another Bayla, but you won't be lonely, and at least she will be young enough for you.

"You have to face the facts, Meiron. Women like Bayla are very rare, and you will probably never meet anyone like her."

Meiron hesitated.

"I promised Rabinowitz that I'd give him an answer."

"Rabinowitz can wait," replied Tziril. "First you must meet Zlateh."

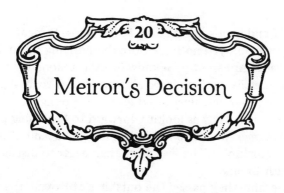

Meiron's Decision

The next morning, Tziril arranged to hire a carriage for her visit to Wilki with Reb Meiron. But as soon as he heard that his aunt intended to make the trip, Nathan volunteered to drive them, and Tziril could not conceal her delight at his unsolicited offer. Quickly, Channa voiced her objections.

"It's really not necessary. Certainly Nathan should have better things to do with his time. Yankel, our hired man, will do the driving."

"Yankel?" Nathan let out a whoop of derision. "The old drunkard will fall asleep before they are half way to Wilki. He always manages to get lost, and what will happen then? I know a short cut that will get us there much faster."

Tziril realized that in many ways, Nathan was still the same playful, affectionate fellow he had been in the days when she had drilled him in the alphabet. He had hated nothing more than to be confined to the schoolroom, and if it hadn't been for her patience and insistence, he might never have learned to read. She had always known that he would never be a scholar, and he never had any desire for learning. It seemed natural to her then, that he would be a favorite with the girls and popular with the young men. Still, she felt a special closeness to this nephew she had helped raise.

But his sister Reizel began to snicker.

"Nathan knows the road all right," she chuckled. "He goes to Wilki often enough!" She drew Hinda aside and whispered to her. The two girls began to giggle.

"Mama is furious. He goes there to see Breina, and thinks he's so smart! He thinks nobody knows."

The next day, Tziril and Meiron set out for Wilki with a tri-

umphant and handsome Nathan at the reins. It seemed to Tziril
that Nathan enjoyed nothing more than driving through the
countryside. Apparently he knew every rut along the way, and
whistled merrily as they drove along a narrow road, deserted
except for a few chickens and ducks. The young man was just
glad to be alive. He was looking forward to beginning a new
life in America, which he would refer to as "a land of unpar-
alleled opportunity;" he was more than eager to discuss his
plans with Breina.

By the time they passed the outskirts of Kovno, the road
narrowed to a single unpaved lane. The wheels of the carriage
began to stick in the pockets of mud left from that morning's
early spring rain. They passed through innumerable villages
and acres of rich farmland, dotted with grazing cattle and
thatched cottages. Chicken and geese scattered to find safety,
and goats leaped from the path of the rattling vehicle. The
weather was clear and mild — a perfect day for an outing —
and the peasants were already bent over their plows in the
April sunshine.

As though to pass the time, Reb Meiron began to compare
this serene yet monotonous landscape with the rugged splendor
of the Caucasian countryside. Tziril nodded in agreement, as
she recalled the vine covered hillsides and the fields of exotic
flowers which could never grow so far north.

"Everything must be in full bloom by now — the orchards,
the vineyards," she sighed. For the first time she realized that
she would never return to Kafkaz again.

When they finally reached their destination, Tziril was a-
mazed to discover that the town of Wilki hadn't changed at
all since she had last seen it. The small, shabby house which
Reb Tevya had occupied since his first marriage seemed as dil-
apidated as the day when she was first introduced to her father-
in-law. Two generations of Wilkimirskys had been born there,
and still it was as though time had stood still.

Her father-in-law lived on the main street, which was
crowded with shops and the stalls of street vendors. It seemed
to Tziril that the whole village had congregated in the small
square between Tevya's house and the synagogue. A stone's
throw away was the mikvah, or ritual bath, and a water pump

in the middle of the square served the community, except for
the few wealthy households which had their own wells.

The arrival of a carriage bringing guests to Tevya's home was
a public event, and a crowd of curious townspeople surrounded
them, following Tziril and her companions all the way to Reb
Tevya's door. Some of the women, pious Jewesses with ker-
chiefs covering their wigs, even went so far as to inquire about
the nature of their business with the venerable Tevya Wilkimirsky. Impatient as ever, Tziril quickly ordered them to disperse
and mind their own business.

Nathan laughed at his aunt's seeming outrage. There was very
little that happened in Wilki that the population didn't learn
about sooner or later.

"Everything is their business," he declared, with a flourish
of his sunburnt arms.

Meanwhile, the commotion had alerted Reb Tevya, who
came running to the door. The crowd didn't seem to bother
him in the least, and he greeted his neighbors and relatives with
an air of nonchalance.

"Why, it's Tziril! My own son Yussel's wife!" he shouted so
that all could hear. He quickly beckoned his guests into the
house and slammed the door behind them, disappointing the
curious who had every intention of following them into Tevya's home, but the crowd seemed satisfied with the old man's
explanation, and began to disperse.

Reb Tevya expressed his joy at seeing Tziril after her long
absence, as well as his pleasure that she had brought along her
distinguished brother-in-law and handsome nephew. He had
already heard about Meiron's arrival in Kovno, and there was
little he didn't know about him.

"News travels fast from shtetl to shtetl," he said. Even in a
small town the size of Wilki, everyone knew what the Jews
of Kovno were doing.

Of course, he wondered why Tziril hadn't brought Hinda —
he was anxious to see his granddaughter. He had heard so much
about how charming she was, and how accomplished in her
schooling. Her ability to learn languages was reputed to be
phenomenal.

Despite his threadbare black caftan, he was still a distinguished man. His beard was snow white and as long and full as those depicted in portraits of the patriarchs. His gray hair radiated like a corona from beneath his frayed velvet skullcap, framing his face like a halo. No one was sure of Tevya Wilkimirsky's age, but even though he was well along in years, he still walked tall and erect, without a cane. Indeed, it seemed as though age had brought him nothing but honor and the respect and love of the entire town.

During the course of his four marriages he had fathered more children than he could count. He had already outlived three wives, and everyone said that he would probably survive the last one, although she was at least twenty years his junior. Although he had never accumulated wealth, he was proud of the fact that no child of his had brought shame to the family name, and he would often boast about this unselfconsciously. He managed to live in relative comfort, though, since the sons in America never failed to send him a monthly stipend. As Reb Tevya Wilkimirsky often remarked, he considered himself blessed.

After greeting his daughter-in-law with an affectionate embrace, he directed his attention to Meiron. Despite the fact that he had known Nathan since he was a small boy, he ignored him completely, for he knew instinctively that Tziril had something important on her mind that concerned Meiron as well as himself.

"My wife is at the market," he explained, ushering the guests into the kitchen. "In the meantime, I'll put on the kettle and we'll have a glass of tea."

Tziril carefully unwrapped a honey cake and a jar of date preserves she had brought in her satchel. "Channa had baked the day before, in honor of their reunion," she told her father-in-law.

Reb Tevya beamed with pleasure.

"Channa is an excellent cook, and in all this time I haven't forgotten how delicious her cakes are. We have to thank God there is a land like America for Jews to run to — my heart breaks for Channa. I know what it means when one's sons have to leave their homes because of the conscription." Tevya sighed with the long suffering look of a sage.

The copper kettle on the stove began to boil, and Tziril brewed tea, which she served in tall glasses. She sliced Channa's honey cake, rich and fragrant with spices and crushed almonds.

As they sipped their tea, Tziril whispered to Tevya that she wanted to introduce her brother-in-law to Zlateh, and needed his approval. He was, after all, head of the family; such respect was his due. She assured him that she personally could vouch for Reb Meiron's excellent reputation and character as well as his ability to provide for a wife handsomely.

"Meiron," she said in a whisper, "is not a man who is easily pleased. He has been giving the shadchen Rabinowitz a hard time for weeks now. You know, it took much persuasion on my part to get him to come here. All I can hope for now is that he will like Zlateh, and that the two of them will come to an agreement that will lead to the marriage canopy."

Tziril continued, this time loud enough for Meiron to hear.

"As his wife, she would live like a queen. Never again would she have to struggle or suffer want. And her daughter would be given a dowry and have many fine suitors."

Old Tevya could hardly believe what he had just heard. There was a catch somewhere, he was certain.

"And the nadon? The dowry?" His voice broke with anxiety, "unfortunately, Zlateh has no dowry."

Tziril cut him short. "Who's talking about a dowry? That's only important for two people starting a life together. But for an established man, like Reb Meiron, who spent a lifetime building for a future – all he seeks is a congenial and honorable companion. Somebody who is still youthful, with whom he can enjoy his remaining years."

Tevya studied Meiron all during Tziril's discourse. It was plain to him that Meiron appreciated Tziril's flattering appraisal of his situation, for he was smiling benevolently. His expression seemed to imply that he was only seeking a chance at the happiness he thought he deserved after years of hard work.

"How clever that Tziril is," Meiron thought. He alone knew what his intentions might have been if she weren't already married, but it was futile for him to think about that, and he wondered what this Zlateh was like.

"If I had been seeking nadon and nothing else," he said, "I

would have been satisfied with the first woman the match-maker introduced me to."

Reb Tevya gave another sigh and closed his eyes as though he were praying. Clasping his gnarled hands, he began to sway back and forth.

"My poor Zlateh," he finally said. "She has been without a husband for too long. She's never had any mazel – no luck at all. To be left a widow with a young child – there could be no worse fate for a woman like her. It's time fortune smiled on her for a change."

Tevya's cheeks were flushed with excitement. He quickly got up from the table..

"You'll have to excuse me. I'll send my neighbor Hersch to fetch Zlateh. She and Breina are working in the chicken market today."

Tziril tore after him. Speaking in a hushed tone she warned him. "Reb Tevya, dear father-in-law, tell Zlateh you have a special guest. Tell her she shouldn't come running over here covered with chicken feathers. She should go home and change, Breina too, they should dress like it's a yomtov in their best clothing."

Chava, Tevya's plump middle aged wife, was unpacking her market basket when Zlateh and Breina arrived, breathless from running and dressed in their best Sabbath finery.

Breina had not expected to see Nathan there, and her color mounted the moment she saw him. Nathan smiled at her, but remained silent, and as though there were a pact between them, a roguish wink was his only greeting. To Tziril, though, it was obvious that his restlessness and boredom had vanished.

Zlateh's thin face was flushed with excitement. In her youth she had been considered the most attractive girl in Wilki, but after many years of hard work and widowhood, there was little beauty left in her high cheekboned face. It was a hard face, with lines of defiance around the mouth, reminders of the years of hardship and loneliness she had known since her husband's death.

She was a tall, thin woman – almost painfully so. Her hair, which had been a lustrous auburn in her girlhood, was now faded and stringy. In defiance of custom, she had refused to wear the wig of the Orthodox matron after her husband's death, and had brought upon herself much censure from the pious.

Her daughter Breina was a constant reminder of all she had lost. The young girl resembled her mother, but she had all the bloom and radiance of youth, and it seemed as though her mother's troubles had left her unmarred. Breina was good natured, a happy girl who responded warmly to her aunt's greeting. She was so glad that her aunt had finally come to visit them after all those years, and asked why she hadn't brought Hinda. But her eyes continued to seek out Nathan's and the look that passed between them was so revealing that Tziril knew at once why Nathan had been so eager to take them to Wilki.

The introductions over, Tziril took Zlateh aside, and in a few carefully chosen words, told her the purpose of their visit.

Zlateh's face was almost expressionless, with her lips tightened into a nervous line. Without hesitation, she replied that she would be honored to have Tziril act as her shadchen. How could she ever be in a position to oppose a match between Reb Meiron and herself? She thanked Tziril for her interest in her welfare.

Within minutes, her workday drabness vanished, and Tziril could see a trace of the lively, popular girl her sister-in-law had once been. Zlateh even began to smile.

"Tziril," she finally said, "I just can't tell you how grateful I am. This is the happiest day I've known since my husband died – he should rest in peace. Perhaps my luck is going to change now!"

But Meiron was unaware of the presence of his proposed bride, and gazed in rapture, as though struck by a supernatural force, at her lovely daughter.

"This one," he announced. "I'm not interested in Zlateh. She's a fine woman to be sure, but I think it's her daughter who will suit me better. I feel strangely drawn to her."

Breina was terrified. She remained frozen on the worn settee, pale with the shock of it. Then her eyes met Nathan's. He started motioning toward the door, as though he were telling her to meet him outside – and quickly. But Zlateh grasped her arm with a strength that made escape impossible.

The look Nathan gave Breina brought Tziril to the verge of tears. Yet, stronger than her pity for Breina and Nathan was her sympathy for Zlateh, whose hopes had been shattered again. Zlateh, however, had command of her wits, despite the fact that no one would have been surprised had she given way to hysterics.

"Breina is exactly what I've been looking for. Breina – a beautiful name," whispered Meiron to Tziril. "I wanted someone lively who would fill my days with joy and bring back my youth. I feel like the day when I first met Bayla!"

"But I brought you here for Zlateh!" Tziril retorted. "I've already spoken to her and her father. How can you shame them this way?"

"Breina is not for you. Can't you see she's much too young? Her head is full of all sorts of romantic foolishness. What kind of life could you have together? There are just too many years separating you. I can't imagine what's happened. You always had such good common sense!"

"But she's the one I want! Speak to Zlateh. Tell her I want to marry Breina. I'm sure Zlateh is a smart woman. Tell her she'll never regret it, and her life will change for the better. I promise she'll lack for nothing as long as she lives."

Zlateh listened to Tziril's explanations and excuses. "Breina," she repeated. "Breina." Then, after a long moment she said, heavily, "So. Let him marry Breina." Her eyes narrowed to slits as she tightened her grip on her daughter's arm.

"I've got good news for you!" Zlateh's voice was harsh. "Breina, do you hear? Let me be the first to wish you mazel tov! You are going to be a bride, my daughter!" Then she was overcome by a fit of sobbing.

Nathan was dejected during their ride home to Kovno. Tziril had to tell herself over and over again that she wasn't to blame and that he would recover from his diappointment. Breina was not for him, and Channa would never have permitted him to marry her anyway.

"Not in a million years," her sister would have said.

Zlateh had done her best to induce Meiron to remain overnight, and it was almost as though she were afraid to let him out of her sight. He promised to return in time for the signing of the engagement contract, and it was agreed that the wedding would follow almost immediately.

Tziril blurted out the whole story to Channa the moment they reached home. Though she sympathized with Nathan, she agreed with Channa that Breina would never have been a suitable wife for him.

To the great amusement of Channa and her family, Reb Meiron enjoyed the role of the happy bridegroom. The old man had never believed anything so wonderful could happen to him, and the change in his outlook was remarkable. But Nathan was bitter and remained secluded in his room for days.

It didn't take Meiron long to prepare for his return to Wilki. He thanked his hosts effusively for everything, and made a donation to their synagogue in Reb Yosef's honor. As an afterthought, he sent a gift of cash to Rabinowitz the shadchen, since he felt that the man deserved something for his trouble.

But he had one more favor to ask of them. Could Reb Yosef recommend a jeweler? He wished to buy a ring for his bride, the finest ring money could buy. Also, a gift for Zlateh would be a good idea, he decided. Perhaps a gold watch and chain would be suitable.

Reb Yosef suggested a jeweler, and then proceeded to accompany the bridegroom to the shop.

"He wanted to buy everything in sight," Yosef reported to his wife that evening. "Nothing was too good or too expensive."

That was the last that anyone in Kovno saw of Reb Meiron, Zlateh and Breina. It was the baker whom Zlateh had worked for who told Tziril and Channa about the wedding.

He reported that Zlateh had been in good spirits on her daughter's wedding day, and seemed to be the typical happy mother of a daughter who was marrying well. She had been ecstatic about the gifts Meiron had lavished on them, and everything had gone smoothly, too smoothly. All Wilki had been invited to the feast. The night before the wedding, Zlateh had accompanied her daughter to the mikvah, and Breina had been docile and obedient on her wedding day.

"But then," the baker continued, " after the ceremony,

just as she and her husband were being led to the feast, the bride threw herself on the floor at her mother's feet and screamed that she didn't want to leave her. Like a mad woman! Breina — that girl wailed that she would die in London, so far from home. The poor girl, I guess had never been away from her mother. 'Why are you sending me away with this old man?' she kept screaming."

Tziril and Channa stared in disbelief, while Hinda listened with horror, though, her cousins seemed amused.

"It can't be true," Channa finally said.

"Every word," assured the baker. "You know Zlateh's temper. Can you believe that instead of slapping Breina soundly and telling her to behave, she also began to scream and carry on? 'Life without her child, her only comfort would not be worth living,' she kept shrieking. 'What will I do if you take my only child away?' "

"And then what happened?" ventured Hinda, who could hardly control her sense of outrage. With growing indignation, she saw that her cousins were stifling their laughter with difficulty, except for Nathan, who had stormed from the room, slamming the door behind him.

How could they laugh? Why on earth did they think it was so hilarious? How could her Aunt Zlateh have permitted such a thing — to force her pretty, young daughter who was only a few years older than Hinda to marry an old man she didn't know? Hinda began to weep.

"But Mama," she sobbed, "How could my grandfather Tevya, whom everyone says is such a saint, allow it?"

"Sha! Hush!" snapped Tziril. "Let him finish."

"So you want to know what happened next? That's the best part," the baker told them as he prepared to depart.

"Wilki will never forget it. Reb Meiron — there's a wise man for you — a real chacham — he settled everything, one, two, three. He told Zlateh there was no call for lamentations. He wouldn't think of separating a mother from her only child. He didn't see any reason why Zlateh couldn't come with them to London. She would be such a help to them while they were getting settled. He even promised her she could live with them as long as she wanted to.

"You know," continued the baker, as he slipped into his jacket, "It didn't take long for Zlateh to pack. When the couple left after the feast, Zlateh went with them." He turned to Tziril as he stood in the doorway.

"You know what I think?" he said. "Strangers who didn't know them would have thought Zlateh was the bride, after all. It's too bad, though, about Breina. That laughing young girl we all knew is gone forever."

Later that evening, Hinda asked her mother if she thought what they had done to Breina was right. Tziril paused to collect her thoughts, and it occurred to her for the first time that as her daughter grew older, her questions became more difficult to answer.

"This is the way life is," she said. "A time comes when a girl should get married. It's unfortunate, but I guess this just had to be."

Hinda's rebelliousness would not let her rest. She couldn't hold back her feelings any longer.

"Mama, you could never do that to me!" she cried. "I'd die first! Or I'd run away. You could never do that to me! How I hate that old man Meiron!" She burst into sobs.

Tziril was shaken. "You have nothing to fear, my child," she assured her. "I promise I will never let such a thing happen to you."

Reconciliation

Before she felt that she was ready to face her husband, the day Tziril had been dreading for so long arrived. Just the day before, she had received an urgent message from Yussel, who had arrived in Hamburg by steamship. If the trains were on schedule, he would reach Kovno that evening. Reb Yosef and Nathan had already left to meet him at the station, and as the hour drew near, Tziril could not hide her misgivings from her sister's knowing eye.

Channa could only pity her, for Tziril was terrified, and it was plain that she dreaded the moment when she would finally meet Yussel face to face.

"What will I say to him?" she asked Channa over and over again. "What can he say to me? He will treat me like a stranger or worse."

She hadn't been able to swallow a mouthful since the previous evening, and more than once Channa inquired whether she was intending to fast all day.

"Tziril, you really should know better," she kept repeating. "Please eat something. Besides, what good will fasting do you at this point? You need your strength."

By this time. Tziril had become totally unnerved, and could only answer that she knew without being told that Yussel would denounce her on the spot and reject her utterly. She had given up hoping that there ever could be a reconciliation, and by now she didn't think she had even the strength to try.

It grew dark, and Channa lighted the lamps. She glanced impatiently at the clock, wondering why her husband hadn't sent a message if Yussel's train had been delayed. She sighed

with annoyed disappointment. The festive meal she had prepared to celebrate Yussel's homecoming would probably be
ruined. But on impulse, she decided that there was no reason
to delay their dinner any longer.

"Tziril! Reizel! Feivel! Hinda! Come!" she called. "Sheindel
and Moshe! Hurry up! We'll eat now. There's no sense waiting."

Tziril refused to sit down, and offered instead to help Channa serve the meal. But one look at her and Channa ordered her
to leave the kitchen and try to compose herself. Tziril's hands
shook so badly she could drop the soup tureen before she was
halfway to the dining room.

Just as they were finishing their soup, the voices of men
were heard outside as they unloaded Yussel's massive trunk
from the carriage. Everyone grew quiet at the sound of their
approaching footsteps on the front stairs. Hinda was struck
with shame and sorrow at the sight of her mother, who had
crept fearfully to the kitchen door at the first sound of
Yussel's voice. In all her life, she could not remember seeing
a grown woman look so small and beaten! Tziril cowered in
the corner as though she expected a blow; her head was bowed
in shame, her cheeks streaked with tears.

Although she didn't recognize him at all, Hinda knew instinctively that the tall man with the clipped red beard was her
father. He stood on the threshold, unsmiling and stern, and
stared at the young people seated around the table. Without a
trace of emotion in his eyes, his gaze wandered from one girl
to the other.

Suddenly he pointed a finger at Hinda.

"This one is mine!" he bellowed. "I crossed the ocean to
see her! Nobody else!" His voice faltered, but he hurled himself across the room and half dragged Hinda from her chair.
In an instant, he was holding her in an embrace that nearly
choked her. He kissed her as though he had forgotten the meaning of restraint.

Hinda was terrified and shocked at this unaccustomed display of feeling, and she fought to escape from his grasp but
Yussel still clutched her and turned to the others who were
watching with open mouths.

"Yes!" he roared again. "It was to see my child that I returned!"

Then, with a look of scorn, he directed his gaze toward Tziril, who cringed in the doorway. She knew that he had seen her the moment he entered the room, although he had made no sign of recognition. Again, he repeated, as though to dispel any hopeful thoughts she might possibly have, "It was for my Hinda that I risked coming back here — not for her! Never!"

Stifling her cry, Tziril fled from the room. In the silence that followed, they could hear her footsteps as she ran up the stairs, and the shaking of the ceiling above them as she slammed her bedroom door.

Hinda wept as though she had suffered an irrevocable loss. She tore from her father's embrace and ran after her mother.

"Mama! Mama!" she shrieked, as she clambered up the stairs. Then they all heard the door to Tziril's bedroom slam once more.

The tension mounted in the dining room as Yussel ran after Hinda up the stairs. Then there was silence.

In a calm voice, as though nothing the least bit out of the ordinary had occurred, Channa turned to her husband.

"You had a hard day, Yosef, and in this heat too. You must be famished! Everybody eat! You, too, Nathan. The food is getting cold."

❧

No one saw or heard either Yussel or Tziril until the following afternoon, and it was not until then that Channa's daughter Reizel told her mother that late the night before, after the family had retired, Hinda had crept into the extra bed that had been prepared for her in her cousin's bedroom. Tziril and Yussel were left alone, and the quiet that prevailed the next morning was reassuring. Channa had not known that her good-natured brother-in-law was capable of such anger although, as she whispered to her husband, it was not unwarranted. Besides, she added philosophically, a man without a temper was not much of a man.

When Tziril and Yussel appeared long after the noon meal had been cleared away, it was a chastened, solemn looking Tziril, a strangely quiet woman who came into the kitchen to brew tea for her husband. She was like someone who had sur-

vived an ordeal. No one said a word about Yussel's rage of the
evening before and it was as though nothing had ever happened.

"And where is Hinda?" asked Channa, sounding casual about
the fact that the three of them had slept through breakfast and
lunch.

"Hinda?" Yussel beamed. "She's still sleeping, I think. I'm
starving! I feel as though I haven't eaten for forty days."

Channa excused herself, and went to heat up the remains of
the noon meal for Tziril and Yussel. In a moment, he was at
Channa's side and whispered something to her.

"That Hinda," he confided. "She's a girl with every imaginable virtue. Can you imagine, Channa, she was the peacemaker?
She was the one who made sholom between Tziril and me!"

✿

Later in the day, after the men returned from evening prayers, Yussel showed his citizenship papers. He was now an American citizen, protected by the American flag. He had officially changed his name to "Joseph Friedman," and so his visa
and papers read.

"The Kovno police will have a hard time connecting the
American, Joseph Friedman, with that old runaway conscript
Yussel Wilkimirsky," he said with his old smile.

To everyone's amazement, Yussel was seriously interested in
the drucke which Tziril had inherited, and deeply regretted
that he had not had the opportunity to meet Reb Meiron or
Bayla. He could not understand why his father had allowed
his niece Breina to marry such an old man. Of course, Zlateh's
motives were clear.

"They'll get his money," he said. "That's what Zlateh was
probably after in the first place. Who else does the old man
have now? They'll get every kopeck."

"Meiron is no fool," Tziril objected. "He's a fine, decent
person, a real mensch. But he was foolish to decide on such a
young wife. I'm sure Zlateh won't find him a fool, though.
And Yussel, you have to remember that he was a good friend
to me, almost like a father, and he taught me how to run the
drucke. His last words of advice to me were that we should
set up a business in Telschi."

But Telschi would have to wait. First Yussel would have to visit his family in Wilki, since he hadn't seen his father in years. Since he was planning to spend several days with old Reb Tevya, he decided to take Tziril and Hinda with him.

The next week however, when Tziril and Yussel visited the city of Telschi, they both were favorably impressed. Telschi had become a thriving metropolis, with a large and prosperous Jewish population engaged in all sorts of commerce and small business. They were certain that the drucke would prosper there. Most importantly, Tziril was overjoyed that Yussel had lost his old fear of the police after living in America for so many years.

He had his citizenship papers, and would never again have to live in terror of discovery. Of course, a time would come when they would all return to America, since Russia was really no place for a Jew. By this time, even Tziril agreed. They were aware that there would be problems in establishing their business in Telschi, and Yussel was sure that it would be difficult for them to operate a printing press since he was an American citizen, even if the business were to be in Tziril's name with Yussel registered as her employee. Moreover, though it did not present an immediate problem, he could never be sure how long he could hide his true identity.

"It would be the height of folly," he told Tziril, "to tie up all our money in Telschi." Although he had changed his name, there could be a time when he would be forced to leave. But first they would establish themselves as printers. Yussel saw the drucke as a commodity that, if properly handled, could one day be disposed of at a handsome profit. In its present state, unassembled and crated, it was almost worthless.

"No man in his right mind would give a kopeck for it," he said.

From their first day in Telschi, Hinda was occupied with making new friends at the girls' gymnasium where she was enrolled. To her delight, the curriculum was more extensive than that of the school she had attended in Kafkaz, and Russian, German, French and mathematics were among the required courses. Though the school originally had been established under Jewish auspices, it was now government controlled, which accounted for the predominance of secular subjects.

Tziril and Yussel, on the other hand, were not as elated a-bout their new home. Telschi already had an established government-subsidized printing business and, they soon learned, the competition was keen. They rented a small shop on the outskirts of the residential area, with living quarters on the second floor. Tziril hung Bayla's copper pots on the white-washed kitchen walls, and found a place for her sister's old samovar. The brass challah pan was set to rest on top of an oak chest of drawers in the high ceilinged kitchen which also served as their dining room and parlor.

As soon as they were settled, Yussel made a trip to Wilki to seek the assistance of Moshe, an old friend who had once been a fellow apprentice at Frumkin's. He was certain that Moshe would be willing and able to reassemble the drucke. According to Yussel, anybody trained by Frumkin was bound to be an expert in any mechanical problem that might arise and, as he had expected, Moshe was glad to help. In no time, they had the printing press assembled and in working order, and Tziril and Yussel were ready to open their doors for business.

But as the weeks and months passed, very little business came their way. Before long, Tziril realized that at best it would be a slow and difficult process to attract a profitable clientele. Meanwhile they resigned themselves to operating at a loss. Though Yussel had returned to Kovno with a respectable sum of money, their resources dwindled faster than they had anticipated.

Yussel became impatient, and began to insist that there was not enough business in Telschi to justify an additional printing establishment. The competition was too firmly established, and held a monopoly on all government contracts, despite the fact that their competitor's presses were running day and night, due to the volume of government material. Occasionally, they were so overloaded with work that they would bring what they could not handle to them.

Yussel chafed at his inactivity and complained that life in Telschi was confining and dull. He didn't seem to fit in with the elite of the community, but had little in common with the city's working people. He began to feel trapped, and to miss his friends and relatives in America, and the freedom of movement he had enjoyed there. Tziril was worried, for once again Yussel developed a morbid fear of the officials who checked on them periodically, asking all sorts of questions. It seemed inevitable to him that one day they would discover that he was the absent conscript, Yussel Wilkimirsky.

Tziril could not dispel his fears. In vain she pointed out that the printing press was in her name, and that she was the sole proprietor and that he was "just an apprentice." No matter how often she tried to reassure him, Yussel was convinced that before long his past would catch up with him. Just when they least expected it, some informer would precipitate his arrest and downfall.

He became sick with anxiety every time a stranger entered their shop, and Tziril soon realized that the time had come for them to dispose of the printing press. But the drucke was a valuable piece of machinery, and of far higher quality than the one operated by their competitor. The rival printing company was aware of this, and was eager to acquire it — in fact, they had already made an offer, which Tziril considered inadequate. She shrewdly decided that if they could hold out long enough, the competition would meet their price, although she didn't think she would ever get what the press was worth.

They had been in Telschi for less than a year when Yussel returned to America. It was agreed that Tziril would arrange as best she could for the sale of the drucke, and would join him in New Jersey. Operating the huge machine had seemed a simple task when she had assisted Reb Meiron, but she had since learned that it was quite another matter when she was responsible for making it a paying proposition. Besides, her husband was just not cut out for that kind of work, and she herself found little pleasure in running the business alone. It had become a burden and a constant source of worry, with no one to share in the work.

Channa and her family had already departed for New York, and Tziril decided that there was no longer any reason for her to remain in Russia. In America she would begin again with a new occupation. She would become a winemaker! This was something she knew she would enjoy, and Yussel would find winemaking simple in comparison to running a printing press. With renewed hope, she wrote to Yussel that she would be joining him as soon as arrangements could be made, for this separation would be their last.

22
A
Stormy Leave-taking

Although Hinda missed her father tremendously after his
return to America, the prospect of leaving Telschi forever left
her with a lump in her throat. She hated the idea of leaving
behind the friends she had made and the school at which she
excelled. Hinda was most reluctant to leave Rosa Schmidt,
who had become her closest friend.

Over the past year, her friendship with Rosa had developed
into a sisterly closeness. They would discuss their plans for
the future in the eager tones of girlish hope. Both Hinda and
Rosa were students at the gymnasium, and studied, ate, and
even went to the synagogue together.

Like Hinda, Rosa was an only child, and this contributed to
their intimacy. Occasionally, they were even able to persuade
their mothers to allow them to spend a night at the other's home.

Tziril had welcomed her daughter's friendship with Rosa
from the beginning, for she had always been aware of Hinda's
loneliness and need for companions of her own age. Besides,
Rosa was the daughter of a prosperous apothecary who was
descended from a long line of well known rabbis. Her father
was bringing much needed business to the drucke, and had
Tziril been in a position to pick a companion for her daughter, Rosa would have been an ideal choice.

Saturday afternoon was always a special time of the week
for them — the only time in fact, when there were no lessons
or household chores which needed attention. Hinda and Rosa
were free to take long walks together along the river road to
the waterfront park, where they would meet their friends and
classmates. Arm in arm they would stroll, exchanging con-
fidences and bits of gossip.

The park was a popular meeting place for the young of Tel-schi. Every Sabbath afternoon, crowds of young people would gather, and there would be laughter and good spirits, even a-mong strangers. Many of the interesting people Hinda met were non-Jews, young men in soldiers' uniforms who were ca-dets at the local military academy. Compared with the serious minded and bookish Jewish boys of her age, these were "men of the world." These dashing cadets were excitingly blond and blue eyed, men who really knew how to pay compliments! To Hinda and Rosa, it didn't seem important that they were gen-tiles. They became friendly with two young cadets, although they knew that never in a lifetime could they ever have more than a casual acquaintance with them. It was exciting, though, for they were having what the romantic novels they read called a "flirtation."

One Saturday afternoon, not long after Yussel's departure, Tziril was awakened from her customary Sabbath nap by a loud knock at her door. There was an unexpected visitor, whom she knew only slightly – the mother of one of Hinda's classmates. All Tziril remembered of the daughter was that Hinda disliked her intensely.

In her most gracious tone of voice, Tziril invited the woman into her house, wondering what had brought her there, but the woman refused to be seated. Without any preliminaries, she declared that she had come to inform Tziril that her daughter and Rosa Schmidt were secretly meeting cadets from the military academy.

"Every Saturday afternoon they sneak off, both of them, It's a scandal the way these Jewish girls from pious families behave on the holy Sabbath!"

Tziril regarded her guest with horror. She was so furious that she could have taken that overdressed woman, arrayed in her best clothes and all her jewelry, and thrown her out the door.

"How dare you say such things! Hinda is a respectable Jew-ish daughter and a good student! You don't know what you are talking about. May such things as you say about others be said about your own daughter!"

"So, if you don't believe me, you can go and see for your-

self! Right now they are probably carrying on. And that Rosa
Schmidt is no better. My own daughter has told me plenty! I
only felt it was my duty to warn you," and she stomped toward the door with her nose in the air.

"*A gut Shabbos* to you, Mrs. Wilkimirsky." And she
slammed the door behind her, her plumed bonnet nodding in
disgust.

Tziril threw on her best Sabbath bonnet and her striped
shawl and tore out from her house. Never before had she permitted Hinda to spend so much time with a friend, but she
had been so proud of the closeness between Hinda and Rosa.
Rosa was the granddaughter of the reknown Rabbi Techeskel
of Cracow, and a polite, soft spoken girl who had won all sorts
of medals at the gymnasium. Young as she was, she was betrothed to a rabbinical student, whom she would be marrying after she completed her studies. Besides, Tziril had been
printing advertising circulars for her father's apothecary shop.

It was hard to believe that a girl from Rosa's background
could behave in so disreputable a fashion – imagine, a girl betrothed to a rabbinical student! And as for her Hinda, if what
the informer had said was true, her reputation would be utterly ruined.

A short, stocky figure of a woman, Tziril hurried to the
park along the shady river road, which was crowded with Sabbath pleasure seekers. All the benches were filled with well
dressed Jews, who were enjoying the weekly respite of the
Sabbath afternoon. Tziril became breathless and red faced
from her unaccustomed pace. Since she saw no sign of Hinda,
she began to run.

All at once, she spied her and Rosa, just ahead of her, strolling along at a deliberate and leisurely pace. Their carefree
movements were so gay, so unfettered by public opinion and
the mores of their parents. Suddenly they were approached
by two young cadets who appeared seemingly from nowhere.
To Tziril's dismay, the young men greeted them as though
Hinda and Rosa were old friends, and continued along with
them just a few yards ahead of Tziril. All she could think of
was "This can't be – not my Hinda and the Rabbi of Cracow's
granddaughter!"

Tziril rushed forward, but before she could overtake them, each girl's waist had been encircled by the arm of a uniformed cadet — the dreaded Russian soldier, of whom young Jewish girls had been taught from early childhood to beware.

She was almost paralyzed with shame when she heard the juicy giggles of Hinda and Rosa. In a moment, though, Hinda sensed that they were being followed, and her laughter stopped short. Who could that be, calling "Hinda!"? It came from directly behind them. Before she could turn her head, Tziril's voice had filled her with panic.

"Oh no! It's my mother!" she whispered to the young man at her side, frantically trying to remove his arm from her waist. He laughed mischievously, and glanced over his shoulder at the red faced, stocky woman who was running after them. But Tziril caught up with them and without a word of warning, grabbed Hinda by her braid and yanked her head back with an almost ruthless lack of concern.

There was a roar of laughter from the crowd which had gathered behind the enraged mother. By this time, everyone was howling uproariously — even the cadets. Only Hinda and Rosa stood there, blushing and panicstricken.

Hinda ran all the way home. She would never forgive her mother! She didn't see how she could go to school the next day. How everyone would laugh at her!

When Tziril herself returned home after a talk with Rosa's mother, she found an hysterical, weeping daughter who would not speak to her. But Tziril's rage had, if anything, increased by this time, and she felt no pity for Hinda who had disgraced her so. The girl was terror stricken! She had never seen her mother so angry. Tziril approached her and slapped her face repeatedly — something she had never done before.

The next week she sold the drucke to her competitor at a better price than she had ever hoped to receive, and made arrangements to leave Telschi at once. She couldn't trust herself to handle Hinda alone anymore. She really needed Yussel now, she decided. Hinda would listen to him and respect his opinion. In a fever of activity, she worked day and night packing their belongings and disposing of those possessions she would be unable to take with her. She swore to herself that nothing less important than Hinda's future wellbeing could have induced her to leave her home with such haste.

Before the week ended, they were ready to depart for America, and Rosa Schmidt and her mother came to pay them a farewell visit. Hinda and Rosa cried in each other's arms, for though it was left unspoken, they knew that they would never see each other again. Rosa confided to Hinda that her parents were furious at her behavior, and were forcing her to marry her fiance long before the appointed date. She was terrified, since she didn't even know where she would be living after her marriage, although she had heard that her betrothed was considering an appointment in Belgium. She didn't know a soul there, and probably would die of loneliness. Hinda promised to write as soon as she reached America, and tried to comfort her friend, but her words were empty and without effect.

After a few days had blunted the edge of Hinda's embarrassment, she realized that her mother had a justifiable cause for her anger and haste; but she still questioned the severity of her punishment. With a heavy heart, she embraced Rosa for the last time, believing she could never again find such a friend.

The Voyage

Tziril and Hinda found themselves steerage passengers a-board the *Rotterdam*, a large steamship of the Holland-Amer-ican Line. Immigration to the United States was beginning to reach its peak, and the competition between the various trans-atlantic companies for the steerage trade had never been more fierce. That year the Holland-American Line was featuring a special low fare — seven dollars a head.

Jewish immigration was at an all time high, and the hold of every vessel was filled to capacity. Most of the voyagers had been sent their passage money by relatives who had already settled in America.

"What Jew," read advertisements in New York and Phila-delphia, "cannot afford a paltry seven dollars to aid a needy relative or co-religionist from home to find freedom and safe-ty in the *goldene medina*?"

They all brought their cherished possessions: feather beds and heirloom candlesticks of silver and brass. The men carried prayerbooks, talithim and worn leather phylacteries in frayed velvet bags, as well as their odds and ends of clothing in flimsy suitcases bound with rope. Years later, Hinda would tell her children and grandchildren when they exclaimed in disbelief at photographs of the newcomers, "Yes, we weren't much better off than that."

Tziril had had a large wooden chest built, in which she packed her bedding and Bayla's copper and brass, in addition to many years' worth of correspondence from Bayla and Yussel. Family portraits and her ketuba, or marriage contract, were carefully placed in the safest inner compartment. She had also seen that the wax flowers Hinda had made at the gymnasium were carefully preserved in their glass boxes. Hinda had won a major prize in the last term's exhibition, and Tziril was very proud of this example of her daughter's handiwork.

Once more, she packed her traveling satchel with her well worn prayer books, and enough food for the duration of the trip. Although the food served to steerage passengers was advertised as being kosher, Tziril had brought along a substantial quantity of black bread and salt herring.

Those last few days in Telschi had been one of her most trying experiences. She was anxious to be with Yussel again, and the episode with Hinda and the cadets had made her more eager to leave. Although Telschi had been an unfortunate experiment which had ended in the kind of disillusionment she had not been prepared for. It had little to do with their business reversals; the main problem was Hinda. Tziril was convinced that Telschi was not a good place to raise a young, impressionable and beautiful daughter.

Influenced by her more cosmopolitan friends, Hinda had undergone a great change. She had begun to read widely, beginning with novels and romances, and finally books that were disapproved by the State. More than one of her classmates had been caught distributing forbidden pamphlets, and there were rumors that someone she knew had been exiled to Siberia.

To her dismay, Tziril discovered too late that Telschi was not a bit like Kovno. Her daughter had begun to question every possible tenet of Jewish Orthodoxy, and Tziril often found herself at a loss for answers. As a girl in Kovno, Tziril had never dreamed of the relative freedom of the Jewish youth of Telschi, where parents seemed to have no control over their rebellious offspring. The intellectual climate of the times was no help at all to an anxious parent. Hinda's friends saw emigration from Russia not as an opportunity to live as pious Jews without harassment, but as a flight from parents, religion, and the circumscribed routine of Eastern European Jewry.

Still, Tziril did not feel as though she were totally to blame. Among her daughter's contemporaries, parental authority was a subject open to question, if not ridicule. Tziril had discussed the situation at length with Rosa

Schmidt's mother, and it seemed as though every parent was having the same problem. Thus, Tziril was convinced that what Hinda needed was Yussel's presence.

To Hinda, however, life alone with her mother was confining and depressing. Since she had been separated from Rosa, Telschi had become a lonely place — desolate. She and Tziril quarreled constantly, and there was no one who would listen to her side of an argument.

Hinda was sure that she would never find another friend like Rosa. They had spent their noon hours at the gymnasium reading books together: Tolstoi, and the stories of Isaac Maier Dik, a leader of the Jewish Enlightenment who was feared and despised by her mother's generation for his liberal views. Hinda remembered the hours when they had read poetry aloud, and the musical sound of Pushkin's words and Rosa's clear voice.

At the same time, she yearned to be with her father again. Yussel had humor and understanding, and felt a sympathy with the needs and desires of his daughter's generation. Besides, Hinda hoped that once they were together, her mother might be happier and her stern outlook would soften once more in the presence of her husband. Still, she was haunted by the shame of that miserable Sabbath when her mother had publicly disgraced her.

But once she and Tziril boarded the *Rotterdam*, her worries of the past few weeks ceased to have much significance. Even the fact that she would probably never see Rosa again lost its impact. Hinda didn't mind the cramped steerage quarters where she and Tziril slept, and she found the very thought of the long ocean voyage most exhilarating, despite the fact that her mother had panicked the moment she lost sight of the docks of Bremen.

❧

They were scarcely a day out of port when almost everyone became seasick, and no one more than Tziril. They ran into foul weather, although the captain refused to worry about the huge waves that lashed at the decks. Tziril refused to eat the food offered by the steward, claiming that it couldn't be kosher, and starvation would be preferable. Hinda finally coaxed her into eating a little black bread and herring.

In the men's half of the steerage quarters, groups of the Orthodox donned prayer shawls and davened. Before long, many of the women, wearing pious matrons' wigs, joined in the prayers, weeping in unison with the swaying chant of the men. Tziril's prayer book never left her hands that first night at sea. Over and over again, she repeated the prayer for fear of drowning on the high seas. She expected the worst. It would take a miracle if they didn't drown before morning, for as the hours dragged on, the intensity of the storm only increased.

Toward dawn, she again became violently seasick, and Hinda half carried her back to her bunk, and remained until her mother finally began to doze. As she looked around, she noticed for the first time that most of the people traveling with them in steerage were young and unencumbered by parents. When she approached a group of young girls sitting in the corner of the cabin, she could hear them laughing at the "antics" of the pious, amusement mingling with their scorn. She joined their circle without being invited, but soon discovered that none of them had met before the voyage, although they now seemed to have become the closest of friends.

They compared experiences. It seemed that they had all left their parents and homes behind. There had been no future for them in Russia because they were Jews, and they were attempting to escape from both their inhospitable homeland as well as the world of the shtetl.

All at once, Hinda's new acquaintances decided that the steerage cabin was too crowded and depressing, and someone suggested that they all move to the hold where they could talk to some of the young men from the other side of the steerage. Hinda discovered that the boys of her age voiced the same opinions as their female counterparts, but only with more vehemence. One could say that the young men of her generation felt more burdened by the old ways than the girls, since the many religious obligations of the pious were, for the most part, a male responsibility. She discovered that they considered the Law of Israel as rigid and unbending as the ukases of the Czar. She was glad her mother was not in hearing range of this.

Despite the frequent storms, from the first night after the *Rotterdam* sailed from port, the sound of guitars and mandolins was heard in the ship's hold from sunset until the early hours of the morning. The young people passed the long nights singing and dancing, unmindful of the deafening thunder and the gales that rocked the *Rotterdam*, threatening to split the vessel in two.

Hinda recalled her first crossing of the Black Sea when she was a child and it seemed to her that the Black Sea had been a smooth and tranquil lake compared with the turbulent Atlantic.

Despite the crowding and discomfort, she enjoyed the voyage and to Tziril's dismay, spent each day looking forward to the merriment of the evening. Tziril, on the other hand, had not been able to accustom herself to the motion of the ship, and was wretchedly ill most of the time.

One night, she was unable to sleep, even for an hour, and could feel herself literally shaking with chills. She called out to Hinda, but noticed that her place beside her was empty. Hinda was nowhere in sight, and Tziril found it impossible to remain in her bunk.

The other women tried to comfort her, and one of them attempted to spoonfeed her some weak tea, which she obtained from the steward. Another ran to find Hinda.

Finally, Hinda appeared. She wrapped the shivering Tziril in a blanket and led her back to her bunk, which served as her bed, closet, baggage compartment and kitchen. All eyes were upon them, since no less than three hundred other women shared the cabin with them. As Hinda never forgot, their quarters were so primitive that no cans or receptacles had been provided for waste. Fortunately, Tziril had the foresight to bring her own chamber-pot, but the stench in the steerage was still nauseating.

As she ministered to her mother, Hinda could still hear the strumming guitars in the background. She had pity for her mother, but there seemed to be nothing she could do for her. She regarded Tziril's face anxiously; at least she had finally fallen asleep, though there was not a trace of color in her cheeks. Hinda became alarmed.

"Mama, are you sleeping?" she whispered. There was no response. Suddenly, Tziril snored loudly. Satisfied, Hinda tiptoed out of the cabin, and returned to the hold. Within minutes, she joined the crowd that had gathered around the musicians. Though she was exhausted, she found the atmosphere exhilarating, for she had discovered that there was something magnificent about the way in which the waves tossed the steamer as though it were a scrubbing pail. The pale, flickering light below decks illuminated the faces of her companions with an eerie glow, making it all seem like a scene from some shadow world where everything lacked substance.

She wore her heavy, fair hair in long braids tied with bright ribbons, hanging well below her waist. Her face was flushed with pleasure, and anyone could tell that Hinda had never been among the seasick in the women's cabin. The storms and rough seas failed to frighten her and besides, she was too busy dancing to worry. Soon she would be with her father again who would enjoy her accounts of the storms at sea and the friends she had made aboard the *Rotterdam*. He would laugh with her when she told him how she had danced by the hour while the older generation had been too ill to sit up.

He would be a captive audience for her tales of poetry and dance partners, and she could picture his smile when she repeated the compliments that had been showered upon her. There had even been a proposal of marriage! She could never tell her mother any of these things!

Hinda, however, did feel a twinge of guilt at the thought that had her mother not been sick, she would never have been allowed to join the nightly festivities, though Tziril had never, in so many words, forbidden her to leave the women's half of steerage. The greater part of Hinda's enjoyment lay in the knowledge that for the first time in her life, she was free from her mother's surveillance. Over the past few years she had grown to deeply resent Tziril's incessant warnings and lectures about the relationship between "A young girl's conduct and public opinion."

"One's reputation," Tziril had often warned her, "depends upon the good opinion of others. A good name is one of the most important things in life for a woman, Hinda. Without it you can ruin your life.''

Hinda was sick and tired of being told what she could do and what she could not. It was all so tiresome and unnatural. She wished she could be as casual about the opposite sex as the young women she met aboard ship. Though they were free to come and go as they pleased, they didn't do anything Hinda considered wrong. She wished that her mother would come to realize this, as well as the fact that in 1885 it took more than a little dancing and flirtation to ruin one's reputation.

She was entranced by her new friends. They were all so ambitious, and both men and women, she had discovered, were planning to attend night school while earning a living – it didn't matter at what – during the day. Many of them were planning to send for their parents or younger brothers and sisters as soon as they could afford it. They all had dreams of becoming respected professionals, and law, medicine and journalism were their ultimate goals. For Hinda, it was a minor revelation just to be in their company and listen to their conversations.

She even became acquainted with the musicians who enlivened the long journey, making everyone forget the terrible accommodations and the food that was simply inedible. There was no privacy in the steerage, not even a place where one could be alone to pamper a queasy stomach. But while the musicians played, the youth on board forgot the discomfort and the unpleasantness.

That journey left Hinda with memories besides those of dancing while her mother was seasick. As luck would have it, that crossing of the Atlantic, among other things, was one of the longest on record at that time. And more than that, there were snoopers and busybodies, who every so often sought her out, as if to remind her that she had a sick mother who needed her constant attention.

These pious folk had nothing good to say about the young people in their midst, but it seemed as if most of their scorn was reserved for her: the cold, unfeeling daughter of the pious and respected Tziril Wilkimirsky.

"A girl with a heart of stone," they called her, "who dances and carouses while her mother, you should pardon the expression, vomits out her guts. That Hinda is always running off with her friends, leaving her poor mother to be cared for by strangers as ill as herself.

And that was not all. Hinda would never forget that after the first storm had abated, the immaculately groomed captain had given the first class passengers a tour of the ship, including what Hinda could only surmise to be an inspection of the foul smelling human cargo in steerage. These well fed and sumptuously dressed people had literally held their noses all through the tour, and had stared at the inhabitants of that open drain, expressing their opinions among themselves in shocked whispers.

The question at hand was whether or not these wretched specimens of humanity, reeking of herring, perspiration and stale vomit could ever be transformed into acceptable citizens of the great United States of America.

Of course, there was something radically wrong with their laws if such ignorant folk as these were allowed to pass through the sacred portals of New York!

Jersey City

Among the shuffling throng that was herded into the great dome of the Immigration Center at Castle Island were Tziril and Hinda Wilkimirsky. Mother and daughter were loaded down with baggage and barely managed to drag their assortment of trunks and parcels through the closely packed crowd.

Hinda clung to Tziril like a frightened child, although she towered over her by at least half a foot. She was terrified that the pushing and shoving would separate them, and she would be lost. In the crowded, airless depot, they were ordered to form a line. Everyone was required to submit to a physical examination. Their eyes were checked, and those unfortunate immigrants afflicted with the dreaded trachoma were to be shipped back to their land of origin immediately.

Panic spread along the endless line of exhausted voyagers. Not to be admitted to the "golden land" would be an unspeakable tragedy, and the next few hours seemed longer than the entire journey. Slowly the column of people moved through the examining room, which became the impersonal witness to so many heartrending scenes, and the anguish of the rejected.

Somewhere beyond the iron mesh barriers, impatient friends and relatives paced the floor of the dimly lit waiting room. More than once, Hinda cried out that she could hear her father calling their names.

"Papa! Papa!" she called back every few minutes. "We're here! I can't see you, but we're here. Mama and I — we're here!"

They wept with relief when they finally passed successfully through customs and the physical examination. Exhausted but with rising spirits they found Yussel and followed him to the rented wagon where his cousin Velvel was loading their belongings. Yussel assured them that the trip to their new home in Jersey City would be a short one. Their whole mishpocha awaited their arrival, but Yussel reassured Tziril that he had made them promise not to come until the next day. Tziril needed to rest before she could even think about receiving guests, even if they were family. The relatives, however, had brought food to their new home and had even set the table.

"Just think, Tziril. Freshly baked bread, wine, fish – a feast!" Yussel said. "Enough to feed the Czar's army."

On their way to Jersey City, he told Tziril in detail about his plans for the future. He had arranged with his employer, Louis Max, to take a week or two off from work until his family was established in their new home and had become oriented to their new surroundings. Max had been sympathetic. An immigrant himself, he knew that everything would seem strange to the newcomers for a while.

Yussel told Tziril that Louis Max was a wonderful man to work for. He had at least forty glaziers in his employ, for there was much building going on in Jersey City. Even after Yussel returned to work, he was able to spend a considerable time at home with Tziril and Hinda, since Max's glass company was within walking distance of their home on Steuben Street.

Now that Tziril had at last arrived, Yussel planned to establish his own glazing business in their own home. For some time now, in addition to his regular employment, he had been taking odd jobs such as installing windows and plate glass in store fronts. Max had agreed to be his supplier and would give him all the credit he would need to get started.

"You will have to meet him soon," Yussel told her. "Such a fine man. I couldn't have picked a better boss. He even gave me a bottle of schnapps to celebrate your arrival!"

Tziril listened attentively. Yussel's scheme fit right in with her own plans. She was determined to establish a winemaking business once they were settled and would need his help. She envisioned a dual business under one roof. Bayla and Meiron had been able to make such an arrangement work, and profitably. In their early years in Kafkaz, Bayla had done an extensive business making and selling wine, while her husband had busied himself with the drucke. It was good, Tziril decided, that Yussel had a trade which would provide for them comfortably while she established herself in her new home, for one could not become a successful winemaker overnight. Such an undertaking would take time. But she was confident that, like Bayla before her, she would be a success in her own right. Hadn't her sister made wine? And before that, her father's family had been vintners for generations. She felt that it was in her blood, and that she was bound to succeed.

❧

It took them an hour to reach the two story frame building on Steuben Street where Yussel rented a small flat. Their house was one of a long row of similar dwellings, closely built in a straight line. As she followed him up the stairs, all Tziril could think of was whether or not there was a cellar. She couldn't live in a place without a cellar — where would she make her wine?

Yussel surveyed the feast spread out on the table with satisfaction, but Hinda said that she wasn't hungry. First, she wanted to bathe and cleanse herself of the odor of the steerage which, she said, had followed her all the way from the *Rotterdam*. She couldn't wait to wash her hair.

Their four room lodgings contained just the bare essentials, but Yussel proudly pointed out the running water that gushed from a tap in the kitchen, which was something they hadn't had in Russia. What intrigued Tziril the most was the small gas stove for cooking and baking — the first she had ever seen. Of course, there were no indoor plumbing facilities, but she hadn't expected that convenience. The only difference, Yussel explained light heartedly, was that the out houses in Jersey City were never as cold as those in Kovno.

Tziril forced herself to wait until morning to inspect the cellar, which proved to be rat infested and crammed from floor to ceiling with all sorts of rubbish. Despite the squalor, there was already a tenant, a junk dealer, who had set up a housekeeping of sorts in the middle of the clutter. With a trace of belligerence, he told Tziril and Yussel that he did, in fact, pay rent, and that the old broken tubs, furniture and rusty stoves were the source of his livelihood.

"So, Yussel, we will just have to move," was Tziril's comment. She needed a place where a winepress could be installed, as well as storage place for barrels and bottles. In the meantime, she refused to even unpack her trunk.

But nothing could be done about moving until after the Sabbath, and Tziril consented to unpack Sabbath clothing for Hinda and herself, as well as her brass candlesticks and a heavy copper pot. She began to prepare for her first Sabbath in America on Thursday morning, and while Yussel shopped for the fish and poultry, she prepared the dough for the huge Sabbath loaves, and made the noodles with Hinda's help.

The lighted candles on the table that Friday evening had a special significance for them. After blessing the wine, Yussel exclaimed that it was the happiest moment he had known since his arrival in America almost a dozen years before. But from Tziril's point of view, not to have prepared a Sabbath meal for her husband would have been unthinkable under any circumstances. Besides, as she reminded Hinda, the day of rest had to be honored for its own sake.

The following week they moved to Seventh Street. Yussel rented the entire first floor of a newly renovated, five family brick house. The rooms were airy and comfortable, and there was a front entrance to their apartment, as well as a back door leading directly from the kitchen to the clean, whitewashed cellar below.

Their landlord, a pleasant mannered Italian carpenter, agreed to rent them the cellar for an extra fee, and to build shelves and partitions as well. There would be a special compartment where Tziril could install a winepress, and more than adequate storage space for barrels and wine racks.

Their new neighborhood was reminiscent of Kovno. Only a block away, on Henderson Street, one could hear Yiddish and the familiar Polish dialect spoken by many people in Kovno. The signs on the shops were in Polish and Yiddish, as well as English. Everyone did most of their marketing at the numerous outdoor stalls, where the squawking of fowl awaiting the slaughterer's knife was enough to drown out the voices of the customers. Hinda could not get over how much Henderson Street reminded her of the marketplace in Kovno.

And there were familiar faces as well. Everywhere they went, Tziril and Hinda encountered people they had known in Kovno, Wilki or Telschi, who greeted them, eager for news of friends and relatives they had left behind.

One of their closest neighbors was Etta Teresa, a distant relative of Yussel's who lived on the opposite side of Seventh Street. Ever since she had first met her in Wilki, Tziril had never been on good terms with her, and Etta Teresa's overtures of friendship had only aroused Tziril's instinctive distrust. After Tziril's arrival in Jersey City, Etta seemed to think that she was entitled to be taken into the former's confidence, since she had "befriended" Yussel in Tziril's absence, and he had often had his meals at her house.

Etta Teresa was an untidy, toothless woman with sparse gray hair pulled tightly back from a prematurely lined face. Invariably, she wore a bedraggled looking shawl that enveloped her withered frame almost completely. According to Hinda, she resembled a "shriveled-up mummy," especially since it was impossible to tell what she was wearing beneath her shawl.

Tziril soon learned from her husband that Etta's husband, Itzig, was a notorious gambler, who spent most of his time at the racetrack. Their undersized and scrawny sons were always with him, and it was the father's ambition that they train as jockeys.

Everyone knew that Itzig had been arrested several times, although no one was sure why. He had a bad reputation, however, just as he had had in Wilki, where it had been rumored that he was a horsethief. Yussel had always felt sorry for Itzig's wife and children, and since Etta was part of his mishpocha, he had pity on her. He had never eaten a meal in her home without paying her for it, and had given gifts of clothing and pocket money to her boys. It was a sin, he said to Tziril, not to show kindness to someone as unfortunate as his cousin.

Velvel's wife Soreh Ruchel was another member of Yussel's large family whom Tziril had grown to distrust. It was almost ironic that Soreh Ruchel and Etta Teresa were enemies, even though everyone knew that the two of them never kept any secrets from each other. Soreh had grown stout since Tziril had last seen her, but her strident voice and aggressive manner hadn't changed a bit. Everyone was afraid of her sharp tongue, and it was said, that compared to Soreh Ruchel, Etta Teresa was a saint.

"But that Soreh Ruchel," Yussel would say, "she can be deadly as a snake. Don't try to be too friendly with her, Tziril. She has a way of tearing one's reputation to shreds."

Even her husband Velvel found her impossible to live with, and consequently he spent as little time as possible in his own home. It was a rare evening when Velvel did not come to visit Yussel, who would often comment that, "It's almost as though Velvel has forgotten he has a home."

Of the two, Tziril found Etta Teresa the more offensive, and Hinda was also finding it increasingly difficult to be polite to her. Etta would come barging into their house without even a pretense of knocking, and Hinda complained that Etta was beginning to spend all her time either in their kitchen, or watching them from her front window.

Etta Teresa seemed to know exactly when Tziril and Yussel left their house, and would pelt them with questions the moment they would return.

Where had they gone? Why? Why was Tziril wearing her best Sabbath bonnet in the middle of the week? Of course, that meant they had gone to New York and had had important business to attend to. Etta wondered why they were all so secretive where she was concerned.

One thing aroused her curiosity – the daily presence of carpenters in their cellar. She could hear them hammering all the way across the street, right in her own kitchen! One day, she chanced to see a wagonload of barrels and demijohns being delivered to Tziril's front door, and she was immediately consumed with inquisitiveness and envy.

"That Tziril," she fumed, the next time she saw Soreh Ruchel. "That woman is lucky beyond her desserts!"

Etta had never been able to find out anything from Yussel about the sale of the drucke, and as she listened to the carpenters at work, she was convinced that Tziril had come to America with a fortune – otherwise, why would her husband have welcomed her back after her seeming desertion? Of course, this new development at the "Friedmans' " was reported to

Soreh Ruchel that very afternoon.

"So, Tziril is really serious about making wine, is she?" replied Soreh, who was not surprised. "Just who does she think will buy? Everyone I know makes their own. They're bound to lose every penny.

"Besides, you know as well as I do that you can't trust her. Even Tziril's own husband never knows what's going on with her. Imagine, her running off to Kafkaz like that! It was a scandal, a *shandeh!* Let me tell you that in Kovno no one had any doubts that she was unfaithful to poor Yussel.

"And that Hinda — she's just like her mother — flighty and too good for everyone else!"

Soreh Ruchel was forever comparing Hinda unfavorably with her own daughters who were "industrious" and saved every penny they earned for their dowries. Their husbands would be lucky — that is, if they ever managed to find husbands. It occurred to her that someone should tell Yussel about his daughter's bad manners and superior airs. Etta Teresa volunteered to speak to him.

Later that week she approached her cousin.

"Tell me, Yussel," she said. "Just why is your Hinda so special? Do you think it is right for a young girl to give herself such airs, looking down her nose at everyone? Why do you let her sit around all day, idle and shiftless, when she could be out earning money like Soreh Ruchel's girls, and helping her parents?"

"Listen to me, Etta," was Yussel's defense. "My wife and I are busy people. Hinda helps her mother look after the house. And please, we have no time to bother with your questions. Why should it concern you, anyway?"

Tziril had overheard their conversation, and could not hold back her annoyance.

"My daughter," she retorted, "went to the gymnasium in Telschi and studied languages. We didn't give her a fine education so she could work for a few pennies a day in a sweatshop!

"Besides, how can you say that Hinda is 'idle'? She goes to night school. She goes to the library. She is learning English. In fact, she is taking private lessons now, and will soon be speaking the language like a native — not like you, a greenhorn!"

But Etta Teresa thought she knew better.

"That's what you say." she replied. "Your Hinda spends all her time in the stores on Newark Avenue buying fancy clothes! You and Yussel must have money to burn! Tell me, Tziril, what sort of wife will she make for a young man struggling to make his way in America?"

Later, Etta complained to Soreh Ruchel that Yussel hadn't even said a word in her defense. He hadn't even offered her a glass of tea. Imagine! Yussel, for whom she had cooked meals that were fit for a king!

⁂

Hinda would have been the last to deny that Newark Avenue, with its rows of modern shops, was an exciting new world to explore. She enjoyed going from store to store, examining the merchandise and comparing prices. But even more than these new experiences, she loved to visit Manhattan with her parents, when they would go to see Channa and her family who were living on East Broadway.

With the exception of Reizel, who now called herself "Rosie," most of her cousins were working in the garment district. Sheindel, the youngest girl, had married and moved upstate, while Feigele, busy with her husband and children, did not visit her parents too often. But the boys were attending night school, and Moshe, Channa's second son, hoped to become a lawyer.

Although she enjoyed visiting with her cousins, Hinda found her aunt's appearance depressing. Channa had aged considerably, and always looked anxious and worn. She would sigh continually as she bemoaned the loss of their wealth and position, and the fact that their living quarters in New York were little better than the slums on the wrong side of the River Niemen.

Channa's major source of worry was her daughter Reizel, who couldn't seem to accustom herself to their reduced circumstances. When it came to selecting a husband, the girl was impossible to please, and it was her mother's opinion that she would probably live out her days as an old maid if she didn't stop thinking that no man was good enough for her. A discontented and bitter young woman, Reizel or "Rosie," had hated New York from the day she had arrived.

Tziril sympathized with her sister. She had problems of her own with Hinda, who was even more rebellious and unpredictable. Tziril did not forget Hinda's behavior on the *Rotterdam*.

Reizel, "Rosie," and Hinda, were closer now than they had been in Kovno, and both girls looked forward to their Sunday visits. Together they roamed through Hester and Delancey Streets on the Lower East Side, which was invariably crowded with Sunday shoppers. Rosie would lend Hinda the fashion books she would borrow from a neighbor who was a dressmaker.

Much to her dismay. Hinda soon realized that she looked nothing like the stylish models in the illustrations, and that even her cousin Rosie, who could hardly speak a word of English, looked more "American" than she did. Rosie had told her that her new dress had been made by the dressmaker next door, and Hinda decided that she was definitely dissatisfied with the ready-made dresses she had bought on Newark Avenue. She didn't want to be seen in them, even though her father had helped in their selection. After a glance at the fashion illustrations, Hinda knew that her own clothes were ill fitting and unbecoming, and she begged her cousin to lend her a fashion book.

By this time, Hinda read English with comprehension, if not ease. That night in the privacy of her bedroom, she studied the instructions that were printed under each picture. She soon understood that each dress could easily be duplicated, if one knew how to sew and bought the right patterns and material.

The pattern, she explained to her skeptical parents, contained all the necessary information for making a dress. But without being told by her cousin Rosie, she knew that it was almost impossible to duplicate the style exactly unless one's clothing was made by an experienced dressmaker.

Tziril was annoyed at Hinda's vanity, and told her sharply that her ready-made clothes were suitable and modest. Besides, they could not afford such extravagances as garments made by a dressmaker. But to Hinda's surprise, the following day, Yussel took her shopping for dress material and a pattern, and on

Sunday, Rosie's dressmaker was only too happy for the extra work.

It didn't take Hinda long to realize that she would need money of her own if she wished to look like the models in the fashion magazines. One day, she noticed a sign in the window of a millinery shop on Newark Avenue that read: "Help Wanted. Knitters and Crocheters." Impulsively, she entered and told the proprietor that she was interested in a position. She was immediately ushered into a back workroom where a dozen girls and women were knitting woolen caps. She was given a crochet-hook and wool and told to copy a sample. Within minutes, she was hired and informed she could begin work the next day.

By the time she reached home, her mother was frantic with worry. When Tziril heard Hinda's news that she had found work at Drachman's Millinery Shop, she immediately objected.

"Never! No!" she said. "My daughter doesn't have to sit all day crocheting in some dark, back room. Never — not while your father and I are alive. I don't care how much money you'll make!"

Hinda reluctantly advised her new employer that her family objected to her working for him. However, Mr. Drachman was eager for her services. Her work, he said, was exquisite and none of his regular help did such fine crocheting. Perhaps her parents wouldn't object to her doing some crocheting at home.

While the weather was pleasant, Hinda worked outdoors, surrounded by an audience of young girls who enviously watched her nimble fingers as they wove cap after cap. Among them was Etta Teresa's youngest daughter, Annie. Soon they were all begging Hinda to teach them to crochet, and as soon as they could obtain wool and crochet-hooks, they sat and worked together under Hinda's guidance.

Annie insisted on sitting next to Hinda and proudly announced to the others that the "teacher" was her cousin. The child elbowed the other girls out of her way until they were forced to make room for her in the favored position. Patiently, but without success, Annie attempted to follow Hinda's instructions.

Hinda had always felt sorry for Annie, who seemed to be

an unhappy and maladjusted little girl. She was constantly quarreling with the other children, and was teased unmercifully by the boys. At least once a day she would run to her in tears, to complain about her troubles with the teachers who always "picked on her."

Most of the time, though, Annie whined about her mother's constant screaming and nagging. Hinda felt drawn to the child and pitied her, for she sensed that under little Annie's bad manners and unpleasant temper was an affectionate and warm-hearted little girl who needed an understanding friend.

Apparently from nowhere, suitors for Hinda began to appear. Two of them were shipboard acquaintances from the *Rotterdam*, with whom she had danced on the voyage across the Atlantic. Tziril and Yussel made them welcome, even though Hinda had informed her father that she wasn't seriously interested in anyone yet. But she did enjoy their company and continued to accept their invitations to theaters and places of amusement. Actually, Hinda was surprised at the fact that her parents were being so hospitable.

She was proud of their home. She made curtains for all the windows and kept the glass spotlessly clean. The brass and copper in the kitchen were always brilliantly polished, and Tziril had given her wax flowers a place of honor on top of a chest of drawers in the sitting room. Tziril told everyone who admired them that if their home was clean and attractive, it was due mostly to Hinda's diligence and imagination.

From her first day in America, Tziril had made it clear to everyone that she had no time to waste on such trifling details as polishing the brass and copper. The time was fast approaching when she would be making an important announcement to the Jewish community: Tziril and Yussel, winemakers, were opening their doors for business!

Tziril
the Winemaker

After months of waiting, after innumerable interviews with local rabbis and leaders of the Jewish community, and endless discussions with suppliers, Tziril's request for permission to make wine for the rituals of home and synagogue was granted. At last, she was awarded the rabbinical seal of approval known as the hechsha.

A hechsha was not easily acquired. In order to qualify, one had to measure up to the most rigid standards of Orthodox Judaism and to be a strict Sabbath observer with a spotless reputation.

Neither Etta Teresa nor Soreh Ruchel considered Tziril worthy of such a highly coveted honor. They both agreed that her past actions did not warrant this official sanction, and shook their heads at the deference which the local rabbinical council displayed.

"Don't they realize that Yussel threatened to send her a *get* and divorce her?" Soreh had asked. "What about all that time she spent traveling around with her brother-in-law? Everyone knew what they were up to!"

But for Tziril, the hechsha was a symbol of victory over the enemies who had tried to destroy her name. She knew who her enemies were — those so-called "relatives" who had tried every possible means to besmirch her reputation and destroy her marriage. In the end, it was they who had failed, and Tziril savored her "triumph" to the fullest.

During one of their interviews, she had told the rabbinical council with candor that she admitted to having often defied public opinion and had, indeed, gambled with her husband's devotion. But there had been a reason. From the first, she had not wanted to leave Kovno, since she had heard that America was a treife land, where the young renounced their sacred heritage without a moment's regret.

To a man, the council could not deny her allegations. They could only sympathize with her reluctance to settle in a place like Jersey City where, until recently, there was neither a synagogue nor a ritual bath. It was noted that only in the past year had it been possible to buy kosher meat without traveling a considerable distance. Besides, as one of the rabbis pointed out, even the Talmud had exonerated a wife who refused to leave the Holy Land and follow her husband into the diaspora.

When the rabbis visited her winery, their favorable initial impression was confirmed. The walls of the cellar had been given a fresh coat of white paint, and all the equipment was new, including the barrels, wicker covered demijohns, and the presses themselves. It was quite easy for Tziril to prove to their complete satisfaction that no one who was not strictly Orthodox had even set foot on the premises, let alone handled the equipment, for as yet, she hadn't even removed the labels of the rabbinically approved distributor who had sold her the entire outfit. Later that evening, Tziril and Yussel, who had been thoroughly investigated as to their sobriety and moral character, successfully answered to an oral examination which testified to their knowledge of Jewish law and tradition.

They received a most favorable recommendation from the highly respected rabbi who served their congregation. Both Tziril and Yussel were, by this time, members of the Burial Society, which Yussel had helped organize. He had done a great mitzvah, he told the rabbinical council, since he had settled in Jersey City against even his own inclinations, for at that time there hadn't been even a minyan of ten Jews with whom to pray.

But the final test was the sampling of the wine itself. One by one the rabbis and prominent members of the Jewish community tasted Tziril's trial vintage.

"Superb!" they all declared. Tziril's wine was far better than that of the New York State winemakers who had established their industry almost a generation earlier. After supervising the winemaking process from start to finish over several months, they unanimously decided to grant the hechsha to Tziril and Yussel.

At the early morning service the next day, Yussel announced that he and his wife would host a kiddush, or reception, for the entire congregation on the following Sabbath, in gratitude for the favorable decision.

As they anticipated, it was a memorable kiddush! The synagogue was packed with Sabbath worshippers, and the entire congregation toasted them after the service with their own wine. In honor of the occasion, Tziril and Hinda had baked long loaves of honey cake and almond bread, in addition to the stacks of flat kichel to be eaten with the mounds of chopped herring. Tziril at last had established her name in her new home, and would soon be known to all Jersey City as "Tziril the Winemaker."

The following week was the busiest she had ever known. Not only were they besieged with customers, but a large wagonload of grapes which they had ordered some time before, in anticipation of the rabbinical council's approval, was delivered. Work had to begin at once to assure a plentiful supply of new wine for the Passover.

Tziril and her two hired assistants worked late into the night. The mashgiach, or ritual inspector, came daily because with him present, there could be no doubt as to whether their wine was kosher.

Their first major customer was the sexton of the Bayonne synagogue, who had been entrusted with the task of selecting the wine for his congregation's Passover use. Tziril beamed at Yussel with satisfaction when she told him how much the sexton had ordered that afternoon.

With growing envy, Etta Teresa watched from her lookout across the street, and became increasingly jealous with every customer who passed through Tziril's front door.

"How could Yussel have done this to me?" she wondered. Apparently, he forgot all she had done for him while that selfish wife of his had left him to his own devices. She had waited on him hand and foot!

The fact that he had paid for his meals and had regularly bought gifts for her children was not remembered. "I helped him out of the goodness of my heart," she told herself.

More than anything, she coveted Tziril's winemaking formula, especially since Tziril refused to even discuss the process with her. Etta Teresa even had offered to bring them customers if they would only take her into the business.

But when she approached Tziril after the kiddush, offering to join them, she was rebuffed. They did not need a partner. Tziril declared that the formula for her wine had been a family secret for generations, and that her fondest hope was that when her daughter Hinda married, her son-in-law would learn the art of winemaking. Only Hinda and her children could share in the knowledge of that formula, for it was their heritage, and there was no room for outsiders in the family business. Someday, Tziril emphasized, it would make their fortune, just as it had in the days when her ancestors had cultivated the grape in Kafkaz after their exile from Spain.

There was nothing but praise for her wine, as congratulations literally "poured in" from all sides, even from her non-Jewish neighbors who had also become steady customers. Etta Teresa noticed with dismay how good business was before each Sabbath, and during the week before the High Holy Days there was a long line in front of Tziril's home from morning until evening.

She also began to observe Hinda's activities more closely, who sometimes could be seen carrying a stack of books to or from her home. On sunny afternoons, she could be seen crocheting on the front steps, surrounded by a circle of neighborhood children, who apparently adored her, Etta's daughter Annie, among them.

She also began to notice the young men who came to call on Hinda.

"So, one isn't enough?" she muttered disapprovingly. Often she saw Hinda leaving the house with one of her admirers — and never the same one.

One evening, Etta Teresa summoned up her courage and crossed the street to pay what she called "a friendly visit" to an astonished Tziril and Yussel. They could only wonder what had brought her to their door again, after it had been made clear that her presence was less than welcome. But Etta did have a certain kind of personal magnetism, and when it suited her purpose she could be agreeable and disarming. With a broad smile that displayed the gaps between her discolored teeth, she told them she had come to prove what a true friend she really was.

"I've come to do you a favor," she announced. "There is a most eligible bachelor, a distant relative by marriage, to be exact, and I think it is time to introduce him to your Hinda."

"Who?" Yussel demanded suspiciously. He knew of no "eligible bachelor" in his mishpocha who could answer to Etta's description: wealthy, handsome, and above all, single. Only out of curiosity he permitted her to continue.

She explained. Since her arrival in Jersey City, she had supplemented her husband's gambling winnings by peddling small trinkets to the Poles who lived on Steuben Street, and for years she had been buying her wares from Hymie's on Houston Street.

"Hymie," she began.

"Hymie?" Yussel roared with laughter. "Don't tell me Hymie is in the mishpocha. So, Hymie is an 'eligible bachelor'? Now I have heard everything!

"But Hymie has a brother," she replied.

"But Hymie in the mishpocha?"

"Of course," answered Etta Teresa. "His father was a Rosenblum, a first cousin of Reb Yosef. Hymie's brother is also called Nathan, named for the same relative as Channa's oldest son. He has a business in Sharon, Pennsylvania."

"And so Hymie is related?" Yussel was amazed. "I never realized that, not even when I bought from him when I was a peddler."

"Listen," said Etta, "Both of you. I see Hymie every week. His family wants Nathan to marry and settle down as soon as possible. He lives among *goyim*. Tell me, who can he meet in Pennsylvania? He has a fine business — a department store, in fact. I thought of Hinda right away. Hymie was very interested, and he'll tell his brother the next time he sees him. Nathan is in New York every other week on business, you know.

"But first, let me ask you one thing—is it serious with any of Hinda's young men?"

"Nothing. They are all just friends," Yussel scoffed. "She goes with them to the theater and to lectures. This is America and Hinda learns fast. But she's a good, hard working girl who's entitled to a little sociability and amusement."

"That's all I wanted to know," replied Etta as she departed. "I'll be seeing Hymie on Sunday and I'll tell him we've got a girl for Nathan."

Hinda showed a lively interest when her mother told her the purpose of Etta Teresa's visit. The next morning as she sat outdoors with her needlework, she noticed that, as usual, she was being watched.

Etta's surveillance didn't bother her in the least, as she sat there wondering what her new suitor would be like. Although he had been described to her in glowing terms, she wasn't sure she would like him, even if he was well-to-do. He was almost twice her age, and certainly much older than the young friends, whose invitations to concerts and plays she always accepted eagerly.

Each of these young men, in turn, were devoted to her, and they had all been lavish with their compliments. Her father had begun to warn her that she was "playing a dangerous game" and that she should not trifle with the affections of so many worthy young men. On the other hand, Tziril advised her to accept one of them and send the others away, or else she would soon lose her good name and be an old maid as well.

All that week, Etta Teresa was a constant visitor. It was not easy to turn her away, even though she had developed the habit of calling at the most inconvenient times. Tziril dreaded her knock on the front door. What business of Etta's was it how their business was doing? How many quarts of wine they sold every week? Yussel agreed, but Tziril realized that until Hinda and Nathan were formally introduced it would be a good idea to tread warily and not arouse Etta's temper.

Yussel made inquiries about Hinda's prospective suitor and learned from reliable sources that he was everything Etta Teresa claimed: handsome, prosperous, and eager to marry a girl from a good Jewish family.

But Tziril soon became even more suspicious of Etta's motives. What was that woman really after? Tziril had never treated her with warmth and had only become angry every time she meddled in their affairs. Furthermore, she remembered Etta's unsavory comments about Hinda and her friends who were, after all, decent boys from good families, from social circles too high for Etta to have known their parents.

More than once, Tziril wished she had never heard of Nathan Rosenblum, or of Etta's offer to introduce him to her daughter. If her efforts as a matchmaker were successful, Tziril was certain that Etta would demand an exorbitant shadchen's fee, and perhaps a share in their winemaking business as well.

Although a fee was never paid until after the wedding, one day Tziril asked Etta Teresa what compensation she would want for her trouble.

Etta smiled. "We'll discuss that after the wedding. There's plenty of time — first let them get to know each other and get married. That's what's important.

"But remember one thing, Tziril. It's not as though I were introducing your Hinda to a pants presser or a peddler. You know, I have arranged several successful marriages. This is one of the ways I help support my children."

But Tziril detected a sharp note of cunning beneath her smile.

A Successful Introduction

Tziril, who had never been lavish with her praise for anyone, had to admit that Nathan Rosenblum really did measure up to Etta Teresa's glowing description.

He was tall, well groomed and youthfully lean, with thinning black hair and a carefully groomed mustache. He was a man with an ingratiating manner, and seemed both sufficiently mature and young enough to capture Hinda's fancy. His gait and clothing announced his prosperity, as did the diamond ring on the little finger of his right hand.

Hinda was quite impressed with his command of English, and had blushed with pleasure when he complimented her on the progress she was making with the language. She soon decided that his mustache was very becoming, and that he had excellent taste in clothing — for a man, anyway. Of course, they were both aware that they were distantly related, and he told them all once again how he had been named for the same ancestor, a great grandfather, as her cousin Nathan. He smiled broadly as he spoke, displaying a mouthful of expensive, gold bridgework.

The evening after their formal introduction, Etta Teresa came running to Tziril's door in a state of great jubilation.

"It's all been such a success!" she announced. She had every reason to congratulate herself. That morning she had paid a call on Hymie, and had been told that Nathan was literally charmed with Hinda and her family, and had even gone as far as to admit that Hinda was, indeed, a beautiful girl, despite the fact that she was a little too thin for his taste. But she was intelligent, he had decided, and besides, she had the most beautiful teeth and eyes he had ever seen. Beauty and youth were extremely important to him.

It was no surprise to anyone, then, when the following week, Nathan Rosenblum made two additional visits to Jersey City, bearing boxes of candy and glazed fruit, and elaborate assortments of pastry, which Tziril accepted most graciously. Confident that he had won the approval of Hinda's parents, he departed, certain that his purpose had been accomplished.

Tziril had no words to describe the impression that Nathan Rosenblum had made upon her. He spoke earnestly to both her husband and herself, and told them everything — how he had never married because he had nursed his mother during her final illness, and how he had built his business upon the foundation his father had established. Though he was a bachelor without parents, he had always been close to his family, and spent much of his free time with his brother and sisters and their children.

His brother Hymie and his wife had accompanied him on his last visit, although Hymie's wife had scarcely uttered a word all evening. Mrs. Rosenblum was a shy but sincere woman who had worn herself out helping her husband in the store and looking after their children.

Hymie greeted Yussel as an old friend, and remarked how well he remembered him from his immigrant days.

"And to think we were related all that time," he said. "And maybe, alevai, we will really be in the same mishpocha now! Remember Yussel, the first time you came to my store? I outfitted you with a peddler's pack and a whole stock of merchandise — and on credit yet!

"When I see what a success you and your wife have made of yourselves, I know that a little luck makes a gamble into a mitzvah!"

After the guests departed, Hinda admitted to her parents that none of the young men she knew could compare with Nathan Rosenblum. She had always enjoyed their company, of course, and they did make her life interesting, but she could never take their attentions seriously. Secretly, she had reveled in the curiosity of her neighbors and delighted in being the subject of so much gossip. Even the youngsters on her block would often ask, "Hinda, which one do you like best?"

Hinda had promised her parents that when she was sure of herself and could make up her mind, she would choose a husband, but up to this point, no admirer had made as favorable an impression as Nathan Rosenblum. She was certain that having met him, she could never consider marrying any of the others.

Still, in the quiet of the long afternoons she kept wondering whether or not Nathan was the one for her. Rosa Schmidt had always told Hinda that in addition to being capricious, she was an incurable romantic. Perhaps her friend was right after all, but she felt sure that before long she would know in her own mind whether or not Nathan Rosenblum was to become the embodiment of her hopes for the future.

※

It soon became common knowledge that Etta Teresa had been responsible for Hinda's introduction to such a promising suitor, and her standing in the community rose to a position higher than she had ever hoped to achieve. People began to notice that even her appearance had improved. She no longer wore the bedraggled clothing that had become her trademark, and she seemed to have grown years younger overnight. More and more frequently, she was approached on the street by mothers of marriageable daughters. After all, if she could arrange such a successful marriage for Hinda, there was no reason why she couldn't manage at least an ordinary one for someone slse.

To her dismay, Tziril was congratulated everywhere – in the fish market and at the synagogue.

"There is nothing to talk about," was her brusque reply to the curious, but her smile gave away what she was thinking. Being somewhat superstitious, she considered it unlucky to announce her daughter's imminent betrothal before it was a fact, and was reluctant even to admit that she was hopeful.

"What better way to attract the evil eye," she reasoned.

She was furious when she found out that Etta Teresa herself had been the source of all the gossip. For the past week, she had been boasting to everyone she met how she had arranged Hinda's introduction to a wealthy man who could have had his pick among all the beautiful and rich girls in the

United States, not to mention Europe. She alone had accomplished this great mitzvah, and now Hinda was practically betrothed to a handsome and prosperous man. Due to her good deeds, that girl had been given the chance of a lifetime!

But soon Jersey City's small Jewish community had something else to talk about. Just as the gossip about Hinda's approaching engagement was beginning to die down, word spread that after all those years, the friendship between Etta Teresa and Soreh Ruchel had come to an end.

Soreh Ruchel had approached Etta in the market in front of all the pre-Sabbath shoppers and had reproached her in scathing terms for not thinking of the wellbeing of her own two daughters. Bitter words passed between the two, with Soreh Ruchel calling Etta a hypocrite, and worse.

"A plague on your head!" she had screamed. "What is this I've been hearing? You know very well you've never had anything good to say about those two before. And now you introduce Hinda to a good prospect! Tell me, how much is Tziril paying you?

"You're no better than your Itzig! Everyone knows he was a horsethief. What will people think of me now? My daughters are ruined and it is your fault. Everyone is saying there must be something wrong with them if you passed them over just like that!"

"I have my reasons," Etta replied. But to Soreh Ruchel no reason could have justified the rejection of her own daughters. She knew she could create the kind of scandal she wanted simply by repeating the stories Etta Teresa had told her about Tziril, not to mention all the things her own husband had told her about his cousin Yussel's wife. Besides, she believed her own daughters were superior to that Hinda, whom Etta Teresa had more than once described as "flat as a board and thin like a consumptive."

What kind of a girl was that Hinda anyway? Everyone knew that she was a fool, was lazy and refused to find a job like everyone else. What could she possibly earn crocheting those little caps? Soreh Ruchel wondered how many she would have to crochet to earn a dollar.

When Etta Teresa's curious friends began to question her

about her break with her lifelong friend, she could not offer them an adequate explanation. How could she tell a mother like Soreh Ruchel that Nathan Rosenblum wanted a young and beautiful wife? As far as she was concerned, Soreh's daughters were already old maids, and far from attractive. One of them had a bad limp. But her friends knew what she was thinking without her telling them, and some of them had no scruples about repeating Etta's unspoken opinions to Soreh Ruchel.

With an air of exaggerated indifference, Tziril listened to different accounts of the quarrel. She refused to discuss it. As she explained to her friends, she was busy, what with her winery and all the cooking and preparations for Nathan's next visit. He was coming the following week, and had hinted that he would bring his sisters.

The gossip only amused Hinda, even though she was the center of attention. She had never liked Etta Teresa or Soreh Ruchel, and the fact that the two were no longer speaking gave her an excuse to ridicule them both.

As usual, Velvel was at their house each evening, and begged Tziril and Yussel not to be upset about his wife's temper. As he explained, she often said things that she regretted later.

My wife is an unhappy woman, with daughters who are not getting any younger. As time goes on this makes her more bitter. All the other girls of their age have found husbands, and it's driving Soreh out of her mind."

Yussel and Tziril pitied Velvel and had let him know that he would always be welcome in their home. Actually, they could not imagine a life without Velvel's nightly visits, when he would sit with Yussel for hours, drinking tea and nibbling Tziril's cinnamon cookies. Velvel had known Tziril long before she and Yussel had met, and once a shadchen had even tried to arrange a match between them. But in spite of this, the friendship between Yussel and Velvel was a close one, even for cousins. Velvel had always had a high regard for Tziril, and respected her opinions regardless of the issue.

Meanwhile, Hinda received letters from Pennsylvania almost every day. It came as no surprise to Tziril when a triumphant Etta Teresa informed her that Nathan was prepared to sign the formal engagement contract known as the adnoyim.

"Start preparing for the adnoyim and the engagement celebration," she told Tziril and Yussel.

Tziril was speechless. Then, close to tears, she and Yussel thanked Etta Teresa for all she had done. The prospective bridegroom was everything a mother could ask for, and more.

But even before relating Etta's news to Hinda, Tziril decided that her sister Channa had to be informed at once. This was a matter that could not wait, for it was a sign of respect for the head of her family. The next day, Tziril and Hinda paid Channa a formal call. Tziril was anxious to have Channa's blessing and approval before the actual signing of the articles of engagement. Her daughter's forthcoming marriage was a joyous event that had long been anticipated.

In Channa's crowded parlor that served also as her daughter Rosie's bedroom, Tziril made her announcement with great solemnity. She emphasized that Hinda was her only child — the only one that the Rabbono Shel Olom had spared for her. Channa listened impassively, without a trace of expression. She had been wondering what unusual business had brought her busy sister to New York in the middle of the week.

"My daughter's engagement is not an everyday occurrence," Tziril told her. "I have come to personally invite you and your family to the tenauim celebration. Channa, you're my only sister. Such a time of joy would not be the same without you!"

Tears welled up in Tziril's eyes. She was well aware of how few true friends she had, even within her own family.

Hinda sat on the sofa with her cousin Rosie, who hadn't offered her congratulations. The great change in her once beautiful aunt saddened Hinda. Channa looked so old and careworn, and bore little resemblance to the handsome, richly attired woman she had admired in her childhood. Her aunt's eyes were lustreless and imbedded in deep folds of wrinkled flesh. Lately, Hinda began to notice a marked resemblance between Channa and her elder sister, Bayla. But unlike Bayla had been, Channa spoke without animation, and permitted Tziril to continue without an interruption. She didn't even have enough curiosity to inquire about the prospective bridegroom.

Finally, Channa ushered them into the kitchen for tea. "Poor Channa," thought Hinda. Everything in her aunt's life had changed, and nothing for the better. Her aunt's small, dark kitchen on the fourth floor of a tenement on East Broadway had a single barred window overlooking an airshaft; there wasn't even a curtain for her aunt. Since they had left their home in Kovno, everything had become so depressing at the Muma Channa's. They all missed the gracious home they had to leave behind!

As she stirred the stew that was simmering on the stove, Rosie had little to say and looked as stolid and unsmiling as her mother. Rosie's sole comment was that their neighbor's daughter had broken her engagement on the very eve of her wedding day after a lavish engagement party and the formal signing of the articles of betrothal.

At this Channa nodded. "Listen to me, Tziril," she said. "It's not lucky to say 'mazel tov' before the wedding. When I see Hinda standing under the marriage canopy with a ring on her finger, then I will wish all of you a hearty 'mazel tov'. But remember one thing. Nothing is certain before the chupah, even if an engagement contract is signed.

Tziril grew pale, as if Channa's warning was a foreboding of misfortune to come, but she put aside the doubts in her mind. Nathan Rosenblum offered more than she had ever hoped for her daughter.

As they rode home on the ferry, Hinda remarked to her mother that Rosie really did have a very dreary life, spending her days caring for her home and waiting on her near invalid mother. Rosie never had a chance to meet young men, and it was no wonder that she was considered an old maid. But Tziril was inclined to be philosophical. As she reminded Hinda, Channa and her family had suffered so many disappointments that they could never find any joy in the good fortune of others, even those who were as close to them as they were.

After all, Channa didn't have too much to be happy about. Her sons' prospects were not too bright, since they never had enough money, and Reb Yosef was no longer the prosperous trader Channa had married so long ago. In fact, he was now an old man. Moreover, they couldn't even survive without financial help from Yosef's eldest sons, Bendit and Shaul, who had been sent to America years before. Even they were only just beginning to prosper to any degree.

Tziril could sense that Channa's lack of enthusiasm about Hinda's engagement stemmed from her disappointment that her two married daughters were leading hard lives, in addition to the fact that Rosie was five years older than Hinda.

But there was still another reason, which Tziril refused to discuss with her daughter — Channa's intense distrust of Etta Teresa, whom she had known years before in Kovno.

Channa had taken Tziril aside and reminded her that Etta's husband, Itzig, had always had an unsavory reputation. Itzig was reputed to have been a horsethief, which to Channa's way of thinking was even worse than being a murderer. To steal a horse was to deprive another man of his livelihood. According to Channa, Etta Teresa was no better. Channa had to admit, even to her overjoyed sister, that she was inclined to view anything involving Etta Teresa with suspicion and distrust.

A Formal Betrothal

For an entire week, Tziril alternately cooked, polished and paced the floor in anticipation of the signing of her daughter's engagement contract. Everyone had been invited to attend: Channa and her family, Velvel and Soreh Ruchel, Etta Teresa, Hymie and his wife, and most important, the sisters of the prospective bridegroom. In addition to the relatives, Yussel had invited the rabbi of their synagogue and several of his close friends to insure the presence of ten men for evening prayers after the signing of the contract.

To the joy and relief of Hinda and her parents, as well as the matchmaker, Etta Teresa, everything went smoothly and the engagement was now a fact. Hinda radiated happiness, and everyone said that they had never seen her look so beautiful as she did that day, in her dress of pale blue silk, with her fair hair piled high on her head. Tziril and her husband, of course, wore their best Sabbath garb, but Tziril had already begun to envision their costumes for the wedding. She fancied herself in stiff black satin with wide panniers, the bodice lavishly trimmed with jet. Yussel would rent a cutaway Prince Albert, striped trousers and a high silk hat. On their daughter's wedding day, a professional photographer from New York would record the grandeur and joy of that occasion for the grandchildren that would be sure to follow.

After the precious document was signed and duly witnessed, Nathan Rosenblum presented Hinda with a costly diamond ring of the finest workmanship, as well as a gold watch and chain. In return, Hinda offered her fiance a heavy gold watch and a chain hung with a locket bearing her likeness in a smiling miniature. All went well, and there was much clasping of hands, and tears and embraces among the women.

Tziril felt an enormous rush of pride as the guests seated themselves at her table, set with a braided challah of majestic proportions, baked fish, roast duck with glazed carrots, noodle pudding, apple strudel and huge decanters of wine. Even the rabbi was in a jocular mood, and whispered to Nathan that he'd be a lucky man indeed, if his bride were half as good a cook as her mother.

After the dinner, while the men retired for evening prayers, Tziril invited Nathan's tall, elegantly dressed sisters to inspect Hinda's trousseau. She opened the large chest that held linens, bedding and a satin covered featherbed, all of which had been itemized in the contract as part of Hinda's dowry.

But there was something about the way in which Nathan's sisters inspected each item and towered over her short, stocky presence that was disturbing to Tziril. One of them stated, matter-of-factly, that if they had their way, Nathan would have waited a bit longer before committing himself to a formal betrothal. Of course, Etta Teresa was to blame.

"That woman and her tongue!" was the elder's comment. "You know, Mrs. Friedman, your daughter is lovely. But she is so young. And they hardly know each other. That brother of mine — he's always in such a rush. I'm sure he's told you he's been engaged twice already. He never bothers to find out if he is suited to the girl. That's his trouble. But we will have plenty of time to plan the wedding, anyway."

But the contract had been signed, hadn't it? And the Articles of Engagement were as binding as the marriage ceremony from the traditional point of view. It was not until the guests departed that Tziril realized the significance of Nathan's sister's words. Nathan Rosenblum had taken his leave without setting a date for the wedding. Tziril had never heard of such a thing!

Could it be that his sisters were unimpressed with Hinda's dowry? Perhaps they were jealous of her beauty and youth. The next morning, Tziril voiced her fears to Etta Teresa, who shrugged off her neighbor's apprehensions as inconsequential. After all, hadn't he given her a ring?

But there were no doubts in Hinda's mind, and she couldn't

remember ever being happier. She looked forward to showing her ring to her night school classmates, none of whom, she was sure, had ever been given such an expensive gift.

Her friends began to call her "Hattie," which, they said, was more "American" than "Hinda." She laughed as she answered their many questions about her fiance and how she had met him. But the young Irish girls especially, and those who had been in the United States since their childhood were almost speechless as they listened to her explanation. Their teacher, Nellie Flanagan, who also tutored Hinda privately in English and Composition, finally could not restrain her misgivings.

"My word, Hattie!" she exclaimed. "Are you really saying that your engagement was arranged by your parents and a professional matchmaker?"

Hinda nodded.

"But you really don't know him!" one of the group blurted out in amazement. "How do you know that you love him? How can you tell that you'll be happy?"

For once Hinda was at a loss for words. She stared at one classmate and then another in disbelief. Finally she looked down at the ring that sparkled on her finger.

"My parents are very pleased," she said thoughtfully. "They tell me he is a wonderful man and that I'm very lucky."

Miss Flanagan broke the silence that followed.

"Oh, Hattie," she said with warmth. "Oh, Hattie, we're sure you'll be happy. Congratulations! Really! You'll be very happy!"

Nathan would be returning in two weeks and Hinda had been invited to join him at a family dinner at Hymie's house. He had also written that he intended to take her to New York to meet his nieces and nephews, some of whom were already married, with small children.

Hinda had no words to describe how much she looked forward to this visit. For the first time, they would be alone together, she and her betrothed, even for a few hours. In accordance with the tradition, she and Nathan had never been permitted to spend any time together. She had never even had a private conversation with him, face to face. In fact, he had hardly spoken with her at all; most of the talk had been between Nathan and her parents.

But Hinda was determined that everything would be different now that they were engaged. Of course, her mother objected.

"Such a thing has never been permitted," Tziril said. "It is unheard-of for a respectable couple to be alone together before they are married. But she sighed in resignation. Everything had changed since her girlhood, and she had doubts as to whether any of the changes were for the better.

❧

The horse-drawn hansom cab waiting in front of Hinda's home aroused the curiosity of the neighbors. The steps of the narrow stoop and the sidewalk were crowded with the small boys who spent most of their time playing in the street.

They followed Hinda and her escort to the carriage.

"Where ya goin' Hinda?" they shouted, almost in unison. "To a wedding? A funeral?"

Hinda could not restrain an amused laugh and the color deepened in her cheeks, Her parents watched her and Nathan from their sitting room window. Their daughter had never looked more lovely, and at that moment they knew a happiness of a kind they had only imagined before.

The eyes of the neighbors as well were on the tall, well dressed man who helped Hinda into the carriage. They had all heard that he was the owner of a department store and extremely well off.

"A lucky girl, that Hinda," they nodded to each other.

As she stepped into the carriage, Hinda saw Etta Teresa watching her from her lookout across the street, her nose thrust through the open window. Etta Teresa was scowling, but Hinda was only amused. Her mother had probably neglected to inform her that Nathan would be calling that evening. Such a slight was bound to throw Etta Teresa into a rage, and Hinda noticed, as their carriage departed, that Etta ran across the street, probably to demand an explanation from Tziril and Yussel.

Under her hooded and fringed plaid cape, Hinda wore her new blue silk dress. Besides her engagement ring, the only jewelry she wore were the watch and chain Nathan had given her. It was the most exciting day of her life — more important even than the adnoyim. As the cab passed her neighbors' homes, she waved gaily to the curious onlookers. Her engagement was the door to a new and adventurous life, without the constant supervision of her parents.

Never before had she traveled to New York in a liveried cab. On her weekly excursions with her parents, they usually walked the short distance to the ferry. Among their circle, it was unheard of to hire a carriage except for a funeral or a wedding.

It was only a short drive to the docks, but once they were on the ferry, Hinda was eager to leave the cab and climb the spiral staircase that led to the upper passenger deck.

"It's such a clear evening, Nathan. We'll be able to see the stars," she said. "I think it is time for the full moon. Have you seen the view from the ferry?"

But theirs was not the only hansom cab on the boat. All around them, people were pouring from their carriages and rushing to the upper deck.

"Look, Nathan!" she exclaimed. "I guess everyone must have the same idea."

Nathan shrugged indifferently.

"I'm comfortable right here," he replied. He lit a long cigar. "I don't see any reason to leave the carriage, my dear."

They were wedged in between a vegetable wagon and a van of cackling chickens enroute to the Washington Street Market. Even their driver had left and was edging his way toward the exit leading to the forward deck.

Hinda felt her face grow hot. She felt like a child who had just been scolded. Suddenly she found herself at a loss for words. For a brief moment her eyes met Nathan's. They were cold, blue eyes, she realized, and those of a man accustomed to giving orders. He moved closer to her. It was something of a shock to her when he reached for her hand and held it possessively. His hand felt moist and clammy.

Instinctively, she wrenched her hand away and wriggled to the opposite end of the seat, gripped by a revulsion of a kind she had never before experienced.

Rosenblum's eyes narrowed. He acted as though he were totally undisturbed by Hinda's response, and made no further attempt to touch her, but only puffed at his cigar. He never did understand young girls. He didn't expect them to be reasonable creatures, or even really intelligent. Most of the young ladies he had encountered had acted in a similar way. They were awkward, excessively shy, and simply baffling, as far as he was concerned. Why had he thought this one would be different? What was Hinda afraid of? Nathan sighed. Of course, he would never want to marry a girl who took his affections and those of others too lightly, but after all, they were engaged, and that in itself should mean something – even to a "well-bred young lady from a good, Jewish family."

Hinda had little to say as they rode through the streets of the Lower East Side. The small shops they passed, reminded Nathan of how his own business had started, and he retold the story of how his store had grown to its present size since his father's time. Like Yussel, his father had begun as a peddler with a pack on his back. Needles, pins and shoelaces had been his stock, and his customers the wives of coal miners in Pennsylvania.

Then, as if apologizing for his bachelorhood, he re-emphasized the fact that he had deferred his marriage for years, sacrificing his youth to his business and his ailing mother.

But Hinda had heard it all before on his first visit. Her mother, of course, had been a most sympathetic listener. There had been complete understanding and rapport between Tziril and Nathan from the beginning. Tears had welled up in her mother's eyes when he had confided that he had vowed to his mother "on her deathbed" that he would seek out and marry a virtuous young woman from a respectable Orthodox home.

As far as Hinda could see, her mother had no doubts whatsoever, that the Master of the Universe, in His infinite wisdom had guided Nathan Rosenblum directly to their door.

28

A Painful Decision

It was long past midnight when Hinda tiptoed to her room, carrying her high heeled slippers so that she would not awaken her parents. But as she passed their door she noticed that their light was still burning. Hinda didn't want to see them tonight if she could possibly avoid it, for she was too confused and depressed. There was so much to think about, and as she reached her bedroom it occurred to her that she had never before realized how much one's life and plans could be changed in a single evening. Was she the same romantic young girl who had stepped into the carriage a few short hours before?

"Goodnight, Hinda," Nathan had said. "Goodnight. I'll be back in two weeks. You'll write to me every day now, won't you?"

More than once he had glanced at his watch. "I really should go. I have to catch the last train back to Pennsylvania, you know. But you'll write to me..."

He nervously checked the time once more as he climbed back into the carriage that had at first seemed to Hinda to be the essence of elegance and sophistication.

She shut her bedroom door with disappointment. She had expected so much from this visit. At last she would have had a chance to be alone with the man to whom she was betrothed. And how had it ended? He had come and he had gone, and there was only the consciousness of a terrible loss. She felt as though all her hopes had betrayed her. No man she had ever known had made her feel so inadequate, graceless and stupid. Her face burned with shame as she threw herself onto her bed.

Nathan's young nieces and nephews had been pleasant and

friendly. but their cordiality had only made her ill at ease, for they were young people of her own age – her own generation. Though they all had great respect for their uncle, they couldn't hide their curiosity and amazement that she, Hinda, was the one he had selected to be their aunt. She was only a young girl, and their contemporary; anyone could tell that Nathan was almost old enough to be her father.

More than anything else, she had wanted to leave and never see any of them again. His sisters had arrived in time for dessert, and had immediately begun to barrage her with questions about her years in Kafkaz. They seemed to know so much about her mother! And their tone implied a kind of criticism Hinda had not been prepared to deal with. Their expensive dresses and gracious manners only half concealed the coarse minded busybodies they really were. They reminded her of Soreh Ruchel and Etta Teresa. What business of theirs was it anyway!

She had hardly tasted the food, and sat for what seemed like hours toying with her napkin.

"Why, Hinda, what's wrong?" Nathan's eldest sister inquired. "You know, our poor mother, may she rest in peace, was like you. She never had any appetite. She died still young, as Nathan has probably told you. She was a frail, sickly creature. When she passed away, there was nothing left but skin and bones. You have the same kind of delicate figure, my dear."

In her room later that evening as she uncoiled and brushed her long hair, Hinda remembered that heartless comment. She could not restrain the tears that filled her eyes as she saw herself in her mirror. The face lighted by the hanging kerosene lamp and reflected from the other side of her chiffonier was not that of a happy young woman.

Now Nathan was gone. There was no rapture, no ecstasy, only doubts, and worst of all, in the morning she would have to tell her parents that she would not be marrying Nathan Rosenblum – not now and not ever. With difficulty, she fought her impulse to run sobbing into their bedroom that moment, and blame them for what she considered to be "a terrible mistake."

She slept late the next morning, since Yussel refused to permit Tziril to wake her. When she finally emerged from her room, Tziril was already serving the noon meal.

Though Hinda was fully dressed, she appeared unkempt. Instinctively, Tziril and Yussel sensed that something had gone wrong the night before, and that Hinda wanted to tell them about it. They had never seen her look in such need of comforting.

Hinda turned her red eyes to Yussel. "Oh *Tateh*," she said in a tired voice, "Oh *Tateh*, I don't want to talk now. I just want some tea."

Tziril and Yussel watched with apprehension as she drank her tea. After a few minutes, Hinda couldn't bear to see them hovering over her with such grave concern any longer. She pushed herself from the table and ran back to her room.

"No, Tziril, not now!" Yussel commanded. "Don't follow her. I don't want you to. She will be all right. Leave her alone now."

Tziril brushed him aside. She found Hinda's door closed, and stood outside and listened. It was ominously quiet, and only Yussel's presence prevented her from entering Hinda's room.

Hinda lay awake that whole night, wondering how she would ever tell them that all their plans for her had suddenly changed. She couldn't even bear the thought of seeing Nathan Rosenblum again. She wished she had never met him, never heard of him. She would have to tell her parents that she would rather die than marry him.

She could visualize their distress and terrible disappointment. Her mother's, in particular! Tziril had been so overjoyed to see her daughter betrothed to a man of substance and position. Nathan was an older man, of course, but what boy of Hinda's age could be so settled and affluent? Ever since her engagement, Tziril walked in a haze of self satisfaction. She had done well for her only child. The moment Nathan Rosenblum had set eyes on her Hinda he had wanted her for his own. Tziril's joy had been so great that she was unable to share it with others, for fear of attracting the evil eye.

Her Hinda was beautiful, desirable and well educated. Tziril and Yussel had spared no expense, and she had been well schooled, both in Kafkaz and at the gymnasium in Telschi.

German, French, Russian — Tziril had told everything to Nathan with pride, and she had shown him the wax flowers, Hinda's creation, that had won her daughter a first prize.

Most of all, her Hinda wouldn't have to sit and languish at home waiting for a suitable husband to present himself, like Channa's daughter Rosie, or Soreh Ruchel's daughters. Hinda knew that her mother had had a bitter girlhood and youth. Her triumph with Hinda was her greatest source of comfort. And Hinda knew that she had no choice but to disappoint her mother.

Early the next morning, she flung open her door and ran weeping into her father's arms.

To please her parents, Hinda promised not to act too hastily. She agreed to see Nathan once more, to make sure and, finally, even she agreed that she owed him, if not herself, that much. There would be plenty of time to think things over and act judiciously. Tziril and Yussel reminded her that an engagement contract had been signed. Under Halacha, religious law, it was binding and could not be dissolved easily. There were formalities that had to be observed. In fact, she was already bound to Nathan Rosenblum as irrevocably as if they had exchanged marriage vows beneath the bridal canopy.

Nevertheless, Tziril and Yussel reassured her that if she refused to change her mind within a certain period of time, they would give their consent to the annulment of the contract, however complicated and embarrassing it might prove to be.

Once she unburdened herself to her parents, Hinda's sense of relief was overwhelming. At last they knew her true feelings. She had a few weeks to think things over and make a final decision. But her mind was made up, and even after her initial disappointment and anger wore off, she was certain that her feelings would never change.

She realized, of course, that her mother was deeply troubled, but this was unavoidable. Tziril went about her work sighing to herself, as though the greatest of all possible calamities had befallen them.

❧

These days, Tziril's biggest problem was avoiding Etta Teresa who was as curious as ever to know the progress of Hinda's courtship. Although she had made no secret of her resentment at not being told in advance of Hinda's recent visit with Nathan's family, she was determined not to let Tziril realize how angry she really was. Etta was by nature suspicious, and always believed that people were keeping things from her. She wondered why Tziril and Hinda were being so evasive. What kind of talk was that!

From Etta Teresa's point of view, there was too much at stake. For one thing, there was her matchmaker's fee for the introduction. They had not discussed it yet, but there was no question in Etta's mind what that fee should be. Of course, she knew that whatever assets Tziril and Yussel possessed were tied up in their winemaking business, but that venture was now thriving. What Etta Teresa had in mind was an arrangement that would give her a share of the profits over a period of time. Every day Etta reproached herself for not going into the winemaking business on her own.

She thought she would have been quite successful, if only she had been given a little assistance at the outset. But Tziril, in her greed and selfishness, had refused to even give her advice. Etta had offered to bring them customers, but those two had wanted no part of her efforts on their behalf, and had refused her suggestions that might have benefited all of them.

More than once she had discussed the matter of her shadchen's fee with Soreh Ruchel before their final quarrel. Etta's friend had always agreed that she was entitled to a handsome commission. Hinda's engagement had been no mean accomplishment, for up to that point, there had been no pleasing Nathan Rosenblum.

Etta had sought the advice of others as well in the matter of her fee. Before long, it had become common gossip that Etta Teresa had had a firm commitment from Tziril and Yussel; after Hinda's marriage, the matchmaker would become a partner in their winery.

Now Etta was troubled. Something was definitely going on behind her back. Where was Hinda hiding herself these days?

No longer did Etta see her sitting on the front steps crocheting, or hurrying off with a stack of library books. Tziril and Yussel were always in such a hurry, and seemed to be constantly disappearing into the winecellar and latching the door behind them. They had no time for her lately, and were always vague in their answers whenever she broached the topic of Nathan Rosenblum.

She could stand it no longer, and one day she paid a surprise call on Hymie, and Etta was amazed to discover that Hymie's brother had been in New York as usual that week — and had already returned to Sharon.

She was aghast. "He didn't even go to see his bride!"

"That's right!" was Hymie's reply. "He wants to teach that girl a lesson. She promised to write. Not one letter did he get!

"My brother is not a man to be made a fool of! But let me tell you something, Etta Teresa. He said he wasn't surprised. He told me that your wonderful Hinda was childish, capricious, and the most spoiled girl he had ever seen!"

"But he seemed to be so taken with her," Etta stammered, "after all, didn't he want a young and beautiful wife?"

"Yes, but he's having second thoughts now. Our sisters say that they wouldn't be surprised if Hinda was sickly like our mother. Nathan wouldn't want a wife who would be bedridden half the time." He shook his head.

"I guess we all wish he hadn't been in such a hurry to give her a ring. But that's Nathan. A man of decision. No fooling around for him!"

It was only a matter of a few days before the small Jewish community of Jersey City — friends, relatives and especially enemies — knew that Hinda's engagement was off.

Hinda's parents had warned her that a broken engagement was bound to be a sordid experience, the subject of conjecture and malicious gossip for weeks to come. The worst of it was that everyone believed, once the contract was nullified and the gifts returned, that the engagement had been called off by the wounded suitor.

Etta Teresa was never more spiteful. She repeated to anyone who would listen how Nathan did not consider Hinda worthy to be his wife. Hinda had been jilted, she told them, and deservedly. Besides, she would add slyly, Tziril's reputation had not helped matters any.

"I don't blame Nathan," she told her friends. "What man would want a woman like that for a mother-in-law? A woman whose husband was all too ready to divorce her, and with good cause!"

It wasn't long before her malicious remarks were repeated to Tziril. The resulting confrontation was so bitter that Tziril ran to the rabbi in tears to bring charges against Etta Teresa. Her husband's cousin spread lies about her that were ruining her business as well as her reputation. Etta added extra bits of gossip to the story of how Tziril had cheated her – an account of the alleged affair between Tziril and her aged brother-in-law, Meiron.

Had Tziril been in Kovno, she would have taken her grievance to the rabbinical court. But in America there was no authority to turn to except the rabbi of the Jersey City congregation. She knew she had cause for bringing suit to the civil courts, but that was contrary to her principles. The one thing she wanted to avoid was bringing shame on their Jewish community. The rabbi understood, and promised to do all he could to help her.

It was no surprise to Tziril, when Etta Teresa dragged Soreh Ruchel into the quarrel as a witness against her. After all, Soreh was Yussel's cousin's wife. Etta swore that Soreh Ruchel had been the source of all her information about Tziril's infidelity, since Yussel had confided in his cousin Velvel during all those years his wife had been in Kafkaz.

"I swear on the lives of my husband and children!" cried Etta. "None of them should live another day if I'm not speaking the truth!"

The local gossips soon discovered another gold mine! Not only did they have Hinda's broken engagement and Tziril's escapades to talk about, but also the latter's charges of libel against Etta Teresa. The word spread that there was to be a rabbinical trial with a committee of rabbis from New York presiding as judges. This would be the first time such an event had taken place in Jersey City.

The Jersey City rabbi disqualified himself, but an impartial council of rabbis agreed to hear Tziril's charges of character defamation against Etta Teresa, who would be given every opportunity to defend herself, and Soreh Ruchel would be summoned as a witness on her behalf.

To everyone's amazement, throughout the hearing, Soreh Ruchel protested that she simply was not involved and knew absolutely nothing. According to her, Etta's testimony that she had been the primary source of information about Tziril's activities was a parcel of lies.

Before the eminent rabbis delivered their verdict, both Etta Teresa and Soreh Ruchel were formally reprimanded. To Etta's dismay, Tziril was exonerated and declared to be an innocent victim of evil minded troublemakers. Moreover, the rabbinical court could only find praise for her decision to refrain from appealing to the civil authorities. Tziril had done what was noble and proper, and had risked her own reputation to avoid bringing disgrace on the Jews of Jersey City, who were only now beginning to make themselves heard as a voice in the community.

29

Alte

As Tziril predicted, Hinda's broken engagement was a devastating experience for everyone involved. The girl could no longer face her neighbors and classmates. The inevitable questioning and sympathy of her well meaning friends was crushing, and she dropped out of night school.

Never again would she permit her parents to arrange a marriage for her, nor would she agree to an introduction to an "eligible bachelor." She vowed that when and if she ever married, she would have only a simple ceremony, and approach the canopy with her parents as her only witnesses. In the future, she would refuse to permit any discussion of dowry, for the memory of her parents' negotiations was enough to make her shudder. It had all been so humiliating.

But as the days passed, her depression only increased. What hurt the most was the knowledge that her broken engagement was regarded by all as a great scandal and a stain on the family name.

Tziril was consumed by her hatred of Etta Teresa and Soreh Ruchel, whom she held responsible for her daughter's misery, as well as the scandalous lies that circulated about her own past. She vowed that she would never forgive either of them and called upon Rabbono Shel Olom to punish them as they justly deserved. Imagine! That Etta Teresa claiming that she had been promised a share in the winery! That lie about her supposed adulterous relationship with her elderly brother-in-law was not only malicious — but preposterous. That aged, infirm old man! He was almost senile!

But Tziril and Yussel were heartbroken. One would think that their world had come to an end. They talked in hushed whispers and walked around on tiptoe, so to speak, to avoid disturbing their grieving daughter. Now and then they changed their tactics and entered Hinda's room and demanded to know how long she intended to sit there alone, not speaking to them, or to any of her friends and cousins who came to commiserate with her and offer their sympathy.

Yussel brought her all sorts of delicacies to tempt her appetite, and the latest fashion magazines and her favorite Yiddish newspapers, but it was no use. The more her parents tried to rouse her from her depression, the worse she felt. Often she would pick up a book or magazine, leaf through a few pages. and then burst into sobbing.

One morning as she gazed vacantly out her bedroom window, it struck her suddenly that spring had come. The last traces of snow had disappeared and the sun shone brilliantly. She sat up straight.

"What a beautiful day!" she said out loud to no one. "What kind of an idiot have I been all this time? I've been acting like a fool!"

How could she spend the first day of spring staring at the wall?

"Why should I feel sorry for myself?" she said. "I only did what I had to do. It was my own decision, this was how it had to be."

And with a burst of energy, she ran to the closet, glanced hastily at the dresses hanging there, some of which she had never even had time to wear, grabbed the nearest frock, and began to arrange her hair before the small mirror above the dresser. She poked around in the bottom of the closet and found the high heeled blue slippers that matched her dress. For a moment, her slim ankles wobbled, but she soon accustomed herself to the shoes. She liked the added height they gave her. As she passed the kitchen her parents turned around, startled at the sound of her step. They stared at her in astonishment as she stood before them with her long plaid cape flung over her shoulders — in their eyes she had never seemed lovelier.

"I'm going to New York," she announced, with a trace of her old defiance, which warned them not to question her. "I read an advertisement in the Forward about a sewing school on East Broadway. A Miss Minna Feigensohn is the director. I'm going to see her. I really hope she accepts me as a pupil. It's a school for pattern designers and dressmakers. Don't worry — it's not too expensive. I just can't spend the rest of my life in my room, sitting and brooding."

Tziril was speechless as Yussel nodded his assent. She regained her composure in a moment.

"You might have time to see your Aunt Channa," was her only comment as Hinda headed for the front door. "Give her a geruss and my love."

With her daughter out the door, Tziril turned to Yussel, who was smiling.

"You don't have to say anything," he told her.

She sighed. "A weight has lifted from my heart. To see her face this morning was like an answer from heaven."

After a brief, business like interview with Miss Feigensohn, Hinda was accepted as a pupil and assigned to a sewing machine. Immediately her teacher began to instruct her in its use. Hinda paused for a moment to take a look around her. There were at least a dozen young women in her class, and from what she could gather, beginners like herself, mostly foreign born. It seemed as though everyone was speaking Yiddish or broken English.

Later, as the girls gathered together to eat their lunches and compare notes about the progress they were making, Hinda introduced herself. She discovered that many of these young women were also attending night school to improve their English, and were eager to get good jobs as dressmakers and designers. They seemed to be both serious and fun loving in their manner and Hinda knew she would enjoy their company at Miss Feigensohn's school.

The afternoon ended too soon. A few minutes before the class was to be dismissed, three young men arrived to pay a call on Miss Feigensohn. The girl on Hinda's left told her that one of them was their teacher's younger brother, and introduces him to Hinda, explaining that he was a rabbinical student at the Reform seminary. Within minutes, his friends approached and asked to be introduced to Miss Feigensohn's new pupil. The three were the closest of friends, explained the spokesman of the trio who introduced himself as Alte Lipschutz.

Hinda was struck by the way he reminded her of the young men she had met on board the *Rotterdam*, and apparently, she made a favorable impression upon him as well. She was flattered when he offered to walk her to the Cortland Street Ferry. It was too nice a day, he said, to be cooped up in the horsedrawn streetcar. In her excitement, she forgot about visiting her Aunt Channa on the way home.

He asked her to call him Alte, and demanded to know all about her.

"I have a class this evening," he explained. "Otherwise I would take you all the way home and you could introduce me to your parents. Besides, I've never been in New Jersey. I'll see you tomorrow, though. I'll meet you at Miss Feigensohn's."

To Hinda's amazement, the next morning, Miss Feigensohn indicated that she had already heard about Alte Lipschutz's interest in getting to know her newest student. The teacher seemed amused, if anything, but she warned Hinda not to take her younger brother's friend too seriously. He was the romantic type, she said, and far from ready to commit himself to any one girl. Her only other comment was that Hinda should not be too disappointed if Alte failed to call for her after class.

"That Alte's always falling in love at first sight," she warned with a trace of cynicism.

Hinda could only guess that her teacher was a woman who had had many disappointments with men. After all, she wasn't young anymore. When closing time arrived that afternoon, and Alte failed to make an appearance, Miss Feigensohn commented dryly that he had never been known for his punctuality, and one could never count on any promise he made. But just as Hinda was preparing to leave without him, he arrived, breathless from running, and announced that he would escort her to the ferry — as he had promised.

As they strolled toward the ferry in the late afternoon sunshine, he told Hinda that he wouldn't have time for supper that night if he wanted to get to his class on time. He was employed as a junior accountant at a dressmaking firm, and attended courses in accounting at the Educational Alliance. He hoped to become a successful manufacturer in the burgeoning garment industry.

Alte Lipschutz had been born in Vilna where he had studied engineering. But because he had been an activist with a student revolutionary group involved in educating the peasantry, his parents had decided that he should be sent to America before he found himself in serious trouble.

"We were only trying to improve things for them," he told Hinda. "We started underground schools to teach them to read and write. My parents were sick with worry, and believed that any day I might be arrested and exiled to Siberia, or worse. Actually they were right. There was one time when I barely escaped being arrested. Of course, I never told them about that!"

As he told her about his life and his decision to come to America, Hinda noticed that he wasn't much taller than she was. Not that he wasn't attractive, though. He had an elegant manner about him, and dressed quite well. His curly brown hair, which was brushed back into a pompadour, added at least another inch to his height, and his full brown mustache made him look mature for his age, and even distinguished. She especially liked his eyes, which changed back and forth from blue to gray.

She sensed right away how sensitive he was about being short.

"My father is a tall man," he told her, a bit apologetically, as though he were aware that his friends always towered over him.

But what impressed her was his talent as a conversationalist. As they walked toward the ferry they discussed every topic under the sun. He was at home with music, poetry, books, world politics and business trends, and had a sense of humor, besides. Except for the fact that he was short, Hinda decided that he was as attractive a "man of the world" as the handsome faces of the male mannequins she had always admired in the fashion magazines.

They were enjoying each other's company too much to part when they arrived at the Cortlandt Street Landing. Alte decided to board the ferry with her and accompany her as far as the New Jersey side of the Hudson, when he would remain on board for the return trip to New York. He followed her to her favorite place on the upper deck.

It was chilly there, and Hinda was glad she was wearing her warm, plaid cape. She slipped the hood over her head to keep her long hair from blowing in her eyes. As though he were an old friend whom she had known all her life, she did not object when he linked his arm in hers.

One thing he let her know was that he didn't approve of her high heeled slippers. He couldn't understand how she walked in them. "A health hazard," he called them.

He asked her if she realized how fortunate she was to have been accepted as a pupil by Miss Feigensohn. Her teacher's family was socially conscious and had great prestige: among them were several famous scholars and well known physicians. Her younger brother, he was convinced, had a brilliant career ahead of him. He expected to marry some time during the next year, and would be continuing his studies at the Reform Theological Seminary in Cincinnati. Of course, his family did not approve, since they were all quite Orthodox, but then Alte's own parents did not approve of his own ideas and ambitions either. The older generation, he said to Hinda, did not realize that especially in America, Orthodoxy was a dying, if not already dead, institution. He was most enthusiastic about his friend, whom he considered to be closer to him than his own brother Velvel, who had emigrated to America almost two years before he himself had left Vilna.

Alte admitted that neither he nor his brother had ever brought any great joy to their father, whom he described as a fanatically religious old fashioned patriarch who had always demanded complete obedience from his family. He was especially strong willed when it came to his sons' education and religious training. Alte's father was a respected Talmudic scholar who had tried, in vain, to mold his sons in his own image, Besides Alte's brother Velvel, there were also two sisters and a younger brother who was a brilliant mathematics student at the university in Vilna.

Their mother, however, was different, and according to Alte, something close to a saint. She always understood her children's needs, and had helped them in any way she could. While his father had sat over his books in the study house, his mother had managed the family business — a successful wholesale grocery business. If it were not for his devotion to his mother, he conceded, he would have left for America even before his brother Velvel. Every day, he said, he missed her more.

As though he wanted Hinda to know everything about him and his family, he told her about his younger brother and sisters as well. The older of his sisters, Sonia, was also a rebel. In her last letter, his mother had written that Sonia was engaged to a lumber merchant who was very wealthy, but without much learning. Of course, to Alte's father's way of thinking, the prospective son-in-law was completely unacceptable; learning was the only worthy criterion.

When Motle, his youngest brother, had chosen secular studies over the Talmud after his Bar Mitzvah, it was a blow their father considered unforgivable, and he had not said a word to his youngest son since. As for Velvel, he had practically disowned him. Velvel had left home with an itinerant cork maker shortly after his fourteenth birthday, and it seemed clear to Alte that his father had driven them all from his home with his tyrannical rule.

Of his entire family, Alte spoke with the most feeling about Pasha, his youngest sister. She was a beautiful child, and his mother had recently sent him a picture of her. Actually he was surprised that his father had allowed Pasha to have her picture taken, and he saw it as an indication that beneath his father's stubborn exterior, there was love and yearning for his sons. This simple act of sending Alte a photograph had been, for his father, like extending his jand in a gesture of peace.

But soon the tide of Alte's conversation drifted back toward himself.

"You know, Hinda," he said, "why I was named 'Alte?' I was born after my mother had had two stillborn children. It's really a very superstitious idea, since 'Alte' means 'the old one.' That way they could be sure that I would live to a ripe old age. When I marry, my parents will go to the synagogue and give me a real name."

Despite his show of amusement at his parents' attempt to foil the evil eye, Alte actually considered this to be a beautiful if archaic custom. He told Hinda that he believed it was, more than anything else, an old fashioned, but lovely expression of parental love. On the other hand, he couldn't emphasize too strongly the fact that he had little respect or enthusiasm for the age old tenets and rituals of the Judaic tradition. With a trace of sadness, he explained that his religious philosophy had been the major cause of his estrangement from his father.

Suddenly, the gates were closing, and Alte and Hinda realized that the ferry would be departing for New York in a few minutes. Alte did not want to find himself stranded on the Jersey side of the river, but as the boat pulled away from the pier, he shouted that he would be sure to meet her the next day.

❧

It was apparent to Tziril and Yussel the moment they heard the excited clatter of Hinda's high heeled slippers on the front steps that their daughter was in a rare good humor. She burst into the kitchen, as breathlessly as if she had run all the way home from the Exchange Place Pier, and announced that she was famished.

Between mouthfuls of Tziril's boiled fish and savory noodle pudding, she related the day's events. Yussel smiled patiently as she described her new admirer, which was something she had carefully omitted the day before.

"He's not as tall as my 'ex' — I mean Nathan — but so lively. Such good company.

"Oh *Tateh*! Are you listening? *Tateh*, stop laughing at me!"

"Yes, Hindele," he answered fondly. "I'm listening. Of course I'm listening."

"Eat," Tziril urged, her face lit up with keen interest.

Yussel was thinking that his daughter hadn't changed at all, in spite of her broken engagement! She was always so impressed with a new admirer, and then seemed to lose interest overnight. He could only think with amusement that this Alte would be no different.

"But *Tateh*," continued Hinda. "I'm telling you. He is different. I learned so much just listening to him. Just imagine — he's related to the Maskil, Isaac Maier Dik, whose books I read in Telschi."

Tziril's forehead wrinkled into a frown. In Kovno, Dik's influence on the young was considered a definite threat. This leader of the so-called Jewish Enlightenment was urging the young to exchange the study of Torah for secular pursuits. The Maskil wanted to raise up a generation of cosmopolitans like himself who would discard their sacred tradition. From the first, Tziril had forbidden Hinda to read his books.

Immediately, she decided that she was not going to like her daughter's new friend.

Suddenly, Hinda changed the subject and began to speak enthusiastically about Miss Feigensohn's school.

"She is such a lady and so well educated. And everyone there is so friendly. Miss Feigensohn's friends are always dropping in. Many of them are young students who work during the day. I think I was lucky to have been accepted as a pupil there."

"And Mama, before long I'll be making my own clothes, and yours too. The teacher has charge accounts at all the major suppliers. We can get everything we need at quite a discount."

But Tziril was more interested in learning about Hinda's new friend Alte, especially his "illustrious" family background. She sighed when Hinda described Alte's father as a learned Talmudic scholar. Of course, the son was nothing like the father — Alte was a "free spirit," a child of the new age. For this was the picture of Alte Lipschutz that Hinda had created: a young man who was a product of the Haskalah movement, or "New Enlightenment" that was having such a profound effect on Jewish youth in Russia, especially in the large cities.

Tziril knew for a certainty that if anything serious ever developed between her daughter and this Alte, he would never be allowed to handle her wine. He was not even a Sabbath observer. Alte Lipschutz was, to her way of thinking, an unbeliever and an apikoros, a heretic, who scoffed at the teachings of the Torah; she decided that their friendship had to be nipped in the bud.

Since Hinda had broken her engagement to Nathan Rosenblum, it had become an obsession with Tziril that any future son-in-law become a business partner as well. Before long, they would need help in enlarging their winery in order to achieve the success she desired. And she wanted it to continue to be solely a family undertaking. Someday, Tziril fervently believed, her wine would become as famous as that of her Sephardic ancestors in Kafkaz.

Bayla had always maintained that their father's secret process was unsurpassable, and that the formula alone was worth a fortune. As her sister lay dying, Tziril had promised herself, indeed she had vowed, that the formula would remain in the family as a heritage for her grandchildren.

She resolved that the friendship between Hinda and Alte would have to be discouraged. She would need Yussel's help in this. His words would reach their daughter, even if her own were to fail. Alte could never find a place in their family. He simply wouldn't fit in with her plans for the future. She would never accept him as a son-in-law, she decided with finality.

And suddenly, Tziril could not even bear to hear his name mentioned, and she demanded to know why Hinda had not visited her aunt.

"There was no excuse!" she said angrily. "Since when is that apikoros more important than your own aunt?"

Hinda was on the verge of tears after such an unexpected outburst from her mother. She could only repeat what she had already told her parents — there just hadn't been time.

"But Mama, he even got on the boat with me and rode all the way to Jersey City. He wants to meet you and the *Tateh*. You will like him. He said he thought very highly of you for sending me to study at the gymnasium."

"Good — very good," countered Yussel with his usual good humor. "Why don't you invite him to spend the *Shabbos* with us? And tell me more about the school. How long will you be going there?"

"Every day for six more weeks. . . "

"I told you I needed you at home on Friday!" Tziril interrupted.

"Of course, Mama. I already told you. There's no class on Friday. Only from Monday to Thursday, and then only a half a day on Thursday. Maybe Thursday afternoon I'll go and visit the Muma Channa."

Tziril didn't even answer. She scowled as she began to clear the table.

30

An Unexpected Encounter

The next day Alte dropped into Miss Feigensohn's school during his lunch hour, just to say "hello," or so he said. He found Hinda busy at her sewing machine, and could only stay long enough to remind her not to leave without him. He would walk her to the ferry that evening.

When he arrived to call for her, he was still in a hurry.

"I can't afford to miss class again," he explained, "or even be late. Soon we will be having our examinations."

That evening, as they walked toward the ferry, he insisted that they speak only in English. "Otherwise, how will we ever learn to speak fluently? We both need practice."

He complimented Hinda on the extent of the English vocabulary she had acquired in so short a time, and predicted that she would be one of those rare people who would ultimately lose their foreign accents.

"You have a good ear," he said. "Like a musician."

Hinda couldn't have been more flattered. She couldn't pretend, especially to herself, that she wasn't enjoying his ardent interest in her. Of course, Miss Feigensohn had warned her that Alte Lipschutz was a romantic and wasn't to be taken seriously, but her teacher had only seen one side of him.

As they sauntered toward the ferry, he told her over and over again, much to her pleasure, that ever since the day he had first met her, he hadn't been able to stop thinking about her. But all too soon they arrived at the landing, and he had to rush off to make his class.

She sat alone on the upper deck of the ferry. She wrapped her plaid cape snugly around her, for the evening wind off the Hudson was sharp, although it was spring. She told herself that it was far too soon to take Alte seriously. She hardly knew him. Over and over again, she reminded herself of her recent disappointment and all the grief it had caused. She had been burned once and that was enough for a lifetime. She was not going to fall into the same trap again — not if she could help it. Still, it was a wonderful feeling to know that someone was so tremendously attracted to her, and more important, someone whom she had discovered for herself, without the elaborate designs of parents and matchmakers.

As for her mother, all she could do was hope she would change her mind, once she actually met Alte. After all, her mother had told her many times how she herself had married Hinda's father without the aid of a go-between. This was something Tziril had always spoken of with pride.

Later that evening, when her parents questioned her about the day, Hinda had little to say. She could only imagine what her mother's reaction would be if she repeated some of the things Alte had said to her on the way to the ferry. Surely she would have been horrified.

Yussel regarded it all as an enormous joke. To his way of thinking, it was simply the way of a healthy young man with a pretty girl. Her good natured father regarded romance as being as natural as breathing: flattery, compliments and ardent words were the language of youth. A man shouldn't always expect to be taken too seriously, though, and a woman should avoid allowing herself to be hurt. Hinda knew that these were the words of advice he would give her, once he stopped laughing, and she decided to remain silent.

But she was haunted by that look in Alte's eyes, beautiful eyes, neither blue nor gray, that beckoned beneath his heavy arching brows that were a shade darker than his curly brown hair. They seemed to be searching for something, while at the same time prodding at her to admit what her feelings for him were.

That night she lay awake, restless and troubled. The memory of the humiliation she had suffered after her broken engagement could not be dispelled. Alte would have to be told about it sooner or later, if anything really serious should develop! And what would he think? She had once read that every man wanted to be the first love in the life of the woman of his choice. But she hadn't been in love with Nathan; she hadn't even pretended to be, and it was only that she had been so happy just to see her parents so ecstatic about their prospective son-in-law and the way of life he would have been able to provide for her. But what would she do, if the simple fact that there had been an engagement, even an arranged one, were to raise all sorts of doubts in Alte's mind?

Moreover, the memory of the bitterness between her mother and Etta Teresa reminded her of the ugly stories that had circulated about her mother's past. Just thinking about that made Hinda cringe in shame. What if those stories should reach Alte's ears? Whom would he believe?

She could no longer resist the temptation to unburden herself to him, and the very next evening she told him the whole story of the weeks of anguish that had followed her broken engagement. Besides, she had to tell him why it was impossible for her to take anyone too seriously just yet. It was much too soon; she would have to be sure this time. She was only beginning to recover from the disillusionment and shame of that first episode.

Alte proved to be all sympathy and understanding. He admitted that he, too, had had disappointments — some that had seemed almost catastrophic at the time. A weaker man might even have ended his life! But, he told her, never before had he felt as completely happy as he did now, in her presence, holding her hand by his side. He was certain that what he felt for her was something permanent, and that before long she would realize, as he did already, that they were destined for each other.

As they lingered in the waiting room at the terminal, he urged Hinda to try to come to New York that Saturday. That was the one day of the week when he had no classes or work; the day was free — a holiday. Besides, on Saturday afternoons all his friends gathered at Minna Feigensohn's.

"Please, Hinda," he urged. "Your parents will understand. Minna has open house every Saturday afternoon, and I know you'd be welcome. Sometimes we dance, or have interesting discussions. And have you ever seen Second Avenue on Satur-

day night when the Sabbath comes to an end? It comes to life!
There is always a dance or a lecture to go to — we can all go
in a group with some of my friends.

"Haven't you ever been to the theater in New York? To a
concert? I hear Kreisler is playing Saturday night at the Academy of Music on 14th Street. Wouldn't you like to go?"

"I'm afraid it's out of the question," Hinda said, wistfully.
She knew she'd never be permitted to travel, or even be away
from home on the Sabbath. Saturday was the holiest of holies
in her mother's house. Besides, how would she ever get back?
The ferry stopped running after midnight.

Alte insisted that Minna would be happy to have Hinda
spend the night with her. He'd speak to her if Hinda wished.
Or maybe, she could arrange to sleep at her aunt's.

"You could go to your aunt's on Friday afternoon, before
the Sabbath begins, and you could stay there until Sunday.
I'm sure your aunt wouldn't mind."

"But I couldn't," Hinda insisted. "My mother would never
permit it. I don't even dare mention it to her."

She described in detail the ritual ordeal of her mother's
weekly preparations for the Sabbath, from which escape was
impossible. Tziril always began her cooking on Thursday, even
though that was when most of the customers purchased their
wine for the Sabbath. Tziril prepared the dough for the golden,
braided challah, spent hours chopping fish, and late at night
rolled and cut the dough for the noodles which would be
served with the chicken soup. Before retiring, she spread the
noodles to dry on the kitchen table overnight.

On Friday, she was on her feet all day. And as for herself,
Hinda's appointed task was the house cleaning: scrubbing all
the floors, scouring the stove, washing windows, polishing the
brass and copper. The linens had to be changed, and freshly
starched curtains hung. Everything had to be as sparkling as
new to welcome the Sabbath Queen.

And her father was just as busy. He usually had wine deliv-
eries to make, sometimes even as far away as Bayonne. Often,
at the last minute, Louis Max, his boss, would summon him
for an emergency window-installation job.

All day *Erev Shabbos*, their home was redolent with the

savory smells of food simmering on the stove, and fresh challah and cake baking in the oven — not to mention the gefilte
fish, made from white fish, pike and even a winter carp purchased live the day before.

Suddenly she paused. Alte was looking at her so strangely.
She was sure she detected tears in his eyes, making them un-
bearably brilliant.

"It reminds me of home," he admitted, "and of my own
mother."

Hinda continued. "I don't dare to speak to my mother until I see her standing in her starched white apron over her best
dress, with a lace scarf over her head, kindling the Sabbath
lights. Not until after she blesses me with a, 'Guten Shabbos,
mein tochter; may you be like Sarah, Rebecca, Leah and
Rachel.' Then it is peaceful in our house at last, and I will be
able to speak to her."

Hinda's first week of classes at Miss Feigensohn's was over.
As usual, she accompanied her parents on their Sunday shopping trip to New York for groceries and whatever else they
needed. Afterwards, they went to Channa's house for their
weekly visit. For once, all of Channa's family were at home.

Channa's second son, Moshe, who had grown so mature and
handsome since his family had left Kovno, greeted them excitedly. He had found a job with a law firm on Second Avenue
and they were encouraging him to study law. The kitchen
table was piled high with his books.

"He's busy all day long, now," his mother said proudly.
"From the job, he goes to law school. The firm is paying his
tuition."

As she exchanged a bit of news with Moshe, Hinda suddenly
found herself wishing that Alte had some of her cousin's
height. Despite his ambitions, Moshe was as lively and fun
loving as always, and as usual, full of compliments for his pretty young cousin.

Hinda thought that every girl Moshe met must succumb to
his charm. He could make any female feel like an irresistible

beauty, whether he meant it or not. Actually, Moshe enjoyed their adulation more than their company, and often boasted that he had never taken the same girl out twice. On one occasion, he told his Aunt Tziril, whom he delighted in shocking, that he loved them all.

"But *Tante*," he said, "I tell you, I have never met a young lady yet who has not been desirable, irresistible, and most important, willing."

Moshe drew Hinda aside. "You know, your friend Alte is a friend of mine," he said. "Wasn't he surprised when I told him we were cousins!"

"I know," said Hinda. "I told him about you, and he said, right away, that you sounded like someone he knew."

But she didn't mention to Moshe that she and Alte had discussed him at length. Alte had admitted that her cousin was quite handsome, clever, and very popular with the girls. Even the most serious minded young women were taken by his devilish charm.

None of Alte's circle were surprised when they learned that Moshe Rosenblum was engaged by the legal firm of Schwarz and Teitelbaum, who had interviewed at least fifty worthy applicants.

"Tell Moshe something, Hinda," Alte had said. "But don't tell him I told you. That cousin of yours is going to have to settle down now and really study. No more fooling around for him if he intends to get ahead in law. Tell him that. Promise. He is very smart, but he should spend more time studying and less time in the cafes on the Avenue."

During the week that followed, Alte had another request to make of Hinda. He wanted her to have a picture taken to send to his parents in Vilna. He had told her several times that he was ready to meet her parents, and hoped that he would have the opportunity to introduce her to his brother Velvel, and his wife, Minnie. Minnie, he told her, was an orphan and had no relatives of her own besides an uncle. Since his arrival in America, Velvel had gone into business as a cork maker, and would soon be doing a good business if he could find a few hundred customers. At present, though, the couple was living in a basement room in the building where Velvel had his workshop. Both of them were working especially hard, since Minnie was expecting their first child. In the meantime, she earned her share of their living by sewing buttons on men's overcoats.

Alte was even more anxious for Hinda to meet his cousin Gregor Lipschutz, for he was closer to Gregor, his wife Rachel, and their children than he was to his own brother. He described Rachel as a brilliant woman who had been a frequent contributor to Yiddish journals in Odessa. She was still greatly admired in the intellectual circles of the Lower East Side. Bessie, their eldest daughter, was attending normal school, and planned to be a teacher.

The following Sunday, after their customary shopping, Hinda and her parents visited Channa and Reb Yosef. To Hinda's amazement, she found Alte at her aunt's house. Moshe had invited him for the afternoon, ostensibly to help him with his English grammar, and Alte had arrived with an armload of books to lend his friend, fully aware that this would be his chance to make a favorable impression on Hinda's parents. Moshe explained to his mother that Alte was a grade ahead of him at night school, and had graciously offered him his services as a tutor.

In the end, it was Moshe who presented his friend Alte to Tziril and Yussel.

"Tante, Vetter," he announced, "I want you to meet my friend Alte Lipschutz. We go to night school together."

Moshe was extremely pleased with himself, and enjoyed Hinda's surprise at finding Alte there. He suppressed his laughter with difficulty as he whispered to Hinda that Alte was certainly more to his liking as a boyfriend for her than that "walking bank account" she had been engaged to.

Moshe's sister Rosie couldn't take her eyes off Alte, although only a few minutes after her cousin's arrival she could sense that Alte was already infatuated with Hinda, and Hinda alone. Actually, their guest paid little attention to any of them, and seemed to have even forgotten about continuing Moshe's English lesson.

As though to further display his friend's talents, Moshe suddenly expressed an interest in having Alte teach him a new dance step that was becoming very popular. It was a very "A-merican" dance, he explained, known as the two-step, and he had recently seen it performed in a vaudeville theater on Broadway. He had heard that Alte Lipschutz was an excellent dancer, and knew all the favorite steps of the day — the waltz, polka, and even this new invention. Hinda and Rosie were delighted, and Yussel, Channa and Yosef smiled encouragingly at the would-be dancers, while Tziril sat alone and glanced disparagingly at the young people from her corner of Channa's sitting room.

Much to Hinda's surprise, before she and her parents departed, Yussel, with the utmost cordiality, invited Alte to spend a Sabbath with them in Jersey City. The fact that her aunt and uncle had spoken in Alte's favor had not hurt matters any. Reb Yosef had reassured Yussel that Alte Lipschutz was a friend and classmate of their son's, and a well spoken young man with fine manners.

"You know, Yussel, his father Reb Yeheschel is still in Vilna. He's a Talmudic scholar, I've heard, and a man of great learning. His wife takes care of the business. Alte's mother is quite a woman. She's a Posner from Minsk — they're an old merchant family from the days of King Sobieski — really wealthy." Reb Yosef had chosen his words carefully and well.

"And you, Tziril, listen to me," Yosef admonished his sister-in-law. "The apple doesn't fall far from the tree. If I were you, I wouldn't try to discourage the attentions of a young man like that."

"If only my Rosie would meet someone like Alte," added Channa.

"And remember, Tziril," Reb Yosef continued, with a sage nod of his grizzled head, "we are now in America . . ."

"Yes!" broke in Tziril. "Yes! We are now in America. An unclean, *treife* land! No place for a Jew!"

Yosef paid no attention to her interruption.

"Our young people are not going to follow the old ways. It is a new world for them. A new beginning. Nothing can be the same as it was in our day. But they are still our children."

Alte accompanied Hinda and her parents to the streetcar. As the horse-drawn trolley approached, Yussel shook the

216

young man's hand and repeated his invitation to spend Shabbos with them.

"Please, be assured that you will be welcome," he said.

But Tziril was far from pleased with the invitation Yussel had so graciously extended, and made no attempt to hide her annoyance. She conceded that Alte was certainly a gentleman, was well educated and had fine manners; obviously his upbringing had left nothing to be desired — but still, Yussel should not have invited him without consulting her first.

Later that night, after Hinda returned, she reproached him bitterly. Alte would never be acceptable to her as a son-in-law, and the last thing she wanted to do was encourage him. But, she agreed, the invitation could not be rescinded.

Once Alte had accepted their gracious offer, there was the awkward question of where their guest would sleep. Tziril insisted all week that she didn't think it proper for him to spend the night, as there were no extra bedrooms. Yussel would have to find accommodations for him with one of his relatives.

Hinda objected angrily, and her father was in agreement — Alte was their guest. What kind of hospitality would it be to send him off to sleep with strangers?

"What's wrong with Alte sleeping on the new horsehair couch in the kitchen?" suggested Yussel. "It was good enough for your nephew Nathan when he came to visit."

Tziril finally relented. Alte would sleep in the kitchen as though he were a close relative, although the thought of him was enough to make Tziril's face redden with anger.

One afternoon during that week, Miss Feigensohn drew Hinda aside and asked to speak with her after class. Thinking that her teacher meant to give her another piece of well intended advice about Alte, Hinda was surprised to discover that she had nothing of that in mind. She complimented Hinda on her progress and told her that she was doing so well that she was going to permit her to make a dress for herself. Minna Feigensohn praised her exceptional skill, and her smooth handling of the sewing machine as though she had had months of practice.

"You really do have a flare of style," she commented. "You know, if you wanted to make a career of it, I think you have the makings of a first-rate designer."

Hinda was almost ecstatic when she repeated Miss Feigensohn's words to her parents that evening. She spent that evening poring over her well-thumbed fashion magazines, trying to decide on a pattern.

She had already promised Alte that she would have a photograph taken of herself, and she decided that she would "sit for her portrait" as soon as her dress was finished. She told her parents that this would be a special dress; it would have to be very beautiful, not to mention stylish. Of course, she would use Miss Feigensohn's charge account when she bought her materials. For once her mother agreed with her; it would be far less expensive than buying something ready-made.

Finally, she made her selection. The dress that captured her fancy was a copy of a recent Paris creation modeled by a willowy blonde.

Hinda showed the illustration to her parents, and declared that she would copy it exactly as it was depicted in the magazine. It was a dark green velvet, with a long-waisted, close-fitting bodice. The collar and cuffs were edges with fine green ruching, and tiny jeweled buttons of a deeper green were sewn from the high neck to the waist. The skirt fell in graceful folds to the mannequin's ankles, with a matching satin sash adding a touch of elegance with its full bow at the waist.

Tziril sighed when she saw the task that Hinda had set for herself. She couldn't believe that it was possible for her daughter to duplicate such an exquisite Paris creation. But it didn't take too much persuasion before Tziril and Yussel decided to give Hinda the money for the materials.

"Go ahead, Hindele. Order it," Yussel said.

"And when you finish this one," Tziril added, "you will make a dress for me. It's been years since I had a stylish new outfit."

But she still was not completely convinced that her daughter had acquired such expertise, but Hinda, after all, was very determined and Yussel reminded her of their daughter's skill.

"She has golden hands. Look at the wax flowers she made, and she was only a child then. If Hinda says she can do it, I believe her."

Hinda laughed as she hugged her father in gratitude.

"Believe me, *Tateh*, it's going to be a splendid dress. And Miss Feigensohn will be there to help me – without her I wouldn't even dare try. And Mama, when my dress is done, I'm going to make you the most beautiful gown you've ever seen. It will be grand enough to wear to my wedding. I already have the pattern picked out."

"Order the material for Mama when you buy your own," Yussel commanded. "And why not? Get it over with. When the dresses are finished, we'll all take a family picture. I'll send it to my father Tevya in Wilki."

31

A "Modern" Courtship

Alte had promised to arrive before Tziril kindled the Sabbath lights, and to please Hinda, he even agreed to accompany
her father to Friday evening services. It was an understatement
to say that he had not been particularly enthusiastic about going to the synagogue; in fact, he had stated bluntly that he
hadn't been inside a synagogue since his arrival in New York.

It was a courtesy he owed his host, and he also would attend the services on Saturday morning, when Hinda and her
mother also went. He made it clear to Hinda that it had no
other meaning for him. Why, he would be ostracized for life if
any of his friends heard about it! But Alte knew that Hinda's
parents, like his, would never change their way of life, and he
didn't expect that of them. All he asked was to be permitted
to live his own life as he saw fit.

The table was set with the best dishes and the candles
glowing by the time Yussel returned from the synagogue with
their guest. Yussel beamed a greeting to his wife and daughter. As he took off his coat, he whispered to Tziril that the
synagogue had been packed that evening, and that everyone
he met had been very curious about the well-dressed young
man who had accompanied him.

"Oy, the questions they asked!" Yussel said with a chuckle.
He was in even better spirits than usual.

"I can just imagine," groaned Tziril. "Plenty of gossip. Who
needs it?"

"So let them talk." Yussel seated himself at the head of the
table, which had been set with their best white cloth. He filled
the wine glasses for the Kiddush.

Despite her reservations, Tziril was touched by Alte's appre-

219

ciation of the invitation that had been extended to him. She was stirred by sympathy for his parents, who probably missed their eldest son terribly. He had been named "Alte" or "the old one." How they must have rejoiced at his birth after the loss of the infants that had preceded his arrival. She, who had lost a child herself, could understand how they must have treasured this son — the first to survive. And more important, she could picture their joy that he had survived to adulthood. How they must long for the day of his marriage when they would go to the synagogue and give his name at last, having won their victory over the Angel of Death.

Perhaps Alte sensed her feelings, for he told her that he, as well as most of his friends, were alone in the new country, and she, as though in answer to this, began to heap his plate with roast chicken and glazed carrots. He smiled his most engaging smile and told her that sitting at her table reminded him of his own parents' home on the Sabbath. It even smelled the same. Tziril's gefilte fish that had preceded the main course, tasted exactly like his mother's and he could almost imagine himself as a boy again in Vilna being served a Sabbath feast by his own mother.

Tziril made no reply. She urged him to have a second helping of chicken, and told Yussel to refill their guest's wineglass.

But when Alte praised her wine in lavish terms, she could no longer restrain her urge to respond to his compliments.

"It's my own," she said. "After the Sabbath, I will show you our winecellar. The formula is a secret. For centuries my ancestors made wine in Spain, and after the expulsion, in Kafkaz. My father's family has been making wine for generations." Her face showed her pride.

The following morning she and Hinda sat in the upstairs women's gallery of the synagogue. They had a good view of Yussel and Alte who stood directly below them in their skull caps and talleisim. The men could not see them, since the *mechitzah* hid the women from their sight. It was possible, however, for the women in the first row of the balcony to peer beneath the curtain and observe unseen the devotions of the men who swayed back and forth in time to the Sabbath chants.

Tziril nudged Hinda when Alte was called to the Torah. Suddenly it occurred to her that not once had Nathan Rosenblum ever honored Yussel by accompanying him to shul. She felt a pang of remorse. Of course, she still regretted her daughter's broken engagement, even though Hinda seemed to have already forgotten her disappointment and sorrow.

Tziril had to admit that this Alte was certainly no ignoramus. He had been taught well, and chanted the blessings as though he were a regular worshipper. And why shouldn't he? He was the son of a scholar – a real Talmud chacham.

Lost in her thoughts, she suddenly realized that the service was almost over. Her problem now was to leave quickly with her daughter to avoid the inevitable questions of the women who would stop to wish them a "Gut Shabbos" as they left the gallery. She didn't quite succeed, however, and every time someone inquired about the handsome young man sitting with her husband, she replied curtly, "An acquaintance; a friend; nobody special." It took a tremendous effort on her part to retain her composure in the face of so much feminine curiosity.

Yussel was extremely pleased with their guest. As far as he was concerned, Alte was a young man he could be proud of, and if Hinda cared for him, he would have no objections. His daughter could do far worse. At the kiddush following the service, he introduced Alte to everyone.

"Can you believe it, Tziril?" he commented. "Etta Teresa even came over and introduced herself. She told Alte that she was one of my mishpocha. Such chutzpah that woman has!"

After the noon dinner, Hinda and Alte excused themselves and left for an afternoon stroll. He reminded her that she had promised to take him up to the top of the hill near her home. As they walked uphill, arm in arm, over the unever cobblestones of Newark Avenue, Alte told her that he felt as though he were leaving the city far behind for a day in the country.

Hinda's hilltop, at the intersection of Newark and Palisade Avenues, was an uncultivated parcel of land covered with trees and wildflowers. A narrow path led to the summit, from which one had a superb view of the Hudson and New York Harbor.

In the early spring sunshine, they could see the beginnings of blossoms on the trees and shrubs. Hinda explained that it was always cool there, even during the hottest days of summer; then her hilltop became a popular gathering place for picnickers and young lovers.

Alte's arm was around her waist. They soon found a smooth flat rock under a willow tree. He had brought along a slim volume of poetry.

"Pushkin," he told her, as he drew the book from his pocket. "Love poems." And he began to read.

Hinda listened. It sounded almost like music, and she was both proud and delighted that she hadn't forgotten her Russian. She murmured, almost shyly, that Pushkin had been a great favorite among her classmates at the gymnasium in Telschi. She felt her eyes grow moist as she remembered Rosa Schmidt and the other friends she had left abruptly behind, but she soon smiled again. She didn't have anyone like Alte in those days. But he soon found himself unable to continue reading, her dark eyes glistened so.

Instead, he began to urge her to spend the following weekend in New York. He was certain that she could make arrangements to stay with her relatives. Next Saturday afternoon, he wanted to take her to meet his cousin Gregor, and in the evening there was a concert.

Hinda was still doubtful that her parents would permit her to spend a Sabbath away from home, and she couldn't promise anything.

"But I'll speak to my father," she said. "He is always so understanding. My mother, though, I don't think she will even listen to me."

Alte seemed pleased all the same. He wanted to show her the museums. Someday, he said, he would take her to the opera. If they sat in one of the upper galleries, it wouldn't cost too much. He explained that just before he left Vilna, he had experienced the thrill of attending his first opera — a splendid performance of Tchaikovsky's *Eugene Onegin*.

More than her company, though, he wanted Hinda to come to know him and all the hopes and plans he had for the future. He was one of a circle of young immigrants who were determined to establish a new and enlightened Jewish community in the New World for themselves and their children. They were determined to discard most, if not all, of the "meaningless rituals" of their ghetto ancestors.

Hinda found herself becoming increasingly apprehensive. She knew for certain that her parents would not approve of Alte's radical ideas, but at the same time she was greatly intrigued and caught up in the spell of his words. It all sounded so marvelous, so idealistic. How he reminded her of those free-spirited young people she had met on board the *Rotterdam*!

Her pleasure was dampened by the knowledge that her parents, especially her mother, would be horrified if they heard him. They'd never permit her to invite him to their home again, nor would they allow her to continue seeing him. It would be a sad end to such a wonderful friendship — or perhaps something more.

Despite Hinda's misgivings, Alte explained his ideas further. He and his friends had a plan; they had already begun to pool their resources. In time, they would buy land and establish a colony of kindred souls. They would all be free-thinkers and liberal-minded men and women.

"We will build homes for ourselves, and a library, and raise our children close to nature. I don't know where — maybe some place far out on Long Island. We'll be far away from the synagogues. No Talmud Torahs and cold, dark cheders for our children!"

Hinda gasped.

"Don't you see, Hinda?" He became impatient. "Through the long, bloody centuries of persecution, we Jews kept ourselves from entering the mainstream of life. The gentiles said we were different — and they hated and feared that difference.

He paused for a moment.

"But now we are Americans. American citizens. Citizens, Hinda! Were we citizens in Russia? I want you to remember that. We are a new breed of Jews. Of course we are still proud of our heritage and traditions. This we can never discard!"

She was deeply moved by his sincerity; his eloquence all but carried her away. Yet she was also seized with a feeling, almost like terror as he concluded his monologue.

"The girl that I marry will have to adjust to this new way of life. No son of mine will be ritually circumcised by an ignorant mohel. It will have to be done by a doctor. No daughter of mine will have her ears pierced. Nor will I arrange to have her married off as soon as she is old enough to put her hair up. Think about it and you will agree that such practices are barbaric – even primitive!"

But all Hinda could say was that he had given her a great deal to think about. She begged him to never, under any circumstances, repeat what he had just said to her parents. It would make them terribly unhappy, as well as outraged.

"And Alte," she said, "I don't want them to make me stop seeing you, I value your friendship too much. And – it is difficult to say this. . . but you are always in my thoughts. But, do you think that what you just said shocked me? I have to be honest with you. No, I wasn't really shocked, but I don't really agree with you either."

She had always thought of herself as being openminded, especially after having spent so many years in Kafkaz, where she had been exposed to a less rigid kind of Judaism than that of Eastern Europe. And in Telschi the students had openly discussed all sorts of revolutionary ideas. She explained to Alte that in spite of her mother's attempt at censorship, she had read many books written by so-called "Enlightened Jews" who had preached assimilation. No, she hadn't been shocked, after all.

Alte left shortly after the Havdalah ceremony which marked the end of the Sabbath, bearing his host's gift of a flask of wine. Hinda retired soon afterward, telling her parents that she was very tired from all the excitement of Alte's first visit. She knew they both had innumerable questions to ask, and what could she have told them? There was no escaping the fact that if she were ever to marry Alte Lipschutz, she would have to compromise to adjust to his way of life. Otherwise, there would never be happiness for either of them.

The following morning, Hinda and her parents left for their weekly trip to New York. But Tziril's mind wasn't on her shopping, for she was deeply troubled by Hinda's seeming infatuation with a young man of whom she could not approve, despite the many points in his favor. She wanted to discuss the matter with Channa. Her sister had married off two daughters, and in her own way was very wise about such things. She would ask Channa's advice.

What really worried her was that Hinda was so close-mouthed where Alte was concerned. She avoided any discussion of him, and Tziril knew for certain that she was hiding something from her. Of course, Yussel was no help at all. He would only smile his secret, knowing smile, and tell her over and over again that she had nothing to worry about.

Channa, though, was in no mood to discuss anything but her own problems. Her daughter Rosie, as she insisted on being called, as though her Yiddish name Reizel weren't good enough for her, had enrolled in night school without consulting her. Channa was distraught. Moshe had egged Rosie on, and now she, Channa, was left alone to run the household without her. Rosie spent the entire day poring over her books.

What disturbed Channa most was that her daughter blamed her for the fact that she had not learned English like her brothers, and hadn't made any new friends in New York. She continually complained that she had been tied down like an old woman. No wonder she was still unmarried! Channa was close to tears as she repeated her daughter's bitter words to Tziril.

"All she keeps saying is "My cousin Hinda can already read and write English! My cousin Hinda has so many friends! She can do as she pleases. She is free. And what do I have? The housework; the cooking; the marketing."

"And now," moaned Channa, "my daughter spends all her time at the library or at school. Day and night. There is no one to help me with the house. So this is what America has done for me!"

That was not all. Rosie was now demanding that she be allowed to attend Saturday night socials which her school was sponsoring, claiming that they were actually classes in English conversation. But she could not fool her mother! There was dancing and all sorts of frivolity. Never would Channa allow her to go among all sorts of questionable people and dance with strange men!

"So I asked Moshe to take her," Channa explained. "But he says he is busy. He's always too busy. Moshe says we should ask Hinda to go with her."

"No, not Hinda," Tziril objected.

"And why not? Hinda could come here for the Sabbath. It would be a pleasure to have her. I promised Rosie I'd speak to you."

Channa was not asking; her tone of voice told Tziril that she was demanding.

It was hard to refuse this request from Channa, and Tziril finally agreed, despite her misgivings. She would permit Hinda to spend the Sabbath with her aunt and cousins this once.

Her only consolation was that Hinda would soon complete her course of study in New York, and would no longer be running off to the city every day. Tziril was determined that once her classes ended, her daughter would remain at home. Lately, Hinda stayed away in New York until late in the evening, and scarcely came home in time for supper. The girl had all sorts of excuses, and told her mother that she was getting special help with her new dress and had already started on Tziril's.

Truthfully, Hinda was progressing well. Her teacher recommended her for a job with a New York designer. Miss Feigensohn had the highest praise for her originality, natural skill and fine workmanship. On numerous occasions, she had complimented Hinda on her personal appearance. She always looked so neat and trim, and Minna Feigensohn was convinced that Hinda had what she called "style." The other girls told Hinda that coming from Miss Feigensohn, this was extremely high praise. As a rule, Hinda was told, their teacher was very critical.

All that week, Hinda dreamed of the coming weekend. She had never anticipated that spending a Sabbath at the Muma Channa's would be such an unexpected pleasure. Alte offered to accompany her and Rosie to the social Rosie's night school was sponsoring. Though he had been planning on a concert, he agreed it would be an excellent idea, and explained to Hinda that he used to attend such gatherings frequently during his first year in America. It would be good for Rosie to go.

He had made several lasting friendships as a result of such school-sponsored events.

That same evening, as he walked her to the ferry, Alte confided to Hinda that he was beginning to lose his respect for her cousin Moshe. He spent too much time in tea rooms, playing cards and gambling, and was beginning to lose his reputation. Alte told her that it was also said that Moshe drank too much and chased women when he should be studying. For a young man who showed so much promise and who had been given such an excellent opportunity to make something of himself, Moshe seemed to be wasting his time. If her cousin didn't change his ways, Alte warned, gambling, liquor and women would be his downfall. Hinda promised to talk with her cousin and then begged Alte to change the subject.

Suddenly, he began to tell her how glad he was that she would finally be coming with him to visit his cousin Gregor and Gregor's family that Saturday afternoon. He had often told her how proud he was of these cousins, and how eager he was for her to meet them. Gregor and his wife Rachel had five children: three daughters and two sons. The young daughters were turning out to be as literary and cultured as their mother, and Alte was sure that Hinda would like them. The girls were also eager to make Hinda's acquaintance.

Finally, Friday afternoon arrived. Hinda reached her aunt's home in time for the blessing of the Sabbath candles. She couldn't help but notice that her aunt was dressed in her old-fashioned Sabbath clothes of black silk, as though she were still in Kovno. Channa still wore the long string of seed pearls that had been her husband's gift when Nathan, their oldest son was born.

That night, after they retired, Hinda confided to Rosie that Alte was taking her to visit his relatives. She hadn't planned to tell her cousin this, but she couldn't resist the impulse to tell someone, and Rosie had always been a good listener.

"Oh, Hinda, why can't I meet someone like Alte?" was Rosie's only comment. She seemed grateful that Hinda and Alte were taking her to the social.

"Your Alte," she said, "he knows everyone who's worth knowing. My brother does too, but Moshe has his own interests. He's always so busy."

She could not admit that her brother was probably embarrassed to take her anywhere. She had been in America several years, and was only beginning to learn English.

But Rosie couldn't hide her feelings of inferiority from Hinda. She began to weep.

"One of these days I will go out and find a job! I don't care what my mother says. I can't stand staying here, scrubbing, polishing, cooking and baking! I had to go to night school.

"You remember, Hinda. In Kovno we had servants. Everyone said I was the prettiest of my sisters. What's happened to me? It's just not fair!"

Hinda agreed with her. Rosie's life had certainly changed, and not for the better. But, Hinda suggested comfortingly, hadn't she started night school, even though her mother had been against it? All Rosie really had to do was change her hair style and wear some of her new dresses. Hinda got up and lit the lamp.

"Come on, Rosie," she said. "Let's get up, it's too early to sleep. I'll help you pick out a dress to wear tomorrow night. You still are pretty, you know."

Rosie's mood began to brighten.

"And you shouldn't worry," Hinda said. "You have a beautiful complexion — flawless. And such lovely blue eyes. The most perfect features in the family.

Rosie seemed to regain her confidence.

"Really, Hinda, do you think so?"

Hinda nodded.

Rosie surveyed herself in the mirror, while Hinda inspected the dress her cousin would be wearing Saturday evening. Rosie towered over Hinda.

"See, Rosie," Hinda said. "Look in the mirror, You are so tall and graceful with such a lovely figure. Such beautiful curves. That's what really fashionable, you know."

Yes, she still is beautiful, Hinda thought with a trace of envy. "Like a Greek statue in a museum," she said out loud.

32

A Different Kind of Engagement

That was a weekend that would live forever in Hinda's memory. By the time she returned to Jersey City, there was no doubt in her mind regarding her feelings for Alte, or his for her. She had promised to marry him before another year had ended.

Of course, by now he had come to realize that her mother had serious reservations about him, although neither Tziril nor Yussel knew just how irreligious Alte was. Hinda was close to tears when she told him that their marriage could easily result in her complete estrangement from her parents. She did care for him — more than she knew how to say — but she loved her parents deeply, and he would have to understand this. To cut herself off from them would break her heart.

Alte was very understanding and promised not to do or say anything that would offend their sensibilities. Still, on one matter he stood firm. After they were married, he would refuse to allow any interference on their part. He and Hinda would live where they wished in a free and independent manner. He warned Hinda that she would have to forget that she was an only child and the center of her parents' existence.

Hinda recalled those long years she and her mother had been separated from her father, and how hard it had been for him to forget, or even forgive. After all that had happened to them, she didn't want to risk losing her father's affection. Yussel still hadn't erased all the loneliness and humiliation of those years from his mind, and as much as he loved Tziril, at one time he had been almost ready to divorce her and leave his daughter behind as well. Even now, Hinda sometimes detected a trace of his old bitterness, and was sure that he had not forgotten. And certainly, she knew he would never let her mother forget.

When Alte called for her early that Saturday afternoon, her aunt and uncle were already taking their customary Sabbath afternoon nap, and Rosie was concentrating on the intricacies of her first grade reader. Hinda whispered to her cousin that she and Alte would be back in plenty of time to take her to the social.

Alte's relatives lived on the top floor of a cold-water tenement on Hester Street. The one advantage, Alte explained, was that all the rooms were bright from the ceiling skylights. Alte's family greeted them noisily, and Gregor's oldest daughter, Bessie, kissed her cousin with delight. Gregor's wife Rachel dominated the conversation. She was a formidable looking woman with wide hips and a stately bosom. Gregor, on the other hand, was a slight, rather stooped man with graying hair. He seemed to be somewhat in awe of his wife; it was clear that he had the utmost respect for her opinions. Her voice was loud, but not unpleasant, and her conversation was punctuated with peals of warm laughter. From the moment they met, Hinda was fascinated by her lively manner and strong personality.

There were no pictures on the walls of Rachel's sitting room, but on every side, shelves overflowed with books and magazines. They were all great readers, Hinda was told, especially Rachel.

A few minutes after their arrival, their hostess announced that they had changed their name from Lipschutz to Wilson; Gregor was now called "George Wilson." Rachel explained that their old name had been an embarrassment to Bessie, a student at normal school, and to their eldest son Louis, who was apprenticed to a printer. It had been Louis who chose the new name.

Rachel insisted that Alte follow their example, and choose a name that was more agreeable and euphonious.

"In the old country, you remember," she said, "Lipschutz was a respected name. It had yichus, a sign of lineage. But here, people think it is disgusting – or so my children tell me."

Before she could make any further attempts to convince

Alte, her daughter Bessie broke in on the conversation and inquired if Alte knew any of the new friends she had made. She knew that he knew many people, especially attractive young men. Among the names she mentioned was that of a young law student she had recently met – to Hinda's astonishment, it was Moshe Rosenblum.

Up to that moment, Bessie had virtually ignored Hinda, but as soon as she learned of the relationship between this Moshe and her guest, her manner changed, and not too subtly.

She smiled her most engaging smile as she tried to draw Hinda into the conversation.

"Oh, he's your cousin? He's so charming. So handsome – an Adonis." She had deep dimples when she smiled, and perfect, evenly spaced teeth.

"Everyone says he's a real charmer! You must bring him here soon."

Rachel was obviously embarrassed by her daughter's extravagant praise of this Moshe and soon told Bessie to keep still.

"If my daughter Bessie says he is so wonderful," she remarked, "then I can be sure he is a ninny – is that how you say it?" She smiled at Hinda who was beginning to blush.

Quite bluntly, Rachel advised her daughter not to make such a fool of herself in front of their guest. But Bessie would not be silenced so easily. Hinda had to admit that she was an attractive girl, even as she noticed how free she was with her affection. Bessie sat on the arm of Alte's chair, playing with his curly hair, and daintily tweaking his nose from time to time. It was evident that whatever else the girl had in her favor, Bessie was quite a tease. Hinda noted approvingly that her younger sisters were more reserved and soft spoken.

Rachel, who insisted that they call her "Mrs. Wilson," served them afternoon refreshments: home made spongecake and tall glasses of tea. She prided herself on being a gracious hostess, and Hinda had noticed the moment she entered their home how orderly and meticulous everything was in spite of the bookish clutter.

She had to admit that she had never met any people in her entire life like the "Wilsons." As they sipped their tea, Rachel discoursed on an article which she had published in a Riga literary journal to which she was a regular contributor.

Without asking for comments from her guests, she proceeded to read them a long letter from another young cousin, who was studying chemistry in Vienna. Hinda was told his name was Chaim Weizmann.

But despite Rachel's effusive manner and booming voice, Hinda soon realized that this large, warm woman was a real personality — what her cousin Moshe would call a "brain." She truly commanded one's respect and admiration.

After they departed, Hinda told Alte that his cousin was the most interesting woman she had ever met. He agreed with her heartily, adding that he wished Hinda had been able to meet his cousins Louis and Fred, also. But their mother had sent them to the library for the afternoon.

※

Hinda had never seen Alte so gay and elegant as at the social that evening. He fit in with all the most interesting people. What pleased her most was that he made sure that Rosie was introduced to all the right people. She was ill at ease and danced poorly, but Alte continued to encourage her, and insisted that he, personally, would teach her the new dances that were now the rage with young people in New York.

"There is no reason," he told her, "why you shouldn't make a charming dance partner, once you have had a little practice." He complimented her on how fast her English was improving. Hinda couldn't help but notice that under Alte's friendly attentiveness Rosie began to lose some of her shyness and reserve.

Hinda was not the only one who noticed the change in Rosie. The next day her entire family felt that there was something different about her. Rosie apologized to her mother for hurting her feelings so deeply. Her life, she said, had not been ruined at all, and she was beginning to take a new interest in everything — even the small details of their own household.

Later in the day, when Tziril and Yussel arrived for their weekly visit, Channa thanked her sister for allowing Hinda to spend the weekend with them.

"You and Hinda," she said. "You have given my daughter back to me."

She also expressed her gratitude to Hinda and Alte. She had only praise for this young man who had been such a "gentleman."

"Oh *Tante*," Rosie commented to Tziril, "that Alte has been more of a brother to me than Moshe!"

But Tziril had missed her daughter, and it had been a dreary Shabbos without her. More than once she wished she had stood her ground and forbidden Hinda to spend the Sabbath away from home. But, as usual, Yussel had been on their daughter's side. Hinda was happy, and that was all that mattered to him. He was certain that once Hinda made up her mind about a young man, she would prove to be a loyal and devoted wife. And more important, with a man who showed her the respect and consideration she deserved, his daughter would be a happy woman.

Having found Alte at Channa's house, Tziril felt herself far from reconciled about her daughter's suitor. After all, she and he husband still knew so little about him. She sought out her nephew Moshe who was spending the afternoon immersed in his books, after Hinda had given him a lecture about his undisciplined habits. Tziril told him that she was deeply troubled about Hinda and her relationship with "this Alte."

Moshe, who delighted in teasing his aunt, praised his friend in the most extraordinary terms.

"That Alte – he's great company. A good card player. He enjoys gambling every so often, and he's always been a great favorite with the ladies, even though he's short. But Tziril..." (Channa's children had always called their aunt by her given name.) As he spoke, his dark eyes twinkled mischievously.

"But Tziril, he's the life of every party. Let me tell you something about this Alte. Don't ever look for him if you need a tenth man for a *minyan!* Not Alte! Look at it this way, though. He's a clever devil. And he's in with a brilliant group of people. Someday they'll all be millionaires, I'm sure."

Tziril hadn't expected any words of comfort from Moshe, and she knew him well enough to realize that his remarks

weren't to be taken too seriously, but the conversation made
her realize more keenly that there was nothing she could do
to keep Hinda and Alte apart. Hinda was completely under
his spell, and Tziril could literally feel the happiness her daughter radiated. Besides, Yussel had nothing but praise for the
young man: he was worthy, intelligent and the son of reputable parents – the father a scholar! What more could Tziril
want?

Every evening Yussel waited impatiently for Hinda's return
from New York. He always said that their house came to life
when their daughter was home.

"She lights up everything – the whole place. Even the walls
have to dance." How could he feel anything but admiration
and gratitude toward a young man who had brought his Hinda
such joy?

Yussel pleaded, even commanded Tziril to show Alte more
hospitality and to treat him with more warmth. He warned
her over and over again that there were certain things a man
could not easily forget or forgive, especially in a future mother-in-law. He reminded her of Hinda's former state and the
weeks of anguish for all of them that had followed the ending
of her first engagement.

Tziril admitted she could never forget this. She still shuddered at the thought of it. Never again, she said would she
ever have the strength to live through such a scandal, and such
a terrible misfortune for her daughter. If Hinda were to suffer
another such disappointment, it would break her mother's
heart.

Yet, she often found herself praying fervently that the Rabbono Shel Olom would watch over her child, and that Alte
would prove himself worthy of his sainted father, devoted
mother, and the great heritage of the people he seemed to regard with such indifference. She prayed that she should live to
bless the day her daughter had met him, and that one day
there would come a time when she would lose the terrible
heartache that engulfed her – that feeling of utter desolation
and disappointment at the thought that this apikoros, Alte
Lipschutz, was her daughter's destined mate.

❧

In the meantime, Yussel and Hinda had their minds on other matters. Yussel promised to buy Hinda a sewing machine as soon as she finished her course with Miss Feigensohn. Hinda had finally persuaded him that it would be a wise purchase that would last her a lifetime.

"*Tateh*, I will even sew beautiful shirts for you. Most of the machines they have now will even make buttonholes. You will see!"

Her green velvet dress was almost finished. All she had to do was sew on the dainty, enameled buttons that sparkled like so many emeralds. Her mother's dress had already been basted together, the skirt gracefully draped over a dressmaker's form. Everyone at the school admired it. That very Sunday afternoon, Hinda announced, she would take her mother to Miss Feigensohn's for a fitting, since her course would be over in two more weeks.

Actually, she could never have made her mother's dress without her teacher's assistance; her own was quite simple in comparison. But Miss Feigensohn had nothing but praise for her patience and skill, especially Hinda's painstaking stitches as she sewed the tiny beads of black jet to the bodice, one by one. The design was exquisite.

Tziril was literally speechless when she arrived for her fitting and was shown her daughter's creation. Not even her sister Channa, at the height of the Rosenblums' prosperity, had had such a dress! Hinda's classmates stood about in awe as she adjusted the hem to its proper length and marked the sleeves.

Afterward, Miss Feigensohn drew Tziril aside and told her that she should be extremely proud to have such a gifted daughter.

"Never, Mrs. Friedman," she said, "never have I seen anyone learn so quickly, and with such natural talent. I will tell you a secret. That dress your daughter has made for you is an exact copy of one worn by Queen Victoria herself. And I will tell you something else. I doubt if the workmanship on the Queen's dress is any better than that on yours."

Later, when Yussel met them at the school, he demanded to see his wife's new gown. Immediately he announced that Tziril must have her picture taken in that dress — they would all have their pictures taken. Hinda would wear her new green velvet and he would rent a frock coat, striped trousers and a high silk hat in honor of the occasion. Hinda agreed and remarked that she was also planning to have a photograph taken for Alte to send to his parents – since he had already written to them about her.

It therefore came as no surprise to Yussel when Hinda approached him that evening, and whispered to him that Alte was coming to have a talk with him. Yes – they were engaged, and wanted to set a date for their wedding.

"*Tateh*," she pleaded. "You must help me. I want Mama to be happy. She acts as though I'm bringing a goy into the house."

Suddenly Hinda smiled. "Besides," she added, "Alte is buying me a ring. Maybe not so grand as the other one, but a ring! When I marry him it will be the happiest day of my life!"

Though there were moments when she remembered the misery that had followed her first disappointment, her present state of mind was the stronger one. Although she hadn't forgotten the gossip and unpleasantness that had once made her too ashamed to show her face, she marveled at the joy that had come into her life since she had met Alte. She had gone from one extreme to the other in such a short time. It was almost like a miracle.

With her parents' permission, the following week she accepted Alte's engagement ring – a modest diamond, actually less than a carat, in a plain gold setting, and later that day she had her picture taken.

Tziril rose to the occasion and accepted what seemed to be the inevitable. She kissed her daughter and warmly congratulated her.

"Mazel tov, tochter! I will welcome Alte into our family. I care only that you are happy, my daughter."

She still had her doubts but, as she confided to Channa, she would try to be thankful for her daughter's happiness, and to make herself believe that Hinda's forthcoming marriage was, in spite of everything, beshert, or preordained. As always, Tziril bowed to the Divine Will.

But no one enjoyed the announcement of Hinda's engagement more than Yussel. He reported to Tziril that the entire community had been taken aback by the news that Hinda was engaged once again. Etta Teresa had been stunned when the word reached her; nevertheless she was not too stunned to embark on another whispering campaign. Word soon got back to Tziril that Etta remarked that it was indeed fortunate for them that Alte's parents lived on the other side of the ocean.

"Otherwise, they'd never consent to their son's marrying a girl whose name had been dragged through the mud."

The portrait of Hinda that Alte finally sent to his parents, along with a long letter telling them of their engagement, was a three-quarter length photograph of his betrothed in her new velvet dress, clasping a single rose in her slender hands.

At last, the letter from Alte's parents that Hinda had been waiting for arrived. He brought it to her himself and read it aloud to Hinda and her parents. It was a loving letter welcoming her into their family. Alte's father sent greetings to her parents as well, and was overjoyed that his son would be marrying a girl who was the daughter of devout, Orthodox parents. Such a young woman, he wrote, would establish a Jewish home for his son in the new country. And above all, he thanked Hinda for sending them the lovely portrait.

But most important, he wrote, that upon receiving his son's letter, he had gone to the synagogue and given Alte a name at long last. He had called his son Abraham, or Avrum, son of Yeheschel and Rivka. No longer would Alte's parents be obligated to elude the Angel of Death with linguistic tricks.

Tziril's eyes overflowed as she listened, and she beamed with pride when she heard the name her son-in-law-to-be had been given. Abraham; it was a good name; it was a good omen, and a sign of a good beginning for her daughter's new life.

That evening, Hinda and Abraham, as he was now called, announced the date set for their wedding: the sixteenth of February, 1890.

33

Hinda's Wedding

In later years, Hinda would describe her courtship to her children and grandchildren as a "storybook romance." Her "betrothed,"as she referred to her fiance, showered her with gifts. Although none of them were valuable in worldly terms, each was accompanied by a note expressing his eternal devotion. She treasured these notes, as well as sheaves of dance and theater programs, all her long life, as mementos of the kind of romance she had always dreamed of.

The days of Hinda's engagement were filled with such a bustle of activity. The young couple spent as much time as they could spare looking for furniture and a place to live. Hinda spent long hours with her new sewing machine hemming towels, pillow cases and sheets. The months passed quickly and before long it was time for Hinda to begin work on her wedding dress, for she insisted on making it herself from start to finish.

As the sixteenth of February drew near, friends and neighbors flocked to her house, eager to see her new sewing machine and the wedding dress she had designed and executed so exquisitely. The admiration and envy of all were aroused by the photographs of the bride-to-be in her green velvet dress, and everyone showered her with compliments on everything – from the way she wore her fair hair piled high on her head, to the single rose she held.

Yussel's pride and joy was the family portrait. Vividly he pictured the excitement it would generate when it arrived in Wilki. How his aged father Tevya would kvell! No one in Wilki could possibly have ever seen anything like it. His Tziril looked almost regal, and Hinda like a princess, while he himself, in a rented Prince Albert and striped pants, was the picture of dignified prosperity, down to the high silk hat held on his knee. Yussel had certainly come a long way from his days as an apprentice at Frumkin's.

By this time, Tziril and Yussel were very aware that their son-in-law-to-be was extremely stubborn in matters pertaining to religion. He often reacted to a simple question as though it were an intrusion into his privacy. They were more than aware that most of his ideas were both alien and unacceptable, and there had been many bitter disagreements, especially between Alte, or Avrum, as he was now called, and Tziril.

He had told Hinda's parents that after their marriage he hoped they would move to some remote country town far from the synagogues and other institutions of the Orthodox. He was determined to raise his children as Americans – they would be the first generation of American-born citizens in the family. It would be more conducive to the happiness of generations to come, he believed, if they could integrate themselves into the mainstream of American life.

"What has Jewish identity ever brought us," he argued, "Except persecution and hatred?"

For this reason especially, Tziril and Yussel were overjoyed when Hinda and Avrum rented a small flat on Mercer Street, within walking distance of their home. It would be almost as though Hinda still lived with them, and to Tziril, this was no small comfort.

"These days we walk softly with a prayer in our hearts," she confided to her sister Channa. Secretly she feared that something might happen at the last minute to spoil her daughter's happiness. "Only the Holy One, blessed be His name, knows how much can go wrong," she often remarked.

She was also disturbed by the fact that Avrum's parents could not be present at the wedding. As the day approached, her future son-in-law presented more and more of a problem. If only his own parents were there to reason with him! He was opposed to the traditional marriage ceremony and stated bluntly that it held no meaning for him. As far as he was concerned, a simple civil ceremony would be more than adequate. Who needed all the fuss and expense when a justice of the peace would do quite nicely? In fact, many of his friends had dispensed with the ceremony altogether. Tziril was horrified when he told her how much he admired the courage and idealism of those free-thinkers.

Yussel advised his wife to disregard Avrum's foolish talk. In the long run, he maintained, Avrum would care more for Hinda's happiness than for his radical opinions.

"He's just a young man letting off steam. He's still so young, and besides, he would be hurting his own parents. Don't forget, his father is a scholar!"

And Yussel proved right, after all. Avrum finally agreed to the things that were most important to his bride-to-be and her parents. There would be a rabbi and a traditional ceremony under the marriage canopy. So what if he insisted on inviting all his "progressive" friends? He had so few relatives. Yussel found it hard to object to an orchestra for dancing, and didn't think it mattered in the least that there would be dances his wife referred to disdainfully as *"goyish."* What really mattered was that there would be a religious ceremony in the traditional manner. Besides, Yussel was sure that between the waltz and the polka there would be plenty of time for a *Yiddishe kazatzky*. He would see to it himself.

He boasted to his cousin Velvel that Avrum had engaged a real dance band conducted by a Professor Wollenberg. "A personal friend of my son-in-law," he assured his cousin. There would be souvenir dance programs specially printed for the occasion, which was something neither of them had ever seen in Wilki.

"Yes, my Hinda will have a stylish wedding," Yussel commented with a touch of pride. "With music no one ever expected to hear at a Jewish wedding. But everything's changed. What can one expect?"

As Velvel later reported to his wife Soreh Ruchel, Yussel didn't seem to be the least bit displeased.

"We're no longer living in the shtetl — this is America," Yussel had added, as though even he was enjoying the idea immensely.

Despite her fiance's numerous disagreements with her parents, Hinda could recall only one serious quarrel with Avrum before their wedding. He had confided to her that his friends were planning to sponsor a dance on the eve of Yom Kippur, the holiest day of the Jewish Year. They had hired a hall next to a synagogue, and tickets and programs had been printed.

When Avrum told her that he had promised to attend and that she would be expected to accompany him, she had actually turned pale in disbelief. She had never even conceived of spending a Yom Kippur Eve in such a sacrilegious fashion. Invariably, she always attended the services with her parents to hear Kol Nidre chanted, and her parents, of course, would expect Avrum to join them this year. Her father had already purchased a seat for him.

With an indignation that Avrum had not before seen in her, Hinda reviled his friends in no uncertain terms for their utter insensitivity and lack of decency.

"How dare they! If you want to go to that Yom Kippur dance, you will have to go without me!"

Avrum was flustered, his face reddened.

"Hinda! Your parents are not going to run my life! I would think that since we are engaged you could at least begin to be on my side instead of jumping every time you are called!"

"Avrum," Hinda wailed. "Please – if you love me, don't go to that dance. And if you must, just remember this, my parents will break our engagement, they will never permit me to marry you. Never!" She could not hold back her tears.

Avrum did spend that Yom Kippur with Hinda and her parents at the synagogue. He actually fasted the entire day, and during the long hours of prayer never strayed from the seat that had been reserved for him along side Yussel.

Hinda never mentioned that quarrel to her parents. Yussel, however, had read about the Yom Kippur dance in the Yiddish newspaper, which had given the incident a great deal of attention. The young people who had attended it had caused an unprecedented disturbance, and several of them had been arrested for disturbing the peace by shamelessly interfering with the solemnity of the Kol Nidre services, and generally creating a nuisance. Despite his liberal attitude, Yussel was shocked to

read the names of the ringleaders – they were all from prominent Orthodox families.

❧

Hinda's parents invited Yussel's mishpocha, with the exception of Etta Teresa, and the entire Jersey City congregation to
the wedding and reception which was to be held at Wood's
Turn Hall in lower Jersey City. Channa and her family represented Tziril's side of the family, and she and Reb Yosef
marched in the bridal procession. Avrum was led to the *chupah*
or bridal canopy by his brother Velvel and his wife Minnie,
and Gregor, Rachel and all their children received invitations,
too.

The cooking for the wedding feast was done in Tziril's kitchen, although a cook was engaged to help with the baking
and roasting. Even the bride-to-be assisted in plucking chickens and chopping the huge mounds of fish. For days, the
aroma of simmering gefilte fish filled the house.

In the days before the wedding, there was a constant stream
of people coming in and out of their home bringing wedding
gifts and offering their services. The apartment sparkled.
Hinda singlehandedly had done all the housecleaning. The
bride had no time for last minute nerves, for in the last days
before her wedding she had hung new curtains and had polished every last bit of copper and brass in her mother's kitchen to a mirror-like brilliance. Everyone who entered declared that the entire place looked and even smelled like a wedding – like a simcha, they all agreed.

Late on the eve of the wedding, Avrum arrived unexpectedly, bringing the souvenir dance programs for Hinda's inspection. He just couldn't wait for her to see them. Printed on the
cover was the legend, "Wedding Reception of Mrs. and Mrs.
Abraham Lipschutz."

Hinda was actually quite relieved when she realized that
Avrum could stay only for a few minutes before he had to
catch the last ferry back to New York. She was exhausted, and
besides, when he had been there the day before, he had made
her promise not to permit her mother to take her to the ritual
bath. But it had been impossible to keep that promise; in her

mother's eyes, her marriage, without the visit to the mikvah, would not have been sanctified.

Hinda had gone without real reluctance, and permitted the bath attendant to clip her finger and toe nails short before the immersion, especially when the older woman reminded her that had she lived in Kovno, she would have had her head shaved as well. Silently Hinda offered her thanks to the Master of the Universe for bringing her to America where she would not be required to wear a wig for the rest of her days.

The bath attendant made certain that her own son was standing by the exit when Hinda and Tziril departed, for it would have been an evil omen had the eyes of a gentile male been the first to see her as she left the mikvah on the eve of her wedding.

After Avrum left, Hinda dropped off to sleep thinking of the dance programs so elegantly printed on the heavy cream-colored paper. She laughed to herself as she remembered the names of the dances: the waltz, schottische, quadrille, lancers, saragossa and Spanish waltz. She had never even heard of most of them, let alone learned the steps, and it amused her to picture her parents' reaction when they saw the stacks of programs bound with tasseled gold cords.

The day of the wedding was crisp and bright with a hint of spring in the air – unusual for February. Hinda and her parents arrived at the Turn Hall earlier than they had planned. As they entered the gas-lit hall, a spirited polka announced their arrival to the many guests who were already dancing. On the small stage, Professor Wollenberg, a tall, distinguished figure with a black beard, dressed in a frock coat and striped pants, led the band with a professional flourish.

But as Tziril greeted her guests and accepted their congratulations, she realized that Channa and Reb Yosef had not yet arrived. She had told them many times how important it was that they arrive early, since Reb Yosef was to be one of the witnesses for the signing of the ketuba, or marriage contract. As she searched among the throng for Channa and her husband, she was overcome by a profound feeling of love for her sister. On this day of rejoicing she was all too aware that whatever happiness she had managed to achieve she owed to Channa

and Reb Yosef, who had given her a home when she had been
left an orphan at the age of eight.

Hinda sat on a special throne-like chair on a raised platform,
surrounded by friends and relatives, as she waited to sign her
marriage contract, before her parents led her to the canopy.

Unexpectedly, she was approached by a woman of her own
age, whom she had met only once before. It was Tamar Yellen,
an old friend of Avrum's with whom he had grown up in
Vilna. Tamar announced that she was getting married the following week and had a request to make.

She was poor and alone, she told Hinda, for her parents
were still in Vilna. Would Hinda let her borrow her wedding
gown? Tamar was a frail, hollow-cheeked girl with fair hair
and large blue eyes; in Vilna she had been considered a beauty.
She had dropped out of medical school to emigrate to the
United States, and now was forced to support herself by working in one of New York's many garment factories.

All Tamar's friends disapproved of the man she was to marry. As far as they were concerned, he was illiterate and un-
couth, in addition to being a butcher by trade. Her well meaning friends had warned her that he had neither culture nor
intelligence, and they could not understand how a girl of her
education and background could consider marriage to a man
who was so inferior.

But without a moment's hesitation, Hinda promised to lend
Tamar her gown and veil.

Suddenly the music stopped. The wedding was about to
begin! The bridegroom, escorted by his brother and sister-in-
law, was led to the marriage canopy. Channa and Reb Yosef
followed Hinda and her parents, as they joined Avrum under
the chupah, as the rabbi chanted an ancient melody from the
Song of Songs.

During her engagement, Hinda had been told many times
over that it was customary for a bride to weep throughout
the marriage ceremony. But it was the happiest moment of
her life, and she could not shed a single tear.

The rabbi began to read the lengthy marriage contract; to
Hinda it seemed to take forever, but she didn't really mind. In
the forefront of her thoughts was her knowledge that hers

would not be a loveless marriage, arranged for the sake of convenience. She was lucky. Not long before, she had heard an old woman refer to such an unfortunate union as a *kalte bet*, and while the rabbi continued his recital, she couldn't help but think that a "cold bed" would have aptly described her fate had she resisted her own impulses and married Nathan Rosenblum. But the rabbi finished at last, and this was not the time for musings on what might have been.

A mischievous smile hovered on her lips as she obeyed the rabbi's instructions to march around her bridegroom seven times. Why and what this act signified was beyond her knowledge. All she knew was that this was the way in which it had always been done; it was the custom.

Her amusement was increased by her awareness that her Alte, or Avrum as he was now called, was annoyed by the whole performance. Suddenly she recalled an old saying that if the bride managed, just once, to step on her husband's foot while she encircled him, he would be her slave for life. With that same smile on her face, she came down so hard on Avrum's foot, that even the rabbi was startled.

Before she knew it, her veil had been lifted and she was sipping the ceremonial wine. Avrum slipped the wedding ring on her finger. The rabbi placed the customary glass under the groom's foot to remind them of the destruction of the Temple – sorrow in the world amidst all the joy. The sound of cracking glass and the loud shouts of "mazel tov" which followed brought Hinda out of her private thoughts. They were married! They were actually married!

The band broke into a lively chorus of *"Chossen, Kaleh, Mazel Tov,"* and suddenly she was in Alte's arms. He kissed her over and over again, holding her so tightly that she thought he would never release her from his embrace. But when she turned to her parents, expecting to see their shocked reaction to what was obviously very unorthodox behavior at a traditional wedding, she realized that they were so busy kissing and embracing all the relatives who were congratulating them, they couldn't do anything but smile.

Professor Wollenberg ordered the guests to clear the dance floor, while Hinda's entire family formed a circle. Everyone clamored for the *Beragus Tanz* to begin. This dance, traditionally performed by the mothers of the newly-married couple, symbolized an end to the usual hostilities between the mothers-in-law once the marriage had become a fact.

Yussel instructed the dapper band leader, and in a few minutes the music began, as though the father of the bride had planned the *Beragus Tanz* all along. Dr. Feigensohn, Minna's brother, who was listed on the dance program as "Master of Ceremonies," led Tziril to the center of the dance floor. Velvel Lipschutz's wife Minnie, as the closest female relative of the groom, was invited to join Tziril as her partner.

But poor Minnie was overwhelmed with shyness, and stood frozen on the outside of the circle while her husband urged her to step forward. "What's the matter with you?" he whispered darkly. "How can you make such a fool of yourself? Of course you can dance. What are you, a dumb cow?"

But I can't," she wept. The expression on Velvel's face was alarming to Hinda, for Alte had told her how rough and demanding his brother could be.

Suddenly, Rachel "Wilson" stepped forward, and with a hearty laugh that even Tziril found irresistible announced that she would dance with Tziril.

To the utter delight of her family, Tziril joyously entered into the spirit of this old folk dance. Of course, she was not exactly a graceful figure, as she gathered up her full skirt around her ankles to avoid tripping, but according to her ultra-Orthodox, traditional point of view, not to have danced at the wedding of her only child would have greatly diminished the joy and significance of the occasion.

Rachel proved to be the perfect partner. In her loud, booming voice, she hurled bawdy insults at her short, stocky partner, as the delighted spectators applauded. Tziril responded with the customary mock-anger and fierce gestures. They were such a comical pair: Tziril so short and stocky, and Rachel towering over her with her wide hips and enormous bosom that even her extra whalebone stays could not restrain from bouncing up and down.

Soon the taunts and insults gave way to menacing gestures, as the pair enacted in pantomime all the disagreements

and quarrels over the wedding arrangements that had gone before. But just when it seemed that they were on the point of
grabbing each other by the hair, they rushed into each other's
arms and embraced in reconciliation, while the wedding guests
shouted their rowdy approval.

The loudest cheers of all, however, came from an uninvited
guest. To Hinda's amazement, Etta Teresa stood in front of
the crowd, drowning out everyone's good wishes with her
hoarse screeching. That woman was determined to flaunt her
unwanted presence. After all, wasn't she part of Yussel's family? He had invited the whole congregation, but her!

Kazatzky followed *Kazatzky* while the tables were set for
the feast. In old-world fashion, Hinda and Avrum were lifted
high on their chairs as the guests danced around them. And
then it was time for the *kosher tanz* – the one dance in which
Orothodox men and women were permitted to dance together.
Each partner held the opposite end of a large handkerchief,
and swayed in time to the music, avoiding all physical contact.

In spite of Avrum's elaborate plans, Professor Wollenberg
was left little time for modern dance music. On the few occasions when the groom's friends were given a chance to try a
waltz or a two-step, Yussel and his friends watched from the
sidelines in amazement, and whispered disapprovingly among
themselves. Is this what America had done to the Jewish
youth of the new generation? The older people were horrified
and averted their eyes from the spectacle of young, unmarried
couples cavorting in each other's arms.

But at ten o'clock, the bride and groom led the procession
of guests into the dining room for the wedding feast, and a
new mood overtook them.

During the main course of roast chicken and sweet carrot
tzimmes, Yussel proudly presented the badchen, or wedding
jester to the guests. After listening to the chunky, bearded
man, pompously decked out in a high silk hat and frock coat,
Dr. Feigensohn nudged Avrum and whispered cynically to the
exasperated bridegroom that this stout, old-world figure
would make an ideal Hamlet

Years later, Hinda described the badchen to her daughters
as a cross between a clown and a well meaning prophet of

doom. Since no traditional Jewish wedding was considered complete without a jester, Avrum had been especially adamant about not having one at his wedding. But here was this overdressed *Purim-shpieler* whom Yussel had engaged to embarrass Avrum in front of his friends — no feature of an Orthodox wedding was more repugnant to them, or subject to more ridicule.

The bridegroom would have put a stop to the nonsense immediately, if Dr. Feigensohn had not restrained him.

"Let the poor man earn his fee," he advised. "He's probably counting on it to pay his rent. Sit back, Alte, and relax. It'll be over in a few minute."

And after a while, even Avrum's "enlightened" friends were enjoying the comic oratory of the badchen, just as they had enjoyed the traditional folk dances. Peals of laughter came from all sides as he quoted prophets and sages, explaining that his task was now to instruct the bride in her marital duties.

"Just listen to Hamlet," Dr. Feigensohn repeated. "Be patient. They all make the same speech, word for word. If you've heard one, you've heard them all."

Meanwhile, the badchen predicted the hardships the bride would suffer during her married life!

"And you will raise children who will be ungrateful. And you will cater to every whim of a self-centered, busy husband who will have no time for you. And don't expect any reward for all of this. No thanks. Not in this life, anyway. Don't be surprised if your daughters grow up wild and run around with *goyim*. Your sons will chase after *shiksas* and break your heart! You are living in America, where anything is possible!

"But remember this. Chastity. Devotion. A life of service. Adherence to the mitzvoth of the mikvah and the Sabbath candles. This is your duty as a true Jewish wife."

At this point in his oration he attempted to console the bride. But Hinda had difficulty restraining her laughter, which broke out so contagiously, one could scarcely hear the badchen's promise above the raucous merriment, that if she proved herself worthy, her daughters would be beautiful and marry young, and her sons would be famous scholars.

It was long past midnight, and the exhausted, but still en-

thusiatic guests began to depart one by one. As they congratulated Hinda and Avrum for perhaps the twentieth time, they
continued to exclaim over and over what a wonderful time
they'd had. It was like being home again, they all said, and
her wedding had revived so many memories of their own
families' celebrations in years past.

With tears in their eyes, some of the young women confided
to Hinda how good it was, after all, to be reminded of their
traditions.

"It was the sort of wedding I'd love to have. Oh, Hinda. I'd
give anything to have my parents with me under the chupah."
Tamar Yellen's blue eyes glistened with tears.

"But at least I'll be wearing your wedding dress. Please,
Hinda. Pray that it will be lucky for me, too."

Just as she was about to leave, Tamar thought of something
else.

"Hinda," she whispered. "Hinda, did you make a wish when
you marched around Avrum?"

Hinda hesitated for a moment. And then she nodded, ever
so slightly, her lips pressed close in a secretive smile.

Epilogue

After my mother's death, we found the dance program from her wedding reception among her treasured possessions. Evidently, it was one of her most cherished momento. Wrapped in discolored tissue paper, it was faded with age. With deep sentiment, she had preserved this crumbling souvenir of the most important event in her life for more than half a century.

Hinda's had been a happy marriage despite tragedy and hardship, and even my grandmother Tziril had been forced to admit that her daughter could not have done better. Their life together was a long and happy one, until her beloved Avrum died shorty after their golden wedding jubilee, while listening to a radio broadcast of *Tosca* one Saturday afternoon. The doctor who was summoned said that my father had "died like a poet."

Her seven daughters, her son and their families, including sixteen grandchildren, were present at her funeral. How ironic it seemed to me that only a few weeks before her death, my mother confided to me that as she had circled her husband beneath the wedding canopy, she had wished for sons.

Perhaps her wish was granted after all. The seven sons-in-law who had admired and loved her were her pallbearers.

GLOSSARY

AGUNAH — A woman whose husband has disappeared and whose death cannot be determined; she cannot remarry in traditional Jewish law until his death is determined. Conservative and Reform Judaism do not observe this tradition. THE AGUNAH by Chaim Grad is a good fictional account of this tradition.

ALEVAI — "so should it be!": an idiomatic expression of consent.

ALTE MOID — Old maid

APIKOROS — Jewish heretic. Derived from the name of the Greek philosopher Epicurus, some of whose beliefs were in opposition to traditional Jewish teachings and attracted some Jews.

BRIS — A Ritual Circumcision performed by a Mohel. Health permitting, the ceremony is performed eight days after the birth of a baby boy.

BUBA MEISSA — Literally "grandmother story" idiomatic: "Old Wives' tale."

CHACHAM — A wise person; sometimes used with mild irony.

CHALLAH — Bread specially prepared to sanctify the Sabbath and Jewish festivals. It originated from that part of the dough given as a gift to the priest in the days of the Temple. The preparation of Challah is particularly enjoined upon women

CHEDER — An elementary Religious school, sometimes attached to the shul or synagogue.

CHEVRA KADISHA — Literally "Holy Brotherhood"; the group who prepare the body of the dead for burial according to Jewish law. Until the 4th Century C. E., the burial of the dead was regarded as the responsibility of the entire community. Today this holy duty is performed by older men and women who are observant in their faith.

CHUPAH — The canopy under which a Jewish wedding takes place. In biblical days, the bride was carried to the home of her prospective bridegroom on a canopied bed or litter. By the middle ages, the bride was led into the synagogue, rather than the bridal chamber, and the chupah at the altar became the substitute for the canopied litter. The chupah can be as simple as a prayer shawl or as extravagant as a flowered arbor.

DAVEN — To pray.

DRUCKE — Printing Press

EMES — Truth. A word usually used for emphasis, rather than literally as "Tell me the truth!"

FORWARD — A Yiddish newspaper in New York City, still in existence.

GEBARNO — A Polish word for Province or governmental unit.

GET — Bill of Divorcement. Jewish laws governing divorce are manifold. To protect the wife, it is unlawful for a man to divorce his wife without her consent. The laws concerning the writing and transmission of the *get* were purposely made exceedingly stringent to prevent possible misuse by the husband of his privilege to annul the marriage.

GOLDENE MEDINA — The Golden Land; usually associated with America, the "Land of Plenty."

GOYIM — The non-Jewish nations of the world , or members of such nations. The word *goy* by itself means "nation."

GERUSS / GRUZE — Greetings, or regards from a friend, etc.; to give a *geruss* is to send regards, or bring greetings.

GUT SHABBOS — Good Sabbath; a greeting on the Sabbath.

HAKNOSES KALAH — The Society to Dower the Bride. The Middle Ages saw a proliferation of societies to meet special social and religious needs. The societies redeemed slaves, ransomed prisoners, etc. This society in dowering the bride, would provide everything from linen, beds, kitchenware, to jewelry lent the bride for the wedding which was also provided.

HALACHA — Those sections of rabbinic literature dealing with Jewish legal tradition. *Halacha* is used in the sense of talmudic law, guidance, traditional practice, the final decision of the rabbinic sages on disputed rules of conduct.

HA SHEM — "God's Name" meaning the Holy One. One of the many terms in which Jews address their God.

HASKALAH — Enlightenment. The movement to acquire western culture and secular knowledge by certain sections of European Jews. The objective was a complete transformation in education and habits of life, and the inadequate Jewish system of education, which shunned secular education.

HECHSHER — A rabbinical endorsement or certification especially of food products that conform with traditional Jewish dietary laws.

KETUBAH — Marriage contract; sometimes regarded as the "Jewish woman's Bill of Rights" it provides for the legal and moral obligations of a husband towards his wife. Originally written in Aramaic, it is usually read at the wedding by the rabbi as part of the traditional ceremony.

KETZELACH — Kittens; an endearing term for small things.

KIDDUSH — Sanctification; A ceremony and a prayer proclaiming the holiness of the Sabbath or Festival; most often chanted over the sacramental wine: "Blessed art Thou, O Lord, our God, King of the Universe, who brings forth the Fruit of the Vine."

KOPECK — A small amount of money in eastern Europe..

KRISHMA — An abbreviation to denote a special prayer, along with the first paragraph of the *Shema* to be recited before going to sleep at night. It is a petition for peace and protection during the night. In Hebrew-Kri-at Sh'ma al Hamitaw.

LANDSLEIT — Compatriots from the same small village or town. Almost similar to "Paisano" for Italians.

L'CHAIM — To Life! Generally to be said with fervor when making a toast.

MASHGIACH — One who supervises the observance of *Kashrut*, the Jewish dietary laws. An inspector authorized to inspect meat stores, bakeries, public kitchens and commissaries to ensure adherence to orthodox Jewish ritual of cleanliness (kashrut)

MASKIL — Title of honor for a learned man; in the nineteenth century it came to designate a follower of the *Haskalah* movement.

MAZEL — Luck, generally considered worth having, no matter who you are.

MAZEL TOV — Good Luck! to be said with gusto, on all occasions of joy, where congratulations are in order.

MECHITZAH — Literally partition. The separation between men and women in an Orthodox synagogue. Usually a curtain.

MELAMED — A teacher of small children.

MIKVAH — Literally: gathering of water. A ritual bath or bathing place for purification in accordance with Jewish law. The water of a *mikvah* must come from a natural spring or river. In cities where water comes from underground pipes, many special technicalities must be observed in its construction. Use of the *mikvah* was prescribed for married women following their menstruation and childbirth. In honor of the approaching Sabbath, bathing on Friday, for both men and woman was a universal Jewish custom. since use of the *mikvah* symbolizes ritual or spiritual purification as well as physical cleanliness.

MINYAN — The minimum number (10) needed for a religious quorum needed for the recital of regular prayers. Until recently only men were eligible to make up this quorum. This tradition is in transition, and women are increasingly being allowed to play a formal part in religious ceremony.

MISHPOCHA — family, clan; a Jewish family or social unit including close and distant relatives.

MITZVAH — a biblical or rabbinic commandment; a good deed; a humanitarian or charitable act. In Jewish tradition to perform a *mitzvah* is to contribute to the upbuilding of a better world.

MOHEL — Circumcisor. The *mohel* is usually subject to regulations to ensure the performance of the operation with adequate precautions.

MALACH HAMOVES — The angel or messenger of death.

MUMA – Aunt

NADON – Dowry. The ancient custom of providing dowries enabled youthful couples to marry long before they were economically independent. The *nadon* sometimes included board and maintenance for a specified time, making it possible for a student to continue at a Talmudic Academy.

PANYA – "Mistress" a title of respect in Polish.

PAYOS/PAYOTH – Earlocks or side curls. The Torah says: "You shall not clip your hair at the temples nor mar the edges of your beard." Yeminites refer to their side curls as *simmanim* (signs) distinguishing them from non-Jews.

POGROMISHKES – Perpetrators of pogroms. "Pogrom," from the Russian, meaning destruction.; organized massacre. In Europe, Jews were the common victims of pogroms. Armenians were also victims of these officially authorized massacres.

RABBONO SHEL OLOM – Literally: Master of the Universe. A name for the Lord.

REB/RABBI – A title denoting respect for the learned Jewish man.

SHABBOS – The Sabbath; the period from Friday at twilight when the candles are lighted and prayers are said, to Saturday evening at twilight when the *Havdalah* candles are lit. "Six days you shall labor and do all your work; but on the seventh day, which is a Sabbath in honor of the Lord your God, you shall not do any work. . . " (Exodus 20:9-10). Linked with the Creation, the Sabbath has been regarded as a perpetual sign between God and the people of Israel, symbolizing the duty of work and the holiness of rest. The Sabbath is the subject of much poetry and has been likened to a bride (Kallah) and also a queen (Malkah).

SHABBOS GOY – Non-Jew who performs tasks forbidden to Jews on the Sabbath. Because the *Shabbos Goy* frequently entered Jewish homes on familiar terms, to light fires or even prepare a meal, they formed a vital link between the Jewish and Christian community.

SEPHARDIM – Denoting Jews who upon being expelled from Spain emigrated east within the mediterranean area. In addition to speaking Ladino as their "home language" they retained what is now called the "Sephardic arrangement of Prayer;" in the 18th century the Hasidic movement adopted this arrangement, hence on many occasions they are referred to as "Sephardim."

SHADCHEN – Marriage broker. The *shadchan's* right to compensation is dealt with in medieval Jewish law codes. Some saintly rabbis regarded the business of matchmaking as a *mitzvah*.

SHIVA/SHIVAH – Seven. The seven-day mourning period follows the burial of an immediate relative. It is observed by abstaining from all ordinary work and diversions. The mourners remain at home, sitting unshod on a low stool. Friends visit the mourner's home

iv

for prayer and condolence during the seven-day period.

SHLOSHIM/SHELOSHIM — the period from the 7th day to the 30th day of mourning.

SHTETL — Place; Jewish small town or small-town community in Eastern Europe.

SIDDUR — Order of prayers: a Jewish prayer book containing both the Hebrew and Aramaic prayers used chiefly in the daily liturgy.

SIMCHA — A joyous occasion such as a wedding, birth of a baby, etc.

STREIMEL — Fur-edged hat worn by Hasidic Jews.

SHUL/SYNAGOGUE — The origin of the synagogue can be found in the period of the Babylonian captivity, 586 B.C.E. By the time of the fall of the Second Temple, 70 C.E., the synagogue was a well developed institution. The function of the synagogue has varied through the centuries, combining the religious, educational and social services in various ways.

TALLEISIM/TALLIT — A woolen or silk prayer shawl. Rectangular or square, with fringes at the four corners. Worn around the shoulders by conservative Jewish men, it is also used to cover the head by the orthodox at certain times. It is worn during the recitation of the of the morning prayers. Before donning the *Tallit*, the wearer pronounces this benediction: "Blessed art thou. . . who hast sanctified us with thy commandments, and commanded us to enwrap ourselves in the fringed grament."

TATEH — An endearing word for Father.

TENAUIM — Conditions: signifies the betrothal or engagement contract and the details and agreements entered into by the parents of the couple.

TREIF — Torn flesh: ritually unclean or unfit according to Jewish law.

VETTER/FETTER — Uncle.

YESHIVA — A school for advanced talmudic study. Also an orthodox Rabbinical Seminary.

YICHUS — Lineage, ancestry, pride in family background.

YIDDISHKEIT — Jewish character or quality. Jewish way of life.

YOM TOV — Literally: good day; a holiday. Used as a greeting during festivals as: "Gut Yom Tov."